FamilyCircle®
Slow Cooker Meals

Meredith® Books
Des Moines, Iowa

Family Circle® *Slow Cooker Meals*

Editor: Lois White
Contributing Project Editors: Carrie E. Holcomb, Spectrum Communication Services, Inc.
Contributing Graphic Designer: Sundie Ruppert
Copy Chief: Doug Kouma
Copy Editor: Kevin Cox
Publishing Operations Manager: Karen Schirm
Edit and Design Production Coordinator: Mary Lee Gavin
Editorial Assistant: Sheri Cord
Book Production Managers: Marjorie J. Schenkelberg, Mark Weaver
Imaging Center Operator: Tony Jungweber
Contributing Copy Editor: Amanda Knief
Contributing Proofreaders: Jeanette Astor, Nicole Clausing, Stacie Gaylor
Contributing Indexer: Elizabeth T. Parsons

Meredith® Books

Editorial Director: John Riha
Managing Editor: Kathleen Armentrout
Deputy Editor: Jennifer Darling
Brand Manager: Janell Pittman
Group Manager: Jan Miller
Senior Associate Design Director: Mick Schnepf

Director, Marketing and Publicity: Amy Nichols
Executive Director, Sales: Ken Zagor
Director, Operations: George A. Susral
Director, Production: Douglas M. Johnston
Business Director: Janice Croat

Vice President and General Manager, SIM: Jeff Myers

Family Circle® **Magazine**

Editor in Chief: Linda Fears
Editorial Director: Michael Lafavore
Creative Director: Karmen Lizzul
Food Director: Regina Ragone, R.D.
Senior Food Editor: Julie Miltenberger
Associate Food Editor: Michael Tyrrell
Assistant Food Editor: Cindy Heller
Editorial Assistant: Katie Kemple
Test Kitchen Associate: Althea Needham

Meredith Publishing Group

President: Jack Griffin
Executive Vice President: Doug Olson

Meredith Corporation

Chairman of the Board: William T. Kerr
President and Chief Executive Officer: Stephen M. Lacy

In Memoriam: E.T. Meredith III (1933–2003)

Pictured on the front cover:
Saucy Pot Roast with Noodles (recipe, page 12)

Contents

Come home to more delicious flavors than ever before!

Looking for an easy way to get dinner on the table tonight? Spend just a little time prepping these weeknight-perfect meals, then let the slow cooker do the cooking for you. From fork-tender roasts and savory soups and sandwiches to mouthwatering casseroles and potluck fare, you'll create food that everyone in your family—kids on up—will enjoy.

Colorful icons on every page help you spot the perfect recipe for the perfect occasion. Here's what each icon represents:

KIDS' FAVORITE!
If you see this symbol next to a recipe, chances are even your pickiest eaters will be eager to give it a try. Whether it's a familiar flavor or something entirely new, it's sure to be a hit with the entire family.

SUPERFAST PREP
Because we know your time is precious, we've marked all the "superfast prep" recipes with this clock symbol. In 20 minutes or less, you'll be ready to turn on the dial and let the slow cooker do its thing.

MAKE IT A MEAL
Preplanned dinner menus include serve-along suggestions to round out the slow cooker meals in this book. You'll find bakery and deli items listed as well as quick recipes from our Sides and Desserts chapter, starting on page 245.

FREEZE WITH EASE
Recipes marked with this icon can easily be frozen for a quick meal another day. Follow our guidelines on page 10 for safe freezing.

Slow-Cooking Basics

Slow-Cooker Features

HIGH- AND LOW-HEAT SETTINGS are a basic feature on all slow cookers. When the cooker is plugged in and the dial is turned on, the heating elements that wrap around the sides of the ceramic liner remain on continuously. On the low-heat setting, the food cooks at about 200°F; on high it cooks at about 300°F. Other convenient features to look for in slow cookers include:

• Removable ceramic inserts: These double as serving dishes and can be used in the freezer, refrigerator and in any oven. They are dishwasher safe, making cleanup easy.

• Keep-warm setting: This setting keeps food warm on low heat after the cooking cycle is complete.

• Programmable control pads: This feature allows cooks to select time and temperature, and at the end of cooking, some cookers will automatically switch to the keep-warm setting.

KEEP THE LID ON: RESIST PEEKING INTO THE COOKER DURING COOKING. BECAUSE THE COOKER WORKS AT LOW TEMPERATURES, LOST HEAT IS RECOVERED VERY SLOWLY. IF YOU MUST LIFT THE LID TO STIR OR ADD INGREDIENTS, REPLACE IT AS QUICKLY AS POSSIBLE, ESPECIALLY WHEN COOKING ON THE LOW-HEAT SETTING. EACH TIME YOU LIFT THE LID, YOU EXTEND THE COOKING TIME BY ABOUT 15 MINUTES.

THE ONE-HALF TO TWO-THIRDS RULE: For best results a slow cooker must be at least half full and no more than two-thirds full. Many of our recipes give a range of cooker sizes (such as 3½ to 5 quarts). Be sure to use a cooker that is within the specified range given in the recipe so the food cooks to the proper doneness.

A low-fat alternative!

Thanks to low, moist heat, slow cooking requires little fat. For low-fat meals, choose lean meat cuts and trim excess fat. Remove poultry skin before cooking. If you prefer to brown the meat before adding it to the cooker, use a nonstick skillet coated with nonstick cooking spray. Before serving the meal, use a slotted spoon to transfer the meat and vegetables to a platter. Pour the cooking liquid into a glass measuring cup and let it stand for 2 minutes. Once the fat rises to the top of the cup, skim off any visible fat with a slotted spoon.

Adapting Favorite Recipes

Use the following tips to make many of your favorite recipes in the slow cooker:

START WITH A RECIPE THAT USES A LESS-TENDER MEAT CUT, such as pork shoulder or beef chuck. These meats typically benefit from a longer cooking time. You need to use extra care with recipes that use dairy products because they can break down during extended cooking. We recommend adding dairy products, such as milk, cream, sour cream or cheese, just before serving.

FIND A RECIPE IN THIS BOOK that is similar to your family favorite to use as a sample. It will give you a good idea of quantities for meat, vegetables and, perhaps most critically, liquid.

CUT VEGETABLES IN PIECES similar in size to the sample recipe you've chosen.

TRIM EXCESS FAT FROM MEAT and, if necessary, cut the meat to fit in the cooker. Place the meat on top of the vegetables in the cooker.

REDUCE THE LIQUIDS in the recipe you are adapting by about half unless the recipe calls for long grain rice.

FOLLOW THE HEAT SETTING AND COOKING TIME recommendations listed in the sample recipe.

THAW MEAT FIRST

Thaw raw meat and poultry completely in the refrigerator or defrost it in the microwave before adding it to the cooker. If the meat thaws as it cooks, it will stay in the bacterial danger zone (40°F to 140°F) for too long.

PLAY IT SAFE

As slow cookers age they can fail to heat properly. A unit in tip-top shape cooks food slowly enough for all-day cooking but hot enough to keep food out of a temperature danger zone (40°F to 140°F) where bacteria will thrive. To find out if your slow cooker is safe, fill the cooker one-half to two-thirds full of water. Heat it on low-heat setting for 8 hours with the lid on. Check the water temperature with an accurate food thermometer. (Do this quickly since the temperature drops fast when the lid is removed.) The water temperature should be about 185°F. If the temperature is lower, replace your slow cooker.

PLAN AHEAD

Prepare some of the ingredients for your slow cooker meal the night before so you can get a head start on prepping the cooker the next morning. Here are some timesaving tips:

Chop vegetables and refrigerate them in separate containers. You can keep chopped potatoes from turning brown by covering them with water. Or if your cooker has a removable liner, place the vegetables in the liner, cover it and keep it in the refrigerator until the next morning.

Assemble, cover and chill liquid ingredients or sauces separately from the solids.

If you'd like to brown ground meat, poultry or sausage the night before, be sure to cook it completely. Cool and store it tightly covered in the refrigerator. For roasts, cubed meat and poultry pieces, it's best to do the browning just before slow cooking because browning only partially cooks the meat or poultry.

THE RIGHT COOKER FOR YOU

The size of slow cooker you need depends on the number of people you want to serve. That is why many cooks own several sizes of cookers. As a general rule:

1½ quart
- Cooking meals for two
- Keeping party foods warm

3½ quart
- Cooking a small roast (2 to 2½ pounds)
- Cooking small batches of soup

3½ to 4½ quart
- Cooking soups, stews, chilis, small to medium pieces of meat, side dishes and desserts

4½ or 5 quart
- Family-size meals, including larger cuts of meat, soups, stews and chilis

6 to 8 quart
- Dinners for company, potluck dishes and party foods, including hot beverages

FREEZE WITH EASE

One of the nice things about cooking many of the recipes in this book is that you can freeze leftovers to reheat and enjoy on busy days. To successfully freeze foods and maintain good flavor, here are a few pointers:

Choose freezer-safe containers or bags. Look for moistureproof and vaporproof materials that can withstand temperatures of 0°F or below and can be tightly sealed. For liquid or semiliquid foods, use rigid plastic containers, bags or wide-top jars designed for freezing. Regular jars seldom are tempered to withstand freezer temperatures.

Cool hot foods quickly. Divide soups and stews into portions that are 2 to 3 inches deep and stir while cooling. Divide roasts and whole poultry into portions that are 2 to 3 inches thick. Place food in the refrigerator. When thoroughly chilled, transfer food to freezer containers. Arrange containers in a single layer in the freezer to allow cold air to circulate around them. Once the food is frozen, stack the containers for storage.

Remove excess air. This will help prevent freezer burn. There is an exception: When freezing cooked food, you'll want to leave about ½ inch of space between the top of the food and the rim of its container. This will provide room for the food to expand while it freezes without breaking the container or causing the lid to pop off.

Be label conscious. Include the name of the recipe, the quantity, the date it was frozen and number of servings.

Thaw and reheat properly. Thaw the food overnight in the refrigerator. Reheat in the microwave or on the stovetop until thoroughly heated through.

MAXIMUM FREEZE TIMES

ROASTS AND MEAT DISHES (COOKED): 3 MONTHS

POULTRY DISHES (COOKED): 4 MONTHS

SOUPS AND STEWS: 6 MONTHS

Meats

28 Mushroom and Onion Sauced Round Steak

Hot and Spicy Sloppy Joes 42

50 Seed-Coated Roast Pork

Lo Mein-Style Pork 60

Flavor-packed meats—classic cuts of beef and pork—fill this chapter to the brim. Find a windfall of ethnic recipes alongside traditional favorite slow cooker roasts, sandwiches and chops.

PREP:
25 minutes

COOKER SIZE:
3½- or 4-quart

COOK:
10 to 12 hours on low-heat or 4 to 5 hours on high-heat setting

MAKES:
6 to 8 servings

KIDS' FAVORITE!

FREEZE WITH EASE

MAKE IT A MEAL:
Lemon-Almond Broccoli (see recipe, page 256)

Purchased cherry pie topped with sweetened whipped cream

This old-fashioned pot roast will have everyone coming back for seconds.

Saucy Pot Roast With Noodles

1 beef chuck pot roast (2 to 2½ pounds)
1 tablespoon vegetable oil
2 medium-size carrots, sliced
2 ribs celery, sliced
1 medium-size onion, sliced
2 cloves garlic, chopped
1 tablespoon quick-cooking tapioca
1 can (14½ ounces) Italian-style stewed tomatoes
1 can (6 ounces) Italian-style tomato paste
1 tablespoon brown sugar
½ teaspoon salt
¼ teaspoon black pepper
1 bay leaf
   Hot cooked noodles
   Celery leaves (optional)

1. Trim fat from roast. If necessary, cut roast to fit into 3½- or 4-quart slow cooker. In large skillet, brown roast on all sides in hot oil.

2. In the slow cooker, combine carrots, celery, onion and garlic. Sprinkle tapioca over vegetables. Arrange roast to cover vegetables.

3. In medium-size bowl, combine tomatoes with their juices, tomato paste, brown sugar, salt, pepper and bay leaf; pour over the roast in slow cooker.

4. Cover slow cooker; cook on low-heat setting for 10 to 12 hours or on high-heat setting for 4 to 5 hours.

5. Remove and discard bay leaf. Transfer roast to cutting board, reserving cooking liquid; slice roast. Skim fat from cooking liquid. Serve beef and cooking liquid with noodles. If desired, garnish with celery leaves.

Per serving: 569 cal., 27 g total fat (10 g sat. fat), 127 mg chol., 693 mg sodium, 48 g carbo., 4 g fiber, 32 g pro.

PREP:
25 minutes

COOKER SIZE:
5- or 5½-quart

COOK:
6 hours on high-heat setting

MAKES:
10 servings

KIDS' FAVORITE!

FREEZE WITH EASE

MAKE IT A MEAL:
Buttery Corn Medley (see recipe, page 257)

Purchased chocolate cupcakes

If you've forgotten how good a succulent, slow-cooking pot roast can be, remind yourself with this classic version.

Classic Pot Roast With Vegetables

1 **large onion, diced**
1 **cup peeled baby carrots, cut into ¼-inch-thick slices**
1 **rib celery, cut into ¼-inch-thick slices**
2 **cloves garlic, chopped**
1 **boneless beef chuck roast (about 3 pounds), tied**
1 **teaspoon extra-virgin olive oil**
1 **teaspoon salt**
¼ **teaspoon black pepper**
2 **cups sliced white button mushrooms**
4 **sprigs fresh thyme**
1 **bay leaf**
1 **cup beef broth**
½ **cup dry red wine**
2 **tablespoons tomato paste**
3 **tablespoons all-purpose flour**
2 **tablespoons extra-virgin olive oil**
   Hot cooked noodles

1. In 5- or 5½-quart slow cooker, layer onion, carrots, celery and garlic. Rub roast all over with the 1 teaspoon olive oil; season roast with the salt and pepper. Scatter mushrooms over vegetables in slow cooker; place roast on top. Tuck thyme sprigs and bay leaf into mixture.

2. In medium-size bowl, whisk together beef broth, wine and tomato paste. Pour mixture over meat.

3. Cover slow cooker; cook on high-heat setting for 6 hours.

4. Remove roast from slow cooker; cover and keep warm. For gravy, pour liquid with vegetable mixture from slow cooker into medium-size saucepan; remove and discard thyme sprigs and bay leaf. Bring to a boil.

5. In small cup, stir together flour and the 2 tablespoons oil until well blended and smooth. Stir flour mixture into liquid in saucepan. Boil, stirring, about 1 minute or until liquid is slightly thickened.

6. Slice roast. Serve with gravy and noodles.

. . . .

Per serving: 545 cal., 30 g total fat (10 g sat. fat), 130 mg chol., 433 mg sodium, 34 g carbo., 2 g fiber, 33 g pro.

Maque choux (MOCK shoo) is a Cajun dish of corn smothered with green pepper, onion and tomatoes seasoned with a little Cajun kick.

Cajun Pot Roast With Maque Choux

1 boneless beef chuck roast (2 to 2½ pounds)
1 tablespoon Cajun seasoning
1 package (10 ounces) frozen whole kernel corn
1 large green pepper, seeded and chopped
1 medium onion, chopped
1 teaspoon sugar
½ teaspoon hot-pepper sauce
⅛ teaspoon black pepper
1 can (14½ ounces) diced tomatoes

1. Trim fat from roast. Rub roast all over with the Cajun seasoning.

2. Place roast in 3½- to 4½-quart slow cooker, cutting to fit if necessary. Add frozen corn, green pepper, onion, sugar, hot-pepper sauce and black pepper. Pour tomatoes with their juices over vegetables in slow cooker.

3. Cover slow cooker; cook on low-heat setting for 8 to 10 hours or on high-heat setting for 4 to 5 hours.

4. Remove roast from cooker. Drain vegetables, discarding cooking liquid. Serve roast with vegetables.

. . . .

Per serving: 255 cal., 5 g total fat (2 g sat. fat), 90 mg chol., 311 mg sodium, 17 g carbo., 2 g fiber, 34 g pro.

PREP:
20 minutes

COOKER SIZE:
3½- to 4½-quart

COOK:
8 to 10 hours on low-heat or 4 to 5 hours on high-heat setting

MAKES:
6 servings

FREEZE WITH EASE

MAKE IT A MEAL:
Refrigerated garlic herb breadsticks, baked

Apple and pear slices

Brownie and Walnut Pie (see recipe, page 274)

MEATS

15

PREP:
20 minutes

COOKER SIZE:
3½- or 4-quart

COOK:
8 to 10 hours on low-heat or 4 to 5 hours on high-heat setting, plus 15 minutes on high-heat setting

MAKES:
12 servings (2 wraps per serving)

FREEZE WITH EASE

MAKE IT A MEAL:
Hot cooked rice

Fortune cookies

Here's a dish sized for a crowd and bound to please. Asian-seasoned roast and crunchy jicama are wrapped in lettuce leaves.

Asian Lettuce Wraps

   1 boneless beef chuck pot roast (about 3 pounds)
1½ cups diced jicama (1 small) or chopped celery (3 ribs)
   ½ cup chopped scallions
   ¼ cup rice vinegar
   ¼ cup reduced-sodium soy sauce
   2 tablespoons bottled hoisin sauce
   1 tablespoon finely chopped fresh ginger
   ½ teaspoon salt
   ½ teaspoon chili oil
   ¼ teaspoon black pepper
   2 tablespoons cornstarch mixed with 2 tablespoons cold water
  24 Bibb or Boston lettuce leaves

1. Trim fat from roast. Place roast in 3½- or 4-quart slow cooker, cutting to fit if necessary. In medium-size bowl, combine jicama, scallions, rice vinegar, soy sauce, hoisin sauce, ginger, salt, chili oil and pepper; pour over roast in the slow cooker.

2. Cover slow cooker; cook on low-heat setting for 8 to 10 hours or on high-heat setting for 4 to 5 hours.

3. If necessary, raise temperature to high-heat setting. Stir cornstarch mixture into meat mixture. Cover slow cooker; cook about 15 minutes longer or until thickened.

4. Using slotted spoon, remove meat from slow cooker. When cool enough to handle, use two forks to pull meat apart into shreds. Return shredded meat to mixture in slow cooker; heat through. Spoon shredded meat mixture onto lettuce leaves. Fold bottom edge of each lettuce leaf up and over filling. Fold in opposite sides; roll up from bottom.

Per serving: 168 cal., 4 g total fat (1 g sat. fat), 67 mg chol., 401 mg sodium, 5 g carbo., 0 g fiber, 25 g pro.

The well-seasoned meat is fall-apart tender, so don't attempt to slice it. Just use two forks to pull it into bite-size pieces.

Savory Beef Sandwiches

- 1 boneless beef sirloin or rump roast (about 4 pounds), cut into 2- to 3-inch pieces
- ½ cup water
- 1 envelope (0.7 ounce) dry Italian salad dressing mix
- 2 teaspoons dried Italian seasoning
- ½ to 1 teaspoon crushed red pepper
- ½ teaspoon garlic powder
- 12 kaiser rolls or other sandwich rolls, split
  Roasted red pepper strips (optional)

1. Place roast in 3½- to 5-quart slow cooker, cutting to fit if necessary. In small bowl, stir together the water, dry salad dressing mix, Italian seasoning, crushed red pepper and garlic powder; pour over roast in slow cooker.

2. Cover slow cooker; cook on low-heat setting for 10 to 12 hours or on high-heat setting for 5 to 6 hours.

3. Transfer roast to cutting board, reserving cooking liquid. Using two forks, pull roast apart into shreds. Serve shredded beef on rolls. Drizzle each sandwich with some of the cooking liquid to moisten. If desired, top each sandwich with roasted red pepper strips.

. . . .

Per sandwich: 361 cal., 8 g total fat (2 g sat. fat), 91 mg chol., 598 mg sodium, 31 g carbo., 1 g fiber, 38 g pro.

PREP:
15 minutes

COOKER SIZE:
3½- to 5-quart

COOK:
10 to 12 hours on low-heat or 5 to 6 hours on high-heat setting

MAKES:
12 sandwiches

KIDS' FAVORITE!

FREEZE WITH EASE

MAKE IT A MEAL:
Potato chips

Purchased coleslaw

Purchased oatmeal raisin cookies

PREP:
25 minutes

COOKER SIZE:
3½- to 6-quart

COOK:
10 to 12 hours on low-heat setting

STAND:
15 minutes

MAKES:
8 servings

KIDS' FAVORITE!

FREEZE WITH EASE

MAKE IT A MEAL:
Creamy Ranch Coleslaw (see recipe, page 250)

Purchased baked beans

Sliced apples and pears served with purchased caramel dip

Brisket benefits from the long cooking time, so simmer it on the low-heat setting.

Tangy Barbecue Beef

2 tablespoons chili powder
1 teaspoon celery seeds
½ teaspoon salt
½ teaspoon freshly ground black pepper
1 beef brisket (about 3 pounds)
2 medium-size onions, thinly sliced
1 cup bottled smoke-flavor barbecue sauce
½ cup beer or ginger ale
8 kaiser rolls or Portuguese rolls, split and toasted
    Leaf lettuce
    Tomato slices
    Hot-pepper sauce (optional)

1. In small bowl, combine chili powder, celery seeds, salt and pepper. Rub brisket all over with chili powder mixture. Place half of the sliced onions in 3½- to 6-quart slow cooker. Place brisket on the onions, cutting brisket to fit cooker if necessary. Place the remaining onions on top of the brisket. In small bowl, stir together barbecue sauce and beer or ginger ale. Pour over brisket and onions.

2. Cover slow cooker; cook on low-heat setting for 10 to 12 hours or until brisket is fork-tender.

3. Transfer brisket to cutting board, reserving sauce mixture; let brisket stand for 15 minutes. Raise temperature to high-heat setting. Halve brisket crosswise. Using two forks, pull brisket apart into shreds. Return shredded brisket to sauce mixture in slow cooker. Heat through.

4. Top bun bottoms with lettuce and tomato slices. Using a slotted spoon, spoon beef-onion mixture on top of tomato. If desired, season to taste with hot-pepper sauce. Add bun tops.

Per serving: 404 cal., 10 g total fat (3 g sat. fat), 72 mg chol., 993 mg sodium, 44 g carbo., 3 g fiber, 31 g pro.

PREP:
25 minutes

COOKER SIZE:
5- to 6-quart

COOK:
10 to 11 hours on low-heat or 5 to 5½ hours on high-heat setting

MAKES:
8 servings

Fresh fennel, tomatoes, olives and Greek or Italian seasoning transform ordinary beef brisket into an exotic Mediterranean treat.

Mediterranean Pot Roast

1 beef brisket (about 3 pounds)
3 teaspoons dried Greek or Italian seasoning
2 medium fennel bulbs, trimmed, cored and cut into thick wedges; or 4 ribs celery, cut into ½-inch-thick slices, plus ½ teaspoon fennel seeds
1 can (14½ ounces) diced tomatoes with basil, oregano and garlic
½ cup beef broth
1 can (2¼ ounces) sliced pitted ripe olives, drained
¾ teaspoon salt
½ teaspoon grated lemon zest
¼ teaspoon black pepper
¼ cup cold water
2 tablespoons all-purpose flour
Pitted ripe and/or green whole olives (optional)

1. Trim fat from brisket. Sprinkle brisket with 1 teaspoon of the Greek or Italian seasoning. Place brisket in 5- to 6-quart slow cooker, cutting to fit if necessary. Top with fennel wedges or sliced celery and fennel seeds.

2. In medium-size bowl, combine tomatoes with their juices, beef broth, sliced olives, salt, lemon zest, pepper and the remaining 2 teaspoons Greek or Italian seasoning. Pour over brisket and vegetables.

3. Cover slow cooker; cook on low-heat setting for 10 to 11 hours or on high-heat setting for 5 to 5½ hours.

4. Transfer brisket to cutting board, reserving vegetables and cooking liquid. Thinly slice brisket. Arrange brisket and vegetables on serving platter. Cover brisket and vegetables; keep warm. Pour cooking liquid into a glass measuring cup; skim off fat.

5. For sauce, measure cooking liquid; add water if necessary to make 2 cups total liquid. Transfer to small saucepan. In small bowl, combine the ¼ cup cold water and the flour; stir into liquid in saucepan. Cook and stir until thickened and bubbly. Cook and stir for 1 minute longer. Serve sauce with brisket and vegetables. If desired, garnish with whole olives.

Per serving: 287 cal., 11 g total fat (3 g sat. fat), 82 mg chol., 750 mg sodium, 8 g carbo., 6 g fiber, 37 g pro.

MAKE IT A MEAL:
Hot cooked noodles

Lemon-Almond Broccoli (see recipe, page 256)

Parmesan Dinner Rolls (see recipe, page 264)

Purchased apple tart served with ice cream

This recipe makes enough for a party. It also freezes well so you could serve half tonight and save the rest for later.

Beef Brisket with Horseradish

2 **cups water**
1 **large onion, halved and sliced**
2 **tablespoons bottled horseradish**
1 **package (2.4 ounces) beef stew mix (goulash) or 2 packages (1½ ounces each) beef stew seasoning**
1 **beef brisket (4 to 5 pounds)**
½ **teaspoon salt**
¼ **teaspoon black pepper**
½ **cup cold water**
¼ **cup all-purpose flour**

1. In 5-quart slow cooker, stir together the 2 cups water, the onion, horseradish and dry beef stew mix. Trim fat from brisket. Add brisket to slow cooker, slicing in half to fit if necessary. Cover slow cooker; cook on low-heat setting for 7½ hours, turning meat once, if possible.

2. Transfer brisket to cutting board, reserving cooking liquid. Cool brisket slightly.

3. For sauce, strain cooking liquid into bowl; discard solids. Skim fat from cooking liquid. Pour strained cooking liquid into saucepan. Stir in salt and pepper.

4. In measuring cup, whisk together the ½ cup cold water and the flour until smooth. Heat liquid in saucepan over medium heat until simmering. Pour in flour mixture in thin stream, whisking constantly. Simmer, whisking constantly, about 3 minutes or until thickened.

5. Slice brisket. Serve brisket with the sauce.

Per serving: 272 cal., 13 g total fat (6 g sat. fat), 91 mg chol., 449 mg sodium, 6 g carbo., 0 g fiber, 30 g pro.

PREP:
15 minutes

COOKER SIZE:
5-quart

COOK:
7½ hours on low-heat setting

MAKES:
12 servings

FREEZE WITH EASE

MAKE IT A MEAL:
Buttermilk Angel Biscuits (see recipe, page 267)

Frozen mixed vegetables, cooked

Purchased spice cake

PREP:
30 minutes

COOKER SIZE:
3½- to 5-quart

COOK:
8 to 10 hours on low-heat or 4 to 5 hours on high-heat setting

BROIL:
2 minutes

MAKES:
8 sandwiches

FREEZE WITH EASE

MAKE IT A MEAL:

Barbecue potato chips

Creamy Ranch Coleslaw (see recipe, page 250)

Purchased sour cream raisin pie

Muenster cheese gives these orange-spiked corned beef sandwiches a hint of nutty goodness.

Citrus Corned Beef Sandwiches

1 **corned beef brisket with spice packet (2 to 3 pounds)**
1 **cup water**
¼ **cup Dijon mustard**
¼ **teaspoon grated orange zest (optional)**
⅓ **cup orange juice**
4 **teaspoons all-purpose flour**
16 **slices marble rye bread or 8 kaiser rolls, split**
6 **ounces Muenster cheese, cut into 8 slices**
Lettuce leaves (optional)
Orange slices (optional)

1. Trim fat from brisket. Rub brisket all over with spices from spice packet. Place brisket in 3½- to 5-quart slow cooker, cutting to fit if necessary. In small bowl, combine the water and mustard; pour over brisket.

2. Cover slow cooker; cook on low-heat setting for 8 to 10 hours or on high-heat setting for 4 to 5 hours.

3. Remove brisket; cover to keep warm. Skim fat from cooking liquid. Reserve cooking liquid; remove and discard whole spices. For sauce, in small saucepan, stir together orange zest (if desired), orange juice and flour. Gradually stir ¼ cup of the reserved cooking liquid into the mixture in saucepan. Cook and stir until thickened and bubbly. Cook and stir for 1 minute longer. Remove from heat.

4. Heat broiler. Thinly slice brisket across the grain. Place bread or arrange rolls, cut sides up, on unheated rack of broiler pan. Broil 4 to 5 inches from heat for 1 to 2 minutes or until toasted. Remove eight of the bread slices or the roll tops from broiler pan. Place sliced brisket on the remaining bread slices or on bottom halves of rolls. Drizzle about 1 tablespoon of the sauce over meat on each slice of bread or roll. Top with Muenster cheese. Broil 1 to 2 minutes or until cheese melts. If desired, top with lettuce leaves and orange slices. Add remaining bread slices or roll tops.

Per sandwich: 464 cal., 24 g total fat (9 g sat. fat), 99 mg chol., 1,539 mg sodium, 33 g carbo., 0 g fiber, 26 g pro.

PREP:
25 minutes

COOKER SIZE:
5- to 6-quart

COOK:
11 to 12 hours on low-heat or 5½ to 6 hours on high-heat setting, plus 30 to 60 minutes on high-heat setting

MAKES:
8 servings

MAKE IT A MEAL:
Rye bread slices served with butter

Sliced pickled beets

Chocolate chip ice cream topped with hot fudge sauce

On a chilly day, this slow-cooker version of the traditional one-pot meal will warm you through and through.

New England Boiled Dinner

½ cup mayonnaise or salad dressing
½ cup sour cream
2 tablespoons horseradish mustard
2 teaspoons chopped fresh chives
6 medium-size potatoes, peeled and quartered (about 2 pounds)
6 medium-size carrots, cut into 2-inch lengths
1 large onion, quartered
3 cloves garlic, chopped
1 corned beef brisket (3 to 3½ pounds)
2 teaspoons dried dill seeds
1 teaspoon dried rosemary
½ teaspoon salt
2 cans (14 ounces each) beef broth
1 small head cabbage, cut into 8 wedges

1. For sauce, in small bowl, stir together mayonnaise, sour cream, horseradish mustard and chives. Cover; chill in refrigerator for at least 5 hours or up to 24 hours.

2. Meanwhile, in 5- to 6-quart slow cooker, combine potatoes, carrots, onion and garlic. Trim fat from brisket. (Discard seasoning packet if present.) If necessary, cut brisket to fit into the slow cooker. Place brisket on top of vegetables; sprinkle with dill seeds, rosemary and salt. Pour beef broth over brisket.

3. Cover slow cooker; cook on low-heat setting for 11 to 12 hours or on high-heat setting for 5½ to 6 hours.

4. If necessary, raise temperature to high-heat setting. Add cabbage wedges to cooker, pushing them down into liquid. Cover slow cooker; cook for 30 to 60 minutes longer or until cabbage is tender. Transfer brisket to cutting board. Thinly slice brisket across the grain. Place brisket slices on a serving platter. Using a slotted spoon, transfer vegetables to serving platter. Serve sauce with brisket and vegetables.

Per serving: 411 cal., 21 g total fat (6 g sat. fat), 86 mg chol., 648 mg sodium, 26 g carbo., 5 g fiber, 29 g pro.

Carrot and lettuce add a fresh note to this
slow-simmered meat and vegetable combo.

Beef Sirloin Fajitas

1 large onion, cut into thin wedges
2 pounds boneless beef sirloin steak
1 teaspoon ground cumin
1 teaspoon ground coriander
½ teaspoon salt
½ teaspoon black pepper
2 medium sweet red or green peppers, seeded and cut into thin bite-size strips
¼ cup beef broth
8 (7- to 8-inch) whole wheat or plain flour tortillas
1 cup shredded carrots
1 cup coarsely shredded lettuce
   Purchased salsa, guacamole and sour cream

1. Place onion in 3½- or 4-quart slow cooker. Trim fat from steak. Rub one side of the steak with cumin, coriander, salt and black pepper. Cut steak across the grain into thin bite-size strips. Add beef strips to slow cooker. Top with sweet pepper strips. Pour beef broth over mixture in slow cooker.

2. Cover slow cooker; cook on low-heat setting for 7 to 8 hours or on high-heat setting for 3½ to 4 hours.

3. To serve, use a slotted spoon to spoon beef-vegetable mixture onto tortillas. Top each serving with carrots and lettuce. Fold tortillas over. Serve with salsa, guacamole and sour cream.

Per serving: 327 cal., 10 g total fat (3 g sat. fat), 70 mg chol., 642 mg sodium, 22 g carbo., 12 g fiber, 33 g pro.

PREP:
25 minutes

COOKER SIZE:
3½- or 4-quart

COOK:
7 to 8 hours on low-heat or 3½ to 4 hours on high-heat setting

MAKES:
8 servings

KIDS' FAVORITE!

FREEZE WITH EASE

MAKE IT A MEAL:
Tortilla chips served with salsa

Fudge Cookies in Chocolate Cream (see recipe, page 276)

MEATS

25

PREP:
25 minutes

COOKER SIZE:
3½- or 4-quart

COOK:
7 to 9 hours on low-heat or 3½ to 4½ hours on high-heat setting, plus 30 to 40 minutes on high-heat setting

MAKES:
8 servings

MAKE IT A MEAL:
Purchased egg rolls with sweet-and-sour sauce

Fresh fruit plate

Thanks to ready-made stir-fry sauce and a slow cooker, this Asian classic couldn't be any easier!

Lo Mein-Style Beef

 2 **pounds boneless beef sirloin steak, cut 1 inch thick**
 1 **tablespoon vegetable oil**
 1 **large onion, sliced**
 1 **can (8 ounces) sliced water chestnuts, drained**
 1 **jar (4½ ounces) whole mushrooms, drained**
 1 **jar (12.1 ounces) stir-fry sauce**
 1 **tablespoon quick-cooking tapioca**
 1 **package (16 ounces) loose-pack frozen broccoli, cauliflower and carrots**
 ⅓ **cup cashews**
 12 **ounces lo mein noodles, cooked following package directions**

1. Trim fat from steak. Cut steak into 1-inch pieces. In large skillet, brown meat, half at a time, in hot oil. Drain off fat. Set aside.

2. Place onion in 3½- or 4-quart slow cooker. Add beef, water chestnuts and mushrooms. In small bowl, stir together stir-fry sauce and tapioca. Pour over mixture in slow cooker.

3. Cover slow cooker; cook on low-heat setting for 7 to 9 hours or on high-heat setting for 3½ to 4½ hours.

4. If necessary, raise temperature to high-heat setting. Stir in frozen vegetables. Cover slow cooker; cook for 30 to 40 minutes longer or until vegetables are crisp-tender. Stir in the cashews. Serve the beef mixture over hot cooked lo mein noodles.

Per serving: 447 cal., 11 g total fat (2 g sat. fat), 95 mg chol., 995 mg sodium, 52 g carbo., 4 g fiber, 35 g pro.

Tender steak, noodles and a wonderfully rich sauce—based on cream of celery soup—team up in this main dish that the family will love.

Round Steak With Herbs

- 1 **boneless beef round steak, cut ¾ inch thick (about 2 pounds)**
- 1 **medium-size onion, sliced**
- 1 **can (10¾ ounces) condensed cream of celery soup**
- ½ **teaspoon dried oregano**
- ¼ **teaspoon dried thyme**
- ¼ **teaspoon black pepper**
- 4 **cups hot cooked noodles**
   Fresh oregano sprigs (optional)

1. Trim fat from steak. Cut steak into six serving-size pieces. Place onion in 3½- or 4-quart slow cooker; place steak pieces on onion. In small bowl, combine cream of celery soup, dried oregano, thyme and pepper; pour over steak.

2. Cover slow cooker; cook on low-heat setting for 10 to 12 hours or on high-heat setting for 5 to 6 hours.

3. To serve, cut meat into bite-size pieces. Toss meat and sauce with hot noodles. If desired, garnish each serving with fresh oregano.

· ·

Per serving: 392 cal., 11 g total fat (3 g sat. fat), 113 mg chol., 483 mg sodium, 32 g carbo., 2 g fiber, 39 g pro.

PREP:
15 minutes

COOKER SIZE:
3½- or 4-quart

COOK:
10 to 12 hours on low-heat or 5 to 6 hours on high-heat setting

MAKES:
6 servings

KIDS' FAVORITE!

MAKE IT A MEAL:
Purchased Waldorf salad

Purchased lemon meringue pie

COOKER SIZE:
3½- or 4-quart

COOK:
8 to 10 hours on low-heat or 4 to 5 hours on high-heat setting

MAKES:
8 servings

FREEZE WITH EASE

MAKE IT A MEAL:

Mashed potatoes

Steamed green beans

Pistachio ice cream topped with toasted sliced almonds

If you like, stir a couple of tablespoons of red wine into the beef mixture just before serving to add even more depth of flavor.

Mushroom and Onion Sauced Round Steak

2 pounds boneless beef round steak, cut ¾ inch thick
1 tablespoon vegetable oil
2 medium-size onions, sliced
3 cups sliced fresh mushrooms
1 jar (12 ounces) beef gravy
1 envelope (1.1 ounces) mushroom gravy mix

1. Trim fat from steak. Cut steak into eight serving-size pieces. In large skillet, brown meat, half at a time, in hot oil. Drain off fat. Set aside.

2. Place onions in 3½- or 4-quart slow cooker. Add steak and mushrooms. In small bowl, stir together beef gravy and dry gravy mix. Pour over mixture in cooker.

3. Cover slow cooker; cook on low-heat setting for 8 to 10 hours or on high-heat setting for 4 to 5 hours.

Per serving: 194 cal., 7 g total fat (2 g sat. fat), 57 mg chol., 479 mg sodium, 7 g carbo., 1 g fiber, 24 g pro.

PREP:
20 minutes

COOKER SIZE:
6-quart

COOK:
7 hours on low-heat or 4 hours on high-heat setting

MAKES:
6 servings

FREEZE WITH EASE

MAKE IT A MEAL:
Sliced mangoes

While this dish can be cooked on the low-heat setting, the texture and color will be better if it is cooked on the high-heat setting.

Asian Pepper Steak

- 2 pounds beef round steak, cut against the grain into ¾-inch-thick slices
- 3 large sweet red or green peppers, seeded and cut into ¾-inch-thick slices
- 2 large onions, halved and cut into ½-inch-thick slices
- 1 can (14½ ounces) stewed tomatoes, drained
- 3 cloves garlic, chopped
- 1 cup beef broth
- ¼ cup light soy sauce
- 2 tablespoons rice wine vinegar
- 2 tablespoons cornstarch
- 1 teaspoon sugar
- 1 can (8 ounces) bamboo shoots, drained
  Hot cooked rice

1. Coat 6-quart slow cooker with nonstick cooking spray. Add steak; top with peppers, onions, tomatoes and garlic.

2. In a small bowl, whisk together beef broth, soy sauce, vinegar, cornstarch and sugar. Pour over beef and vegetables. Sprinkle bamboo shoots over mixture in slow cooker.

3. Cover slow cooker; cook on low-heat setting for 7 hours or on high-heat setting for 4 hours. Serve with hot cooked rice.

Per serving: 415 cal., 6 g total fat (2 g sat. fat), 86 mg chol., 851 mg sodium, 49 g carbo., 5 g fiber, 41 g pro.

For authentic old-world flavor, top these herbed beef sandwiches with roasted red peppers.

Italian Beef Sandwiches

- **6** ounces beef flank steak
- **½** teaspoon dried oregano
  Dash crushed red pepper
- **1** clove garlic, chopped
- **½** cup low-sodium tomato juice
- **¼** cup bottled roasted red pepper strips (optional)
- **2** 4-inch-long pieces French bread, split and toasted
- **¼** cup shredded provolone cheese (1 ounce)

1. Trim fat from steak. Place steak in 1½-quart slow cooker, cutting to fit if necessary. Sprinkle with oregano, crushed red pepper and garlic. Pour tomato juice over mixture in slow cooker.

2. Cover slow cooker; cook on low-heat setting for 7 to 8 hours or on high-heat setting for 3½ to 4 hours. If no heat setting is available, cook for 6 to 7 hours.

3. Remove steak from cooker, reserving cooking liquid. Using two forks, pull meat apart into shreds. If desired, stir roasted pepper strips into shredded meat. Place shredded meat on bottoms of toasted French bread pieces. Drizzle enough of the cooking liquid over meat to moisten. Sprinkle with shredded cheese. Cover with tops of French bread pieces.

Per sandwich: 302 cal., 11 g total fat (5 g sat. fat), 44 mg chol., 442 mg sodium, 23 g carbo., 2 g fiber, 26 g pro.

PREP:
15 minutes

COOKER SIZE:
1½-quart

COOK:
7 to 8 hours on low-heat or 3½ to 4 hours on high-heat setting

MAKES:
2 sandwiches

FREEZE WITH EASE

MAKE IT A MEAL:
Purchased gelatin salad

Purchased double chocolate biscotti

MEATS

31

PREP:
30 minutes

COOKER SIZE:
6- to 7-quart

COOK:
9 to 10 hours on low-heat or 4½ to 5 hours on high-heat setting

MAKES:
8 servings

MAKE IT A MEAL:
Sourdough bread slices with butter

Prepared butterscotch pudding

Couscous flecked with almonds and olives provides a soothing counterpoint to the spicy short ribs, chickpeas and vegetables.

Moroccan-Style Short Ribs

 1 tablespoon dried thyme
 1 teaspoon salt
 1 teaspoon ground ginger
 1 teaspoon black pepper
 ½ teaspoon ground cinnamon
 3½ pounds beef short ribs
 2 tablespoons extra-virgin olive oil
 3 cups beef broth
 1 can (16 ounces) chickpeas, drained and rinsed
 1 can (14½ ounces) diced tomatoes
 1 large onion, cut into thin wedges
 1 medium-size fennel bulb, trimmed and cut into thin wedges
 1 cup chopped carrots
 4 cloves garlic, chopped
 1 package (10 ounces) quick-cooking couscous
 ½ cup sliced almonds, toasted
 ½ cup pitted kalamata olives, halved

1. In small bowl, combine thyme, salt, ginger, pepper and cinnamon; rub evenly over short ribs. In large skillet, brown short ribs, half at a time, in hot oil over medium-high heat. Drain off fat. In 6- to 7-quart slow cooker, combine beef broth, chickpeas, tomatoes with their juices, onion, fennel, carrots and garlic; top with short ribs.

2. Cover slow cooker; cook on low-heat setting for 9 to 10 hours or on high-heat setting for 4½ to 5 hours.

3. Using a slotted spoon, transfer short ribs and vegetables to a serving dish. If desired, spoon some of the cooking liquid over the short ribs and vegetables.

4. Meanwhile, prepare the couscous following the package directions. Stir in toasted almonds and olives. Serve couscous with short ribs and vegetables.

Per serving: 441 cal., 17 g total fat (4 g sat. fat), 46 mg chol., 1,064 mg sodium, 45 g carbo., 6 g fiber, 26 g pro.

Beef short ribs make the perfect comfort meal. These ribs get special treatment with five-spice powder and other Asian flavorings.

Ginger-Orange-Glazed Short Ribs

3 **pounds beef short ribs**
1 **large red onion, cut into wedges**
1 **cup orange marmalade**
⅓ **cup water**
2 **tablespoons rice vinegar**
1 **tablespoon soy sauce**
2 **teaspoons five-spice powder**
2 **teaspoons finely chopped fresh ginger**
½ **to 1½ teaspoons chile oil**
2 **cloves garlic, chopped**

1. Trim fat from short ribs. Set short ribs aside. Place red onion in a 3½- to 5-quart slow cooker. Add short ribs. In medium bowl, combine orange marmalade, the water, rice vinegar, soy sauce, five-spice powder, ginger, chile oil and garlic. Reserve ⅔ cup of the marmalade mixture for sauce; cover and chill. Pour the remaining marmalade mixture over ribs and onion in cooker.

2. Cover slow cooker; cook on low-heat setting for 11 to 12 hours or on high-heat setting for 5½ to 6 hours.

3. For sauce, in small saucepan, bring the reserved ⅔ cup marmalade mixture to a boil; reduce heat. Boil gently, uncovered, for 5 minutes. Remove short ribs and onion from cooker; discard cooking liquid. Serve ribs and onion with sauce.

Per serving: 452 cal., 12 g total fat (5 g sat. fat), 64 mg chol., 385 mg sodium, 58 g carbo., 1 g fiber, 29 g pro.

PREP:
20 minutes

COOKER SIZE:
3½- to 5-quart

COOK:
11 to 12 hours on low-heat or 5½ to 6 hours on high-heat setting

MAKES:
4 to 6 servings

FREEZE WITH EASE

MAKE IT A MEAL:
Hot cooked brown rice

Steamed baby carrots

Lemon-Spice Cupcakes (see recipe, page 271)

MEATS

33

PREP:
25 minutes

COOKER SIZE:
5-quart

COOK:
9 hours on low-heat or 6 hours on high-heat setting

MAKES:
6 servings

Beef ribs take on an exotic flavor in this Korean-inspired dish. To keep it simple, use purchased shredded carrots.

Korean-Style Short Ribs

½ cup reduced-sodium soy sauce
⅓ cup packed light brown sugar
2 tablespoons dark Asian sesame oil
2 tablespoons rice vinegar
2 tablespoons finely chopped fresh ginger
4 cloves garlic, chopped
½ teaspoon red pepper flakes
5 pounds beef short ribs
3 tablespoons cornstarch mixed with 3 tablespoons cold water
1½ cups shredded carrots
3 scallions, trimmed and thinly sliced
1 tablespoon sesame seeds, toasted if desired
Hot cooked rice

1. In small bowl, combine soy sauce, brown sugar, sesame oil, vinegar, ginger, garlic and red pepper flakes.

2. Place ribs in a 5-quart slow cooker; add soy sauce mixture. Cover slow cooker; cook on low-heat setting for 9 hours or on high-heat setting for 6 hours.

3. Transfer ribs to a platter. For sauce, skim fat from cooking liquid. Pour cooking liquid into saucepan. Stir cornstarch mixture into cooking liquid. Bring to a boil over high heat; cook and stir about 2 minutes or until thickened. Stir in carrots. Top ribs with sauce, scallions and sesame seeds. Serve with hot cooked rice.

Per serving: 518 cal., 23 g total fat (8 g sat. fat), 92 mg chol., 829 mg sodium, 43 g carbo., 2 g fiber, 33 g pro.

MAKE IT A MEAL:
Steamed fresh snow peas

Lemon sorbet with crushed amaretti cookies

The refreshing topper for these shanks is called gremolata, typically a mixture of parsley, lemon and garlic.

Wine-Braised Beef Shanks

- **1 cup dry red wine or beef broth**
- **2 tablespoons tomato paste**
- **1 teaspoon dried basil**
- **½ teaspoon dried marjoram**
- **3 cloves garlic, chopped**
- **1 teaspoon salt**
- **1 cup ½-inch pieces rutabaga**
- **4 beef shank cross cuts, about 1½ inches thick (about 3 pounds)**
- **2 leeks, quartered lengthwise and cut crosswise into 1-inch pieces**
- **2 cups sliced carrots**
- **2 tablespoons all-purpose flour**
- **2 tablespoons cold water**

Gremolata:
- **¼ cup fresh parsley leaves**
- **1 tablespoon grated lemon zest**
- **1 clove garlic**

1. In 5½- or 6-quart slow cooker, combine wine or broth, tomato paste, basil, marjoram, garlic and salt. Add rutabaga; top with beef shank cross cuts, leeks and carrots.

2. Cover slow cooker; cook on low-heat setting for 9 hours or on high-heat setting for 5 hours or until beef is fork-tender.

3. Transfer beef and vegetables to serving dish. For sauce, pour cooking liquid into small saucepan. Skim off fat. In small bowl, whisk together flour and the cold water until smooth. Whisk in a little of the cooking liquid. Whisk flour mixture into cooking liquid in saucepan. Cook and stir over medium heat about 3 minutes or until mixture bubbles and thickens. Spoon over meat and vegetables.

4. Gremolata: Finely chop together parsley, lemon zest and garlic. Sprinkle over meat and vegetables.

· ·

Per serving: 541 cal., 23 g total fat (9 g sat. fat), 99 mg chol., 844 mg sodium, 23 g carbo., 4 g fiber, 49 g pro.

PREP:
25 minutes

COOKER SIZE:
5½- or 6-quart

COOK:
9 hours on low-heat or 5 hours on high-heat setting

MAKES:
4 servings

FREEZE WITH EASE

MAKE IT A MEAL:
Hot buttered egg noodles

Purchased lemon cake served with whipped cream and fresh blueberries

COOKER SIZE:
3½- or 4-quart

COOK:
8 to 9 hours on low-heat or 3½ to 4½ hours on high-heat setting, plus 30 minutes on high-heat setting

MAKES:
6 servings

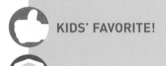

KIDS' FAVORITE!

FREEZE WITH EASE

MAKE IT A MEAL:
Refrigerated biscuits, baked

Easy Apple-Cherry Crisp (see recipe, page 280)

Depending on how much heat you like, choose sweet or hot Hungarian paprika.

Beef Goulash With Noodles

1½ pounds beef stew meat cubes
2 medium carrots, bias-cut into ½-inch-thick slices
2 medium onions, thinly sliced
3 cloves garlic, chopped
1¼ cups beef broth
1 can (6 ounces) tomato paste
1 tablespoon Hungarian paprika
1 teaspoon grated lemon zest
½ teaspoon salt
½ teaspoon caraway seeds
¼ teaspoon black pepper
1 bay leaf
1 sweet red or green pepper, seeded and cut into bite-size strips
  Hot cooked noodles
  Sour cream or yogurt
  Hungarian paprika (optional)

1. In 3½- or 4-quart slow cooker, combine beef, carrots, onions and garlic. In small bowl, combine beef broth, tomato paste, the 1 tablespoon paprika, the lemon zest, salt, caraway seeds, black pepper and bay leaf. Stir into vegetable and beef mixture in slow cooker.

2. Cover slow cooker; cook on low-heat setting for 8 to 9 hours or on high-heat setting for 3½ to 4½ hours.

3. If necessary, raise temperature to high-heat setting. Stir in sweet pepper strips. Cover slow cooker; cook for 30 minutes longer. Remove and discard bay leaf. Serve with hot cooked noodles. Top with sour cream or yogurt. If desired, sprinkle with additional paprika.

Per serving: 356 cal., 11 g total fat (4 g sat. fat), 85 mg chol., 678 mg sodium, 33 g carbo., 4 g fiber, 32 g pro.

PREP:
15 minutes

COOKER SIZE:
3½- or 4-quart

COOK:
10 to 12 hours on low-heat or 5 to 6 hours on high-heat setting

MAKES:
6 servings

FREEZE WITH EASE

MAKE IT A MEAL:

Hot cooked noodles

Buttered peas

Purchased pound cake served with lemon curd and blueberries

This hearty stew is the perfect way to use a small amount of leftover red wine.

Beef in Red Wine Gravy

1½ **pounds beef stew meat**
 1 **cup coarsely chopped onion**
 2 **beef bouillon cubes or one envelope (½ of a 2-ounce package) onion soup mix**
 3 **tablespoons cornstarch**
   Salt
   Black pepper
1½ **cups dry red wine**

1. Cut meat into 1-inch pieces. In 3½- or 4-quart slow cooker, place beef and onion. Add bouillon cubes or dry onion soup mix. Sprinkle with cornstarch, salt and black pepper. Pour red wine over mixture in cooker.

2. Cover slow cooker; cook on low-heat setting for 10 to 12 hours or on high-heat setting for 5 to 6 hours.

Per serving: 215 cal., 4 g total fat (1 g sat. fat), 64 mg chol., 405 mg sodium, 7 g carbo., 1 g fiber, 26 g pro.

Feta cheese, oregano and dried tomatoes load this meat loaf with Mediterranean flavor.

Mediterranean Meat Loaf

- 1 **egg**
- 2 **tablespoons milk**
- ½ **cup packaged plain dry bread crumbs**
- ½ **teaspoon salt**
- ½ **teaspoon dried oregano**
- ¼ **teaspoon black pepper**
- 2 **cloves garlic, chopped**
- 1½ **pounds lean ground beef (93% lean)**
- ½ **cup crumbled feta cheese (2 ounces)**
- ¼ **cup oil-pack dried tomatoes, drained and snipped**
- 3 **tablespoons bottled pizza or pasta sauce**

1. In medium-size bowl, combine egg and milk; beat with a fork. Stir in bread crumbs, salt, oregano, pepper and garlic. Add ground beef, feta cheese and dried tomatoes; mix well. Shape meat mixture into a 5-inch round loaf.

2. Tear off an 18-inch square piece of heavy aluminum foil; cut into thirds. Fold each piece of foil into thirds lengthwise. Crisscross foil strips and place meat loaf in center of foil strips. Bringing up strips, transfer loaf and foil to a 3½- or 4-quart slow cooker (leave foil strips under loaf).

3. Press loaf away from side of slow cooker. Fold strips down, leaving loaf exposed. Spread pizza sauce over loaf.

4. Cover slow cooker; cook on low-heat setting for 7 to 8 hours or on high-heat setting for 3½ to 4 hours.

5. Using foil strips, carefully lift meat loaf from slow cooker. Discard foil strips.

Per serving: 387 cal., 18 g total fat (7 g sat. fat), 158 mg chol., 1,030 mg sodium, 14 g carbo., 1 g fiber, 40 g pro.

PREP:
20 minutes

COOKER SIZE:
3½- or 4-quart

COOK:
7 to 8 hours on low-heat or 3½ to 4 hours on high-heat setting

MAKES:
4 to 6 servings

FREEZE WITH EASE

MAKE IT A MEAL:
Volcano Mashed Potatoes (see recipe, page 262)

Refrigerated corn bread twists, baked

Purchased red velvet cupcakes

PREP:
25 minutes

COOKER SIZE:
6-quart

COOK:
8½ hours plus 30 minutes on low-heat or 5½ hours plus 30 minutes on high-heat setting

MAKES:
12 servings

FREEZE WITH EASE

MAKE IT A MEAL:
Crusty French bread

Shortbread Brownies
(see recipe, page 270)

All you need to round out this dinner is some crusty bread. If your family likes things spicy, pass extra red pepper flakes at the table.

Beef Ragù with Beans

2 large carrots, peeled and coarsely chopped
2 large ribs celery, coarsely chopped
1 large onion, coarsely chopped
4 cloves garlic, peeled
2 pounds lean ground beef (93% lean)
2 cans (14½ ounces each) diced tomatoes
2 cups beef broth
1 can (15½ ounces) white cannellini beans, drained and rinsed
3 tablespoons tomato paste
2 teaspoons sugar
1½ teaspoons dried Italian seasoning
1½ teaspoons salt
1 teaspoon red pepper flakes
For serving:
2 pounds rigatoni, cooked following package directions
Grated Parmesan cheese (optional)

1. In food processor, combine carrots, celery, onion and garlic; cover and pulse until finely chopped.

2. In large bowl, combine finely chopped vegetables, ground beef, diced tomatoes with their juices, broth, beans, tomato paste and sugar. Add half of each: Italian seasoning, salt and red pepper flakes. Stir until combined. Transfer beef mixture to 6-quart slow cooker.

3. Cover slow cooker; cook on low-heat setting for 8½ hours or on high-heat setting for 5½ hours.

4. Stir in the remaining Italian seasoning, salt and red pepper flakes. Cover slow cooker; cook for 30 minutes longer.

5. For serving: Toss beef sauce with cooked rigatoni. If desired, sprinkle with Parmesan cheese.

. . . .

Per serving: 460 cal., 7 g total fat (2 g sat. fat), 41 mg chol., 778 mg sodium, 70 g carbo., 6 g fiber, 29 g pro.

A can of tomato soup brings just the right consistency and homey tomato flavor to these perfectly seasoned sloppy-Joe-style sandwiches.

Cheeseburger Sandwiches

PREP:
20 minutes

COOKER SIZE:
3½- or 4-quart

COOK:
6 to 8 hours on low-heat or 3 to 4 hours on high-heat setting, plus 5 to 10 minutes on low-heat setting

MAKES:
12 to 15 sandwiches

2½ pounds lean ground beef (93% lean)
1 can (10¾ ounces) condensed tomato soup
1 large onion, finely chopped
¼ cup water
2 tablespoons tomato paste
1 tablespoon Worcestershire sauce
1 tablespoon yellow mustard
2 teaspoons dried Italian seasoning
2 cloves garlic, chopped
¼ teaspoon black pepper
6 ounces American cheese, cut into cubes
12 to 15 hamburger buns, split and toasted

1. In large skillet, cook ground beef until cooked through, stirring to break into bite-size pieces. Drain off fat. Transfer meat to 3½- or 4-quart slow cooker. Stir tomato soup, onion, the water, tomato paste, Worcestershire sauce, mustard, Italian seasoning, garlic and pepper into meat in slow cooker.

2. Cover slow cooker; cook on low-heat setting for 6 to 8 hours or on high-heat setting for 3 to 4 hours. If necessary, lower temperature to low-heat setting.

3. Stir in American cheese. Cover slow cooker; cook for 5 to 10 minutes longer or until cheese is melted. Serve meat-cheese mixture on toasted hamburger buns.

Per sandwich: 344 cal., 13 g total fat (6 g sat. fat), 64 mg chol., 662 mg sodium, 28 g carbo., 1 g fiber, 27 g pro.

KIDS' FAVORITE!

MAKE IT A MEAL:
Frozen French fries, baked

Broccoli-Cheddar Salad (see recipe, page 251)

Chocolate chip cookie ice cream sandwiches

PREP:
25 minutes

COOKER SIZE:
5- to 6-quart

COOK:
8 to 10 hours on low-heat or 4 to 5 hours on high-heat setting

MAKES:
12 to 14 sandwiches

FREEZE WITH EASE

MAKE IT A MEAL:

Potato chips

Sliced peaches

Purchased white cake with chocolate frosting

These standout sandwiches get their firepower from a Scotch bonnet chile and black pepper.

Hot and Spicy Sloppy Joes

2 **pounds ground beef**
4 **medium-size onions, cut into strips**
4 **medium-size green peppers, seeded and cut into strips**
2 **medium-size sweet red peppers, seeded and cut into strips**
1 **cup ketchup**
¼ **cup apple cider vinegar**
1 **fresh Scotch bonnet chile, seeded and finely chopped,* or ¼ teaspoon cayenne pepper**
1 **tablespoon chili powder**
½ **teaspoon salt**
½ **teaspoon black pepper**
12 **to 14 hoagie rolls or hot dog buns, split and toasted**

1. In very large skillet, cook ground beef and onion until ground beef is cooked through and onion is tender, stirring to break ground beef into bite-size pieces. Drain off fat.

2. In 5- to 6-quart slow cooker, combine ground beef mixture, green pepper strips, red pepper strips, ketchup, vinegar, chile or cayenne pepper, chili powder, salt and black pepper.

3. Cover slow cooker; cook on low-heat setting for 8 to 10 hours or on high-heat setting for 4 to 5 hours. Serve in toasted rolls or buns.

· ·

Per sandwich: 592 cal., 18 g total fat (6 g sat. fat), 48 mg chol., 1,051 mg sodium, 83 g carbo., 6 g fiber, 27 g pro.

*Note: Because chiles contain volatile oils that can burn your skin and eyes, avoid direct contact with them as much as possible. When working with chiles, wear plastic or rubber gloves. If your bare hands do touch the chiles, wash your hands and nails well with soap and warm water.

PREP:
30 minutes

COOKER SIZE:
3½- or 4-quart

COOK:
5 to 6 hours on low-heat or 2½ to 3 hours on high-heat setting

MAKES:
6 servings

KIDS' FAVORITE!

FREEZE WITH EASE

MAKE IT A MEAL:

Mixed greens with honey-mustard dressing

Root Beer Float Cake (see recipe, page 272)

If there are any of these zesty meatballs left over, reheat them and serve them in hoagie buns for a sensational sandwich.

Home-Style Italian Meatballs

2 eggs
⅓ cup soft bread crumbs
¼ cup finely chopped fresh parsley
¼ cup grated Parmesan cheese
¼ cup finely chopped onion
1 teaspoon salt
1 clove garlic, minced
½ teaspoon crushed red pepper
1 pound ground beef
8 ounces lean ground pork
1 tablespoon extra-virgin olive oil
1 jar (26 to 28 ounces) marinara pasta sauce
½ cup water
  Hot cooked pasta
  Grated Parmesan cheese (optional)

1. In large bowl, beat eggs with a fork. Stir in bread crumbs, parsley, the ¼ cup Parmesan cheese, the onion, salt, garlic and crushed red pepper. Add ground beef and ground pork; mix just until combined. Using a scant ¼ cup mixture per meatball, form mixture into 18 meatballs.

2. In very large skillet, brown meatballs in hot oil. Drain off fat. Transfer meatballs to 3½- or 4-quart slow cooker. Pour marinara sauce and the water over meatballs.

3. Cover slow cooker; cook on low-heat setting for 5 to 6 hours or on high-heat setting for 2½ to 3 hours.

4. Serve meatballs and sauce over hot cooked pasta. If desired, sprinkle with additional Parmesan cheese.

Per serving: 526 cal., 19 g total fat (6 g sat. fat), 139 mg chol., 1,099 mg sodium, 56 g carbo., 4 g fiber, 31 g pro.

Italian-style frozen meatballs and cream of mushroom soup with roasted garlic team up for this sumptuously saucy and super-easy dish.

Meatballs in Tomato Gravy

1 can (10¾ ounces) condensed cream of mushroom with roasted garlic soup
1 cup water
1 medium onion, chopped
1 can (4 ounces) sliced mushrooms, drained
½ cup snipped dried tomatoes (not oil-pack)
½ teaspoon dried basil
½ teaspoon dried oregano
⅛ teaspoon black pepper
2 packages (16 ounces each) frozen cooked Italian-style meatballs, thawed
1 package (16 ounces) heat-and-serve cooked polenta
Fresh basil sprigs (optional)

1. In 3½- or 4-quart slow cooker, combine cream of mushroom soup, the water, onion, mushrooms, tomatoes, basil, oregano and pepper. Stir in meatballs.

2. Cover slow cooker; cook on low-heat setting for 5 to 6 hours or on high-heat setting for 2½ to 3 hours.

3. Heat broiler. Cut polenta into eight slices. Coat unheated rack of broiler pan with nonstick cooking spray. Place polenta slices on prepared pan. Broil 4 to 5 inches from heat about 2 minutes or just until slices start to brown, turning once. Serve polenta with meatballs and gravy. If desired, garnish with fresh basil.

. . . .

Per serving: 440 cal., 28 g total fat (13 g sat. fat), 74 mg chol., 1,442 mg sodium, 24 g carbo., 7 g fiber, 22 g pro.

PREP:
20 minutes

COOKER SIZE:
3½- or 4-quart

COOK:
5 to 6 hours on low-heat or 2½ to 3 hours on high-heat setting

BROIL:
2 minutes

MAKES:
8 servings

FREEZE WITH EASE

MAKE IT A MEAL:
Steamed broccoli

Frozen strawberry yogurt served in waffle cones

PREP:
20 minutes

COOKER SIZE:
3½- or 4-quart

COOK:
8 to 10 hours on low-heat or 4 to 5 hours on high-heat setting

MAKES:
4 servings

FREEZE WITH EASE

MAKE IT A MEAL:
Mesclun salad served with oil and vinegar

Steamed green beans

Wheat bread slices served with butter

Purchased macadamia-white chocolate chunk cookies

The savory flavors of fennel-infused roast and luscious mashed sweet potatoes make a winning combination.

Italian Pork with Mashed Sweet Potatoes

1 teaspoon fennel seeds, crushed
½ teaspoon garlic powder
½ teaspoon dried oregano
½ teaspoon paprika
¼ teaspoon salt
¼ teaspoon black pepper
1 boneless pork shoulder roast (1½ to 2 pounds)
1 pound sweet potatoes, peeled and cut into 1-inch pieces
1 cup chicken broth

1. In small bowl, combine fennel seeds, garlic powder, oregano, paprika, salt and pepper. Trim fat from roast. Rub roast all over with fennel seed mixture. If necessary, cut roast to fit into 3½- or 4-quart slow cooker. Set aside.

2. Place sweet potatoes in slow cooker. Top with roast. Pour chicken broth over mixture in slow cooker.

3. Cover slow cooker; cook on low-heat setting for 8 to 10 hours or on high-heat setting for 4 to 5 hours.

4. Transfer roast to cutting board; slice roast. Using a slotted spoon, transfer sweet potatoes to medium-size bowl; reserve cooking liquid. Using a potato masher, mash sweet potatoes, adding enough of the cooking liquid, if necessary, to moisten. Serve meat with mashed sweet potatoes.

Per serving: 356 cal., 14 g total fat (5 g sat. fat), 115 mg chol., 525 mg sodium, 21 g carbo., 3 g fiber, 35 g pro.

PREP:
30 minutes

COOKER SIZE:
5- to 6-quart

COOK:
11 to 12 hours on low-heat or 5½ to 6 hours on high-heat setting

MAKES:
8 to 10 servings

Perfect for a meal on a blustery day, this pork dish gets its flavor from a wine sauce that's loaded with garlic, rosemary and thyme.

Pork with Parsnips and Pears

1 boneless pork top loin roast (single loin) (2½ to 3 pounds)
1 tablespoon vegetable oil
1½ pounds parsnips and/or carrots, peeled and cut into 1½- to 2-inch pieces*
2 medium-size pears, peeled, quartered and cored (stems intact, if desired) (about 2 cups)
2 tablespoons quick-cooking tapioca
6 cloves garlic, chopped
1 teaspoon dried rosemary
1 teaspoon dried thyme
½ teaspoon salt
¼ teaspoon black pepper
½ cup port wine or apple juice
  Salt
  Black pepper

1. In large skillet, brown roast on all sides in hot oil. Place parsnips and/or carrots and pears in 5- to 6-quart slow cooker; sprinkle with tapioca. Place roast on top of vegetables and pears; sprinkle roast with garlic, rosemary, thyme, the ½ teaspoon salt and the ¼ teaspoon pepper. Pour wine over mixture in slow cooker.

2. Cover slow cooker; cook on low-heat setting for 11 to 12 hours or on high-heat setting for 5½ to 6 hours.

3. Transfer roast to serving platter, reserving cooking liquid; using a slotted spoon, transfer vegetables and pears to serving platter.

4. Slice roast. Season cooking liquid to taste with additional salt and pepper; serve with roast, vegetables and pears.

. . . .

Per serving: 340 cal., 9 g total fat (3 g sat. fat), 78 mg chol., 292 mg sodium, 27 g carbo., 6 g fiber, 32 g pro.

*Note: Cut any thick parsnip or carrot pieces in half lengthwise.

MAKE IT A MEAL:
Steamed Brussels sprouts

Refrigerated biscuits, baked

Coffee ice cream served with pirouette cookies

The sweet-sour flavor comes from a mix of apples, vinegar, wine, brown sugar, caraway seeds and allspice.

Pork Roast and Cabbage

1 boneless pork loin roast (about 2¼ pounds)
¾ teaspoon salt
¼ teaspoon black pepper
6 cups shredded red cabbage (about 1 pound)
1 pound tiny new red potatoes (halve larger ones)
2 Granny Smith apples, cored and cubed
1 cup apple cider vinegar
½ cup dry white wine
½ cup packed dark brown sugar
1 teaspoon caraway seeds
¼ teaspoon ground allspice

1. Season roast with ¼ teaspoon of the salt and the pepper.

2. Add the cabbage to a 6-quart slow cooker. Top with potatoes; spread apple cubes on top in an even layer. Add roast.

3. In small bowl, whisk together apple cider vinegar, wine, brown sugar, caraway seeds and allspice. Pour around roast. Cover slow cooker; cook on low-heat setting for 7 hours or on high-heat setting for 4½ hours.

4. Transfer roast to cutting board. Cover roast loosely with aluminum foil and let stand for 5 minutes. Season cabbage mixture with the remaining ½ teaspoon salt. Transfer cabbage mixture to a platter, reserving cooking liquid in slow cooker. Thickly slice roast; arrange on top of cabbage. Serve warm, drizzled with reserved cooking liquid.

· ·

Per serving: 421 cal., 10 g total fat (3 g sat. fat), 100 mg chol., 403 mg sodium, 43 g carbo., 4 g fiber, 36 g pro.

PREP:
25 minutes

COOKER SIZE:
6-quart

COOK:
7 hours on low-heat or 4½ hours on high-heat setting

STAND:
5 minutes

MAKES:
6 servings

MAKE IT A MEAL:
Sliced Havarti cheese on whole wheat crackers

Purchased fudge brownies with cream cheese frosting

PREP:
30 minutes

COOKER SIZE:
3½- to 5-quart

COOK:
9 to 11 hours on low-heat or 4½ to 5½ hours on high-heat setting

MAKES:
8 servings

FREEZE WITH EASE

MAKE IT A MEAL:

Mixed greens and vegetable salad

Purchased hard breadsticks

Purchased chocolate cream pie

A savory quintet of anise, fennel, caraway, dill and celery seeds creates a crustlike coating for this ultra-tender roast.

Seed-Coated Pork Roast

1 boneless pork shoulder roast (2½ to 3 pounds)
1 tablespoon soy sauce
2 teaspoons anise seeds, crushed
2 teaspoons fennel seeds, crushed
2 teaspoons caraway seeds, crushed
2 teaspoons dill seeds, crushed
2 teaspoons celery seeds, crushed
⅔ cup apple cider or apple juice
½ cup beef broth
1 tablespoon cornstarch

1. If necessary, cut roast to fit into 3½- to 5-quart slow cooker. Remove netting from roast, if present. Trim fat from roast. Brush soy sauce over surface of roast. On a large piece of aluminum foil, combine anise seeds, fennel seeds, caraway seeds, dill seeds and celery seeds. Roll roast in seeds to coat evenly.

2. Place roast in the slow cooker. Pour ⅓ cup of the apple cider or juice and the beef broth around roast.

3. Cover slow cooker; cook on low-heat setting for 9 to 11 hours or on high-heat setting for 4½ to 5½ hours.

4. Transfer roast to serving platter. For gravy, strain cooking liquid and skim off fat; transfer cooking liquid to small saucepan. In small bowl, combine the remaining ⅓ cup apple cider or juice and the cornstarch; add to cooking liquid in saucepan. Cook and stir until mixture is thickened and bubbly. Cook and stir for 2 minutes longer. Pass gravy with pork.

Per serving: 220 cal., 9 g total fat (3 g sat. fat), 92 mg chol., 285 mg sodium, 5 g carbo., 0 g fiber, 29 g pro.

PREP:
15 minutes

COOKER SIZE:
6-quart

COOK:
6 hours on low-heat or 3 hours on high-heat setting

STAND:
10 minutes

MAKES:
8 servings

A touch of vinegar and pumpkin pie spice enhances the peach sauce.

Pork Roast with Peach Sauce

1 boneless pork loin roast (about 3 pounds), tied
¼ teaspoon onion salt
¼ teaspoon black pepper
1 can (15¼ ounces) sliced peaches in heavy syrup
½ cup chili sauce
⅓ cup packed light-brown sugar
3 tablespoons apple cider vinegar
1 teaspoon pumpkin pie spice
1 tablespoon cornstarch mixed with 2 tablespoons cold water

1. Coat a 6-quart slow cooker with nonstick cooking spray. Place roast in slow cooker; sprinkle with onion salt and black pepper.

2. Drain peaches, reserving the syrup. In small bowl, whisk together reserved peach syrup, chili sauce, brown sugar, apple cider vinegar and pumpkin pie spice. Pour over roast; scatter peach slices over roast.

3. Cover slow cooker; cook on low-heat setting for 6 hours or on high-heat setting for 3 hours.

4. Transfer roast to cutting board. Cover loosely with aluminum foil and let stand for 10 minutes. Using a slotted spoon, remove peach slices and reserve. Pour cooking liquid into small saucepan; bring to a boil over medium-high heat. Stir in cornstarch mixture; cook and stir about 30 seconds or until sauce thickens.

5. To serve, slice roast and place reserved peach slices on top. Serve with sauce on the side.

Per serving: 363 cal., 12 g total fat (5 g sat. fat), 103 mg chol., 368 mg sodium, 25 g carbo., 1 g fiber, 37 g pro.

MAKE IT A MEAL:
Hot cooked noodles

Home Run Garlic Rolls (see recipe, page 263)

Chocolate ice cream topped with crushed shortbread cookies

For sandwiches, shred this flavorful pork and serve on buns topped with Muenster cheese.

Sweet 'n' Tangy Pork

1 medium-size onion, finely chopped
1 boneless pork shoulder roast (about 3 pounds)
1 cup apple cider or apple juice
¾ cup ketchup
½ cup bottled chili sauce
¼ cup honey
¼ cup red-wine vinegar
2 tablespoons Worcestershire sauce
3 cloves garlic, finely chopped
¼ teaspoon red pepper flakes (optional)
¼ cup cornstarch
   Kaiser rolls, split (optional)

1. Spread onion over bottom of 5- or 5½-quart slow cooker. Place roast on top of the onion. In small bowl, stir together ½ cup of the apple cider, the ketchup, chili sauce, honey, red-wine vinegar, Worcestershire sauce, garlic and red pepper flakes (if desired); pour evenly over roast.

2. Cover slow cooker; cook on low-heat setting for 10 to 11 hours or on high-heat setting for 5 to 6 hours or until the pork is fork tender.

3. Transfer roast to platter, reserving onion mixture in slow cooker. Cover roast with aluminum foil; keep warm. If necessary, raise temperature to high-heat setting.

4. In small cup, stir together the remaining ½ cup apple cider and the cornstarch until well blended and smooth. Stir into onion mixture in slow cooker. Cover slow cooker; cook on high-heat setting about 15 minutes or until thickened. Thinly slice roast; spoon onion mixture over top. If desired, serve in Kaiser rolls.

· ·

Per serving: 382 cal., 16 g total fat (6 g sat. fat), 104 mg chol., 632 mg sodium, 29 g carbo., 1 g fiber, 30 g pro.

PREP:
20 minutes

COOKER SIZE:
5- or 5½-quart

COOK:
10 to 11 hours on low-heat or 5 to 6 hours on high-heat setting, plus 15 minutes on high-heat setting

MAKES:
8 servings

KIDS' FAVORITE!

FREEZE WITH EASE

MAKE IT A MEAL:
Volcano Mashed Potatoes (see recipe, page 262)

Steamed fresh broccoli

Butter pecan ice cream

PREP:
15 minutes

COOKER SIZE:
3½- or 4-quart

COOK:
7 to 8 hours on low-heat or 3½ to 4 hours on high-heat setting

STAND:
5 minutes

MAKES:
8 servings

This delicious main dish is especially easy since you don't brown the chops.

Cranberry Orange Pork Chops

1 package (16 ounces) packaged peeled baby carrots
8 boneless pork chops, cut about ¾ inch thick (about 1¾ pounds)
1 package (12 ounces) cranberry-orange sauce
2 tablespoons quick-cooking tapioca
1 teaspoon finely grated lemon zest
¼ teaspoon ground cardamom
3 fresh plums and/or apricots, pitted and sliced (about 8 ounces)
   Hot cooked couscous or rice
   Chopped fresh parsley (optional)

1. Place carrots in a 3½- or 4-quart slow cooker. Top with pork chops.

2. In medium-size bowl, combine cranberry-orange sauce, tapioca, lemon zest and cardamom; pour over pork chops.

3. Cover slow cooker; cook on low-heat setting for 7 to 8 hours or on high-heat setting for 3½ to 4 hours. Stir in sliced fruit. Turn off slow cooker; cover and let stand for 5 minutes. Serve with hot cooked couscous or rice. If desired, sprinkle with parsley.

Per serving: 323 cal., 4 g total fat (1 g sat. fat), 55 mg chol., 73 mg sodium, 47 g carbo., 3 g fiber, 22 g pro.

MAKE IT A MEAL:
Quick and Cheesy Veggies (see recipe, page 253)

Purchased white chocolate chip cookies

PREP:
25 minutes

COOKER SIZE:
3½- or 4-quart

COOK:
5 to 6 hours on low-heat or 2½ to 3 hours on high-heat setting

MAKES:
4 servings

MAKE IT A MEAL:
Broccoli-Cheddar Salad (see recipe, page 251)

Rye bread slices served with butter

Purchased cream puffs filled with pistachio pudding

Although six cloves may seem like a lot of garlic, slow simmering mellows them for a pleasantly mild flavor.

Pork Chops with Mashed Vegetables

    4   bone-in pork rib chops, cut ¾ inch thick (about 2 pounds)
    1   envelope (½ of a 2.4-ounce package) garlic and herb soup and dip mix
    1   pound Yukon gold potatoes, peeled if desired and cut into 1-inch chunks
    ¾   pound parsnips, peeled and cut into 1-inch chunks (about 2 medium)
    6   cloves garlic, peeled
 1¼   cups chicken broth
    2   tablespoons butter
    ⅓   cup half-and-half or light cream
        Salt
        Black pepper
    1   tablespoon chopped fresh parsley (optional)

1. Place pork chops on a tray or large plate. Rub pork chops all over with the dry soup and dip mix. Set aside (the mix will moisten as the chops stand).

2. In 3½- or 4-quart slow cooker, combine potatoes, parsnips and garlic; pour chicken broth over. Place chops on top of vegetables in slow cooker.

3. Cover slow cooker; cook on low-heat setting for 5 to 6 hours or on high-heat setting for 2½ to 3 hours.

4. Transfer chops to serving platter; cover and keep warm. Drain vegetables, reserving cooking liquid. Mash vegetables with a potato masher. Add butter. Stir in half-and-half and, if necessary, enough of the reserved cooking liquid to make mixture light and fluffy. Season vegetable mixture to taste with salt and pepper. Discard remaining cooking liquid. If desired, sprinkle with parsley. Serve vegetable mixture with pork chops.

Per serving: 440 cal., 16 g total fat (8 g sat. fat), 94 mg chol., 1,224 mg sodium, 41 g carbo., 5 g fiber, 33 g pro.

For 5- to 6-quart slow cooker: Use 6 bone-in pork rib chops (about 3 pounds), 2 pounds Yukon gold potatoes, 1 pound parsnips (about 3 medium), 8 cloves garlic, 1 can (14 ounces) chicken broth, 3 tablespoons butter, ½ cup half-and-half or light cream and 2 tablespoons parsley (optional). Leave amount of the soup and dip mix the same. Makes 6 servings.
Per serving: 462 cal., 16 g total fat (8 g sat. fat), 94 mg chol., 924 mg sodium, 45 g carbo., 6 g fiber, 34 g pro.

Meaty pork ribs, parsnips and carrots marry beautifully with fruits and aromatic spices.

Spiced Country Ribs

½ pound medium-size carrots, chopped
½ pound parsnips, peeled and chopped
1 large onion, coarsely chopped
1 cup dried apricots (6-ounce package), each apricot halved
½ cup pitted prunes (3½ ounces), each prune halved
2 cloves garlic, chopped
1 cinnamon stick (3-inch)
4 whole cloves
4 whole allspice berries
1 square (6-inch) 100%-cotton cheesecloth
3 pounds pork country-style ribs
1½ cups chicken broth
½ cup orange juice
2 tablespoons balsamic vinegar
1 teaspoon salt
⅛ teaspoon black pepper
¼ cup all-purpose flour

1. In 5- or 5½-quart slow cooker, layer carrots, parsnips, onion, apricots, prunes and garlic. Place the cinnamon stick, cloves and allspice on clean cheesecloth square; tie the ends together with clean kitchen string to form a bundle. Place the ribs and spice packet on top of the vegetables.

2. In 2-cup measure, stir together 1 cup of the chicken broth, the orange juice, balsamic vinegar, salt and pepper until well blended; pour evenly over ribs.

3. Cover slow cooker; cook on low-heat setting for 10 to 11 hours or on high-heat setting for 5 to 6 hours or until the vegetables and ribs are tender.

4. Transfer ribs to large platter, reserving vegetable mixture in slow cooker; cover with aluminum foil and keep warm. Remove and discard spice packet. If necessary, raise temperature to high-heat setting.

5. In 1-cup measure, stir together the remaining ½ cup chicken broth and the flour until well blended and smooth. Stir into vegetable mixture in the slow cooker. Cover slow cooker; cook on high-heat setting for 5 to 10 minutes longer or until liquid is thickened. Spoon vegetable mixture onto platter with ribs.

· ·

Per serving: 622 cal., 23 g total fat (8 g sat. fat), 133 mg chol., 1,094 mg sodium, 61 g carbo., 9 g fiber, 45 g pro.

PREP:
40 minutes

COOKER SIZE:
5- or 5½-quart

COOK:
10 to 11 hours on low-heat or 5 to 6 hours on high-heat setting, plus 5 to 10 minutes on high-heat setting

MAKES:
4 servings

FREEZE WITH EASE

MAKE IT A MEAL:
Golden Green Bean Crunch (see recipe, page 254)

French bread slices served with butter

Assorted fresh berries topped with whipped cream and crushed shortbread cookies

MEATS

57

PREP:
30 minutes

COOKER SIZE:
5-quart

COOK:
7 hours on low-heat or 5½ hours on high-heat setting

MAKES:
8 servings

FREEZE WITH EASE

MAKE IT A MEAL:
Fresh baby carrots served with blue cheese dressing

Purchased tiramisu

Pork Ragù with Pasta

3 teaspoons vegetable oil
2 carrots, sliced
2 ribs celery, sliced
1 large onion, chopped
4 cloves garlic, chopped
2 pounds boneless pork country-style ribs
1 cup beef broth
2 tablespoons tomato paste
1 can (28 ounces) crushed tomatoes
1½ teaspoons dried Italian seasoning
½ teaspoon black pepper
½ teaspoon salt
Hot cooked bowtie pasta

1. In large skillet, heat 1½ teaspoons of the oil over high heat. Add carrots, celery, onion and garlic; cook and stir about 5 minutes or until vegetables are browned. Remove from skillet. Add the remaining 1½ teaspoons oil and the pork ribs; cook about 5 minutes or until ribs are browned, turning to brown evenly.

2. Transfer ribs to 5-quart slow cooker. Top with the vegetables. In small bowl, stir together beef broth and tomato paste; add to slow cooker. Stir in tomatoes with their juices, half of the Italian seasoning and half of the pepper. Cook on low-heat setting for 7 hours or on high-heat setting for 5½ hours.

3. Skim off fat. Using a slotted spoon, remove pork ribs to a platter, reserving cooking liquid; let pork ribs cool. Stir the remaining Italian seasoning, the remaining pepper and the salt into cooking liquid in slow cooker. Using two forks, pull meat apart into shreds. Stir shredded pork into reserved cooking liquid in slow cooker. Serve over hot cooked pasta.

Per serving: 459 cal., 13 g total fat (4 g sat. fat), 73 mg chol., 503 mg sodium, 55 g carbo., 6 g fiber, 32 g pro.

Easier than stir-fry, this Chinese-inspired supper is destined to become a mainstay in your list of fuss-free weeknight dinners.

Pineapple-Ginger Pork

¾ **pound boneless pork shoulder roast**
1 **tablespoon vegetable oil**
⅓ **cup chicken broth**
2 **tablespoons quick-cooking tapioca**
2 **tablespoons reduced-sodium soy sauce**
1 **tablespoon oyster sauce (optional)**
½ **teaspoon finely chopped fresh ginger**
1 **can (8 ounces) pineapple chunks packed in juice**
2 **medium-size carrots, cut into ½-inch pieces**
1 **small onion, cut into 1-inch pieces**
1 **can (8 ounces) sliced water chestnuts, drained**
¾ **cup fresh snow pea pods, halved diagonally**
Hot cooked rice

1. Trim fat from roast. Cut roast into 1-inch pieces. In large skillet, brown roast, half at a time, in hot oil over medium heat. Drain off fat. Set aside.

2. In 1½- or 2-quart slow cooker, combine chicken broth, tapioca, soy sauce, oyster sauce (if desired) and ginger. Drain pineapple, reserving juice. Cover and chill pineapple until needed. Stir pineapple juice into broth mixture. Stir in carrot pieces, onion pieces and water chestnuts. Add meat to mixture in slow cooker.

3. Cover slow cooker; cook on low-heat setting for 6 to 8 hours or on high-heat setting for 3 to 4 hours. If no heat setting is available, cook for 4½ to 5 hours.

4. If possible, raise temperature to high-heat setting (or if no heat setting is available, continue cooking). Stir in drained pineapple and pea pods. Cover slow cooker; cook for 10 to 15 minutes longer or until pea pods are crisp-tender.

5. Serve pork mixture over hot cooked rice.

. . . .

Per serving: 770 cal., 23 g total fat (5 g sat. fat), 110 mg chol., 870 mg sodium, 104 g carbo., 4 g fiber, 43 g pro.

PREP:
20 minutes

COOKER SIZE:
1½- or 2-quart

COOK:
6 to 8 hours on low-heat or 3 to 4 hours on high-heat setting, plus 10 to 15 minutes on high-heat setting

MAKES:
2 servings

MAKE IT A MEAL:
Frozen egg rolls, heated

Amaretti cookies

PREP:
20 minutes

COOKER SIZE:
3½- or 4-quart

COOK:
6½ to 7 hours on low-heat or 3½ to 4 hours on high-heat setting, plus 10 to 15 minutes on high-heat setting

MAKES:
6 servings

 FREEZE WITH EASE

 MAKE IT A MEAL:
Purchased pot stickers

Fortune cookies

Dried Japanese somen noodles have a very fine texture similar to that of angel hair pasta. Look for them wherever Asian foods are sold.

Lo Mein-Style Pork

1½ pounds boneless pork shoulder
2 cups loose-pack frozen sliced carrots
1 jar (12 ounces) teriyaki glaze
2 medium-size onions, cut into wedges
1 cup thinly bias-sliced celery
1 can (8 ounces) sliced water chestnuts, drained
1 can (5 ounces) sliced bamboo shoots, drained
1 teaspoon finely chopped fresh ginger
1 package (6 ounces) frozen pea pods
1 cup small broccoli flowerets
9 ounces somen noodles
½ cup cashews

1. Trim fat from pork. Cut pork into ¾-inch pieces. In 3½- or 4-quart slow cooker, combine pork, frozen carrots, teriyaki glaze, onions, celery, water chestnuts, bamboo shoots and ginger.

2. Cover slow cooker; cook on low-heat setting for 6½ to 7 hours or on high-heat setting for 3½ to 4 hours.

3. If necessary, raise temperature to high-heat setting. Stir frozen pea pods and broccoli into mixture in slow cooker. Cover slow cooker; cook for 10 to 15 minutes longer or until broccoli is crisp-tender.

4. Meanwhile, cook noodles following package directions; drain. Serve pork mixture over noodles. Sprinkle each serving with cashews.

Per serving: 509 cal., 12 g total fat (3 g sat. fat), 73 mg chol., 2,274 mg sodium, 66 g carbo., 6 g fiber, 33 g pro.

PREP:
25 minutes

COOKER SIZE:
5- or 5½-quart

COOK:
5 hours plus
30 minutes on high-heat setting

MAKES:
8 servings

KIDS' FAVORITE!

FREEZE WITH EASE

MAKE IT A MEAL:
Baby carrots and celery sticks served with purchased guacamole and salsa

Frozen vanilla yogurt served with baked cinnamon-sugar pita chips

Serve these amazingly flavorful pork shoulder tacos with sour cream or add other toppers such as scallions, ripe olives, salsa or diced tomatoes.

Mexican Pulled Pork Tacos

- 1 medium-size onion, coarsely chopped
- 1 boneless pork shoulder roast or picnic roast (about 3½ pounds)
- 1 medium-size sweet red pepper, seeded and cut into ¼-inch squares
- 1 medium-size green pepper, seeded and cut into ¼-inch squares
- 1 can (14½ ounces) jalapeño-flavor diced tomatoes
- 2 teaspoons ground cumin
- 1½ teaspoons garlic salt
- 1½ teaspoons dried oregano
- ½ teaspoon cayenne pepper
- 1 can (11 ounces) corn kernels, drained
- 1 jar (4 ounces) diced green chiles, drained
- 3 tablespoons tomato paste
- 16 (about 6-inch) corn tortillas, warmed following package directions
  Sour cream (optional)

1. In 5- or 5½-quart slow cooker, layer chopped onion, pork roast, sweet red pepper and green pepper. In medium-size bowl, stir together tomatoes with their juices, cumin, garlic salt, oregano and cayenne pepper. Pour evenly over the mixture in the cooker. Add corn and chiles.

2. Cover slow cooker; cook on high-heat setting for 5 hours. Transfer roast to cutting board; cover and keep warm.

3. Remove 1½ cups of the cooking liquid from slow cooker and discard. Stir the tomato paste into the vegetable mixture in the slow cooker. Cover slow cooker; cook on high-heat setting for 30 minutes longer.

4. Slice roast. Using two forks, pull roast apart into shreds. Add shredded pork to vegetable mixture in slow cooker; heat through.

5. To serve, wrap the pork mixture in the warmed corn tortillas, dividing the mixture equally among the tortillas. If desired, serve with sour cream.

Per serving: 590 cal., 32 g total fat (11 g sat. fat), 138 mg chol., 836 mg sodium, 35 g carbo., 5 g fiber, 40 g pro.

In the eastern part of North Carolina, the home of vinegar-sauced barbecued pork, coleslaw is a must-have accompaniment.

Pork and Slaw Barbecue Rolls

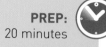

PREP:
20 minutes

COOKER SIZE:
4- to 6-quart

COOK:
10 to 12 hours on low-heat or 5 to 6 hours on high-heat setting

MAKES:
16 servings

- 1 pork shoulder roast or pork shoulder blade Boston roast (Boston butt) (4 to 5 pounds)
- ¾ cup apple cider vinegar
- 2 tablespoons brown sugar
- ½ teaspoon salt
- ½ teaspoon crushed red pepper
- ¼ teaspoon black pepper
- 16 kaiser rolls, split and toasted
  Coleslaw

1. Place roast in 4- to 6-quart slow cooker, cutting to fit if necessary. In small bowl, combine apple cider vinegar, brown sugar, salt, red pepper and black pepper; pour over roast.

2. Cover slow cooker; cook on low-heat setting for 10 to 12 hours or on high-heat setting for 5 to 6 hours.

3. Transfer roast to cutting board, reserving cooking liquid in slow cooker. Skim fat from cooking liquid. When cool enough to handle, cut roast off bones and coarsely chop. In medium-size bowl, combine roast and as much of the reserved cooking liquid as desired to moisten. Arrange pork on roll bottoms. Top with coleslaw. Add roll tops.

- -

Per serving: 272 cal., 6 g total fat (2 g sat. fat), 41 mg chol., 563 mg sodium, 34 g carbo., 1 g fiber, 18 g pro.

FREEZE WITH EASE

MAKE IT A MEAL:
Barbecue-flavor potato chips

Purchased baked beans

Root Beer Float Cake (see recipe, page 272)

PREP:
25 minutes

COOKER SIZE:
3½- or 4-quart

COOK:
10 to 11 hours on low-heat or 5 to 5½ hours on high-heat setting

STAND:
1 hour

MAKES:
6 to 8 servings

FREEZE WITH EASE

MAKE IT A MEAL:
Greens and Berry Salad (see recipe, page 247)

Purchased individual shortcakes topped with canned peach pie filling and drizzled with caramel sauce

Tender red beans go from tame to sassy when mixed with cumin. Serve lime wedges on the side: A spritz of citrus is a nice twist.

Red Beans over Spanish Rice

  2 **cups dry red beans or dry red kidney beans**
  5 **cups cold water**
  ¾ **pound boneless pork shoulder, cut into 1-inch pieces**
  1 **tablespoon vegetable oil**
2½ **cups chopped onions**
  6 **cloves garlic, chopped**
  1 **tablespoon ground cumin**
  4 **cups water**
  1 **package (6¾ ounces) Spanish rice mix**
     Fresh jalapeño chiles, sliced* and/or lime wedges (optional)

1. Rinse beans; drain. In large saucepan, combine beans and the 5 cups cold water. Bring to a boil; reduce heat. Simmer, uncovered, for 10 minutes. Remove from heat. Cover; let stand for 1 hour. (Or omit simmering; in a covered saucepan, soak beans in the 5 cups cold water for 6 to 8 hours or overnight.) Rinse and drain beans.

2. Meanwhile, in large skillet, cook pork, half at a time, in hot oil until browned. Drain off fat. Lightly coat 3½- or 4-quart slow cooker with nonstick cooking spray. Combine the beans, pork, onions, garlic and cumin in the slow cooker. Pour in the 4 cups water; stir.

3. Cover slow cooker; cook on low-heat setting for 10 to 11 hours or on high-heat setting for 5 to 5½ hours.

4. Before serving, prepare rice mix following package directions. Using a slotted spoon, remove beans from slow cooker, reserving cooking liquid in slow cooker. Serve beans over cooked rice. If desired, spoon some of the reserved cooking liquid over each serving. If desired, garnish with chile slices and/or lime wedges.

Per serving: 344 cal., 1 g total fat (0 g sat. fat), 0 mg chol., 450 mg sodium, 68 g carbo., 17 g fiber, 19 g pro.

*Note: Because chiles contain volatile oils that can burn your skin and eyes, avoid direct contact with them as much as possible. When working with chiles, wear plastic or rubber gloves. If your bare hands do touch the chiles, wash your hands and nails well with soap and warm water.

PREP:
25 minutes

COOKER SIZE:
1½- or 2-quart

COOK:
8 to 10 hours on low-heat or 4 to 5 hours on high-heat setting

MAKES:
2 servings

FREEZE WITH EASE

MAKE IT A MEAL:

Potato chips with onion-flavor sour cream dip

Fruit and Broccoli Salad (see recipe, page 248)

Vanilla ice cream topped with sliced bananas and hot fudge sauce

A creamy lime dressing provides a cooling complement to gutsy jerk-seasoned pork.

Jerk Pork Wraps With Lime Mayo

- 1 boneless pork shoulder roast (about 1 pound)
- 1 tablespoon Jamaican jerk seasoning
- ¼ teaspoon dried thyme
- ½ cup water
- 2 teaspoons lime juice
- 4 (8-inch) flour tortillas
- 4 lettuce leaves (optional)
- ½ cup chopped mango or pineapple
- ¼ cup chopped sweet red or green pepper
  Lime Mayo (recipe follows)
  Scallion tops (optional)

1. Trim fat from roast. Rub roast all over with jerk seasoning and thyme. Place roast in 1½- or 2-quart slow cooker. Pour the water around roast in slow cooker.

2. Cover slow cooker; cook on low-heat setting for 8 to 10 hours or on high-heat setting for 4 to 5 hours. If no heat setting is available, cook for 7½ to 8 hours.

3. Remove roast from slow cooker; discard cooking liquid. Using two forks, pull roast apart into shreds. Transfer shredded pork to a medium bowl. Drizzle lime juice over pork; toss to combine.

4. If desired, line tortillas with lettuce leaves. Spoon pork mixture onto tortillas just below the centers. Add mango and sweet pepper. Top with Lime Mayo. Fold the bottom edge of each tortilla up and over filling. Fold in opposite sides. If desired, serve on scallion tops.

Lime Mayo: In small bowl, stir together ¼ cup light or regular mayonnaise, 2 tablespoons finely chopped red onion, ¼ teaspoon finely shredded lime peel, 2 teaspoons lime juice, and 1 clove garlic, minced. Cover and chill until ready to serve.

Per serving: 632 cal., 29 g total fat (8 g sat. fat), 158 mg chol., 1,082 mg sodium, 42 g carbo., 2 g fiber, 50 g pro.

If you like dishes with a fiery kick, use hot-style Italian sausage instead of sweet.

Sausage and Mushroom Pasta

- ¾ **pound sweet Italian sausage (remove casings, if present)**
- 2 **cups sliced fresh cremini and/or button mushrooms**
- 1 **can (28 ounces) crushed tomatoes**
- 1 **can (8 ounces) tomato sauce**
- 1 **can (6 ounces) tomato paste**
- 1 **medium-size onion, chopped**
- ⅔ **cup water**
- 2 **cloves garlic, chopped**
- 1 **tablespoon sugar**
- 1 **teaspoon dried rosemary**
- ¼ **teaspoon black pepper**
  Hot cooked spaghetti or fettuccine
  Freshly shredded or grated Parmesan cheese (optional)

1. In large skillet, cook sausage until cooked through, stirring to break into bite-size pieces. Drain off fat. In 3½- or 4-quart slow cooker, combine mushrooms, crushed tomatoes with their juices, tomato sauce, tomato paste, onion, the water, garlic, sugar, rosemary and pepper. Stir in cooked sausage.

2. Cover slow cooker; cook on low-heat setting for 6 to 8 hours or on high-heat setting for 3 to 4 hours.

3. Serve sausage mixture with hot cooked spaghetti or fettuccine. If desired, sprinkle with Parmesan cheese.

Per serving: 410 cal., 14 g total fat (5 g sat. fat), 38 mg chol., 830 mg sodium, 50 g carbo., 5 g fiber, 18 g pro.

PREP:
30 minutes

COOKER SIZE:
3½- or 4-quart

COOK:
6 to 8 hours on low-heat or 3 to 4 hours on high-heat setting

MAKES:
6 to 8 servings

KIDS' FAVORITE!

FREEZE WITH EASE

MAKE IT A MEAL:
Iceberg lettuce served with ranch dressing and croutons

Refrigerated soft breadsticks, baked

Easy Apple-Cherry Crisp (see recipe, page 280)

MEATS

PREP:
15 minutes

COOKER SIZE:
1½-quart

COOK:
1½ hours on low-heat setting, plus 30 to 60 minutes on high-heat setting

MAKES:
6 servings

KIDS' FAVORITE!

MAKE IT A MEAL:
Greens and Berry Salad (see recipe, page 247)

Refrigerated soft breadsticks, baked

Purchased German chocolate cake

A topping of smoked Gouda cheese and ham makes these baked taters hearty and delicious.

Ham and Broccoli Potatoes

1 **can (10¾ ounces) condensed cream of celery soup or cream of chicken soup**
2 **cups shredded smoked Gouda cheese (8 ounces)**
8 **ounces cooked ham, diced**
1 **package (10 ounces) frozen cut broccoli, thawed**
6 **medium potatoes, baked and split***

1. In 1½-quart slow cooker, combine cream of celery soup, Gouda cheese, and ham.

2. Cover slow cooker; cook on low-heat setting for 1½ hours. If no heat setting is available, cook for 1½ hours.

3. If possible, raise temperature to high-heat setting (or if no heat setting is available, continue cooking). Stir in thawed broccoli. Cover slow cooker; cook for 30 to 60 minutes longer or until broccoli is tender and heated through. Stir before serving. Spoon ham mixture over baked potatoes.

Per serving: 339 cal., 15 g total fat (9 g sat. fat), 53 mg chol., 1,469 mg sodium, 34 g carbo., 5 g fiber, 18 g pro.

*Note: Bake the potatoes while the ham-and-broccoli mixture cooks. To bake potatoes, heat oven to 425°. Scrub potatoes and pat dry. Prick potatoes with a fork. (If desired, for soft skins, rub potatoes with solid vegetable shortening or wrap each potato in aluminum foil.) Bake potatoes at 425° for 40 to 60 minutes or until tender. Roll each potato gently under your hand. Using a knife, cut an X in top of each potato. Press in and up on ends of each potato.

For 3½- or 4-quart slow cooker: Double the recipe. Prepare as directed, except cook soup, cheese and ham on low-heat setting for 3 hours. Raise temperature to high-heat setting and continue as directed.

PREP:
15 minutes

COOKER SIZE:
3½- or 4-quart

COOK:
7 to 8 hours on low-heat or 3½ to 4 hours on high-heat setting

MAKES:
6 servings

MAKE IT A MEAL:
Steamed fresh asparagus spears

Refrigerated garlic herb breadsticks, baked

Shortbread Brownies (see recipe, page 270)

This golden casserole is like macaroni and cheese without the macaroni. Kids will like its rosy ham, soft potatoes and rich cheese flavor.

Ham and Potatoes au Gratin

2 packages (5½ ounces each) au gratin potato mix
2 cups diced cooked ham
¼ cup bottled roasted red peppers, drained and chopped
3 cups water
1 can (10¾ ounces) condensed Cheddar cheese soup
Chopped fresh chives (optional)

1. Lightly coat 3½- or 4-quart slow cooker with nonstick cooking spray. Place dry au gratin potato mixes with contents of seasoning packets, the ham and roasted red peppers in the prepared slow cooker. In large bowl, stir together the water and Cheddar cheese soup. Pour over potato mixture in cooker.

2. Cover slow cooker; cook on low-heat setting for 7 to 8 hours or on high-heat setting for 3½ to 4 hours. If desired, sprinkle with chives.

Per serving: 255 cal., 7 g total fat (3 g sat. fat), 29 mg chol., 2,087 mg sodium, 45 g carbo., 3 g fiber, 15 g pro.

Poultry and Fish

78 Easy Chicken Rarebit

Cacciatore-Style Chicken 82

104 Turkey and Pasta Primavera

Cajun Shrimp and Rice 114

Chicken, turkey and seafood dishes go back to basics—and travel the globe in this inspired chapter of slow cooker dishes. Discover dishes starring potatoes and carrots alongside intriguing recipes using curry, Greek seasoning and cumin.

PREP:
25 minutes

COOKER SIZE:
5-quart

COOK:
5½ hours on low-heat or 3½ hours on high-heat setting

MAKES:
4 servings

Button mushrooms can be substituted for the cremini in this creamy tarragon-infused chicken dish.

Mustard-Tarragon Chicken

  6 ounces fresh cremini mushrooms, cleaned
  4 pounds chicken quarters, skin removed
  1 medium-size onion, sliced
  ½ cup chicken broth
  2 tablespoons plus 1 teaspoon Dijon mustard
  ¾ teaspoon dried tarragon
  ½ teaspoon salt
  ¼ teaspoon black pepper
  ½ cup heavy cream
1½ tablespoons cornstarch
  1 teaspoon chopped fresh tarragon
    Hot cooked rice

1. Remove stems from mushrooms; cut mushrooms into quarters. Place chicken, onion and mushrooms in 5-quart slow cooker. In small bowl, whisk together chicken broth, the 2 tablespoons mustard, the dried tarragon, salt and pepper. Pour over chicken; stir to combine.

2. Cover slow cooker; cook on low-heat setting for 5½ hours or on high-heat setting for 3½ hours.

3. Using a slotted spoon, remove chicken and vegetables; set aside. Strain cooking liquid into a saucepan. Skim off fat. Bring to a boil over high heat, stirring constantly. In small bowl, whisk together the remaining 1 teaspoon mustard, the heavy cream and cornstarch; whisk into boiling liquid. Cook about 3 minutes or until mixture is thickened. Stir in fresh tarragon. Pour over chicken. Serve with hot cooked rice.

Per serving: 694 cal., 27 g total fat (10 g sat. fat), 231 mg chol., 835 mg sodium, 39 g carbo., 3 g fiber, 69 g pro.

MAKE IT A MEAL:
Brownie and Walnut Pie (see recipe, page 274)

Capers and olives are what give this sauce its spirited Southern Italian angle. If you prefer, substitute your favorite pasta for the orzo.

Saucy Chicken With Capers

2½ to 3 pounds meaty chicken pieces (breast halves, thighs and drumsticks), skin removed
¼ teaspoon salt
⅛ teaspoon black pepper
1 jar (26 ounces) pasta sauce with olives
2 tablespoons drained capers
1 teaspoon grated lemon zest
   Hot cooked orzo pasta

1. Place chicken pieces in 3½- or 4-quart slow cooker. Sprinkle chicken with salt and pepper. In medium-size bowl, stir together pasta sauce, capers and lemon zest; pour over chicken in slow cooker.

2. Cover slow cooker; cook on low-heat setting for 6 to 7 hours or on high-heat setting for 3 to 3½ hours.

3. Serve chicken and sauce over hot cooked orzo.

- -

Per serving: 315 cal., 8 g total fat (2 g sat. fat), 77 mg chol., 678 mg sodium, 30 g carbo., 3 g fiber, 30 g pro.

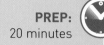

PREP:
20 minutes

COOKER SIZE:
3½- or 4-quart

COOK:
6 to 7 hours on low-heat or 3 to 3½ hours on high-heat setting

MAKES:
6 servings

FREEZE WITH EASE

MAKE IT A MEAL:
Steamed fresh broccoli with lemon wedges

Neapolitan ice cream

PREP:
20 minutes

COOKER SIZE:
3½- to 6-quart

COOK:
6 to 7 hours on low-heat or 3 to 3½ hours on high-heat setting

MAKES:
4 to 6 servings

This no-fuss chicken dish is easy to put together and even easier to enjoy. Freshly grated Parmesan cheese makes it special.

Easy Italian Chicken

½ of a medium-size head cabbage, cut into wedges (about ¾ pound)
1 medium-size onion, sliced and separated into rings
1 jar (4½ ounces) sliced mushrooms, drained
2 tablespoons quick-cooking tapioca
2 to 2½ pounds meaty chicken pieces (breast halves, thighs and drumsticks), skin removed
2 cups purchased meatless spaghetti sauce
Freshly grated Parmesan cheese

1. In 3½- to 6-quart slow cooker, combine cabbage wedges, onion and mushrooms. Sprinkle tapioca over vegetables. Place chicken pieces on vegetables. Pour spaghetti sauce over chicken.

2. Cover slow cooker; cook on low-heat setting for 6 to 7 hours or on high-heat setting for 3 to 3½ hours. Transfer to a serving platter. Sprinkle each serving with Parmesan cheese.

Per serving: 300 cal., 9 g total fat (3 g sat. fat), 94 mg chol., 662 mg sodium, 24 g carbo., 4 g fiber, 35 g pro.

MAKE IT A MEAL:
Hot cooked pasta

Parmesan Dinner Rolls (see recipe, page 264)

Mixed greens with raspberry vinaigrette

Purchased cannoli

POULTRY AND FISH

74

COOKER SIZE:
4- to 5-quart

COOK:
5 to 6 hours on low-heat or 2½ to 3 hours on high-heat setting

MAKES:
6 servings

MAKE IT A MEAL:
Buttermilk Angel Biscuits (see recipe, page 267)

Tossed green salad

Purchased miniature apple tarts

Lemon zest, basil, rosemary, parsley and a crumble of feta cheese flavor this tender chicken. It's lovely with a salad—and bread.

Feta-Topped Chicken

- 1 **teaspoon grated lemon zest**
- 1 **teaspoon dried basil**
- 1 **teaspoon dried rosemary**
- ½ **teaspoon salt**
- ¼ **teaspoon black pepper**
- 2 **cloves garlic, chopped**
- 3½ **to 4 pounds meaty chicken pieces (breast halves, thighs and drumsticks), skin removed**
- ½ **cup reduced-sodium chicken broth**
- ½ **cup crumbled feta cheese (2 ounces)**
- 2 **tablespoons chopped fresh flat-leaf parsley leaves**

1. In small bowl, combine lemon zest, basil, rosemary, salt, pepper and garlic. Rub lemon zest mixture onto all sides of chicken pieces. Place chicken pieces in 4- to 5-quart slow cooker. Pour chicken broth over chicken in slow cooker.

2. Cover slow cooker; cook on low-heat setting for 5 to 6 hours or on high-heat setting for 2½ to 3 hours.

3. Transfer chicken to a serving platter. Discard cooking liquid. Sprinkle chicken with feta cheese and parsley.

· ·

Per serving: 179 cal., 6 g total fat (2 g sat. fat), 97 mg chol., 425 mg sodium, 1 g carbo., 0 g fiber, 29 g pro.

Cream cheese makes the tantalizing sauce for this japaleño-seasoned chicken extra rich.

Jalapeño and Bacon Chicken

- 6 **bone-in chicken breast halves (about 3 pounds total), skin removed**
- 1 **tablespoon chili powder**
- ½ **cup reduced-sodium chicken broth**
- 2 **tablespoons lemon juice**
- ⅓ **cup bottled pickled jalapeño chile slices, drained**
- 1 **tablespoon cornstarch**
- 1 **tablespoon cold water**
- 1 **package (8 ounces) cream cheese, softened and cut into cubes**
- 2 **strips bacon, crisp-cooked, drained and crumbled (optional)**

1. Sprinkle chicken with chili powder. Place chicken, bone sides down, in 4½- to 6-quart slow cooker. Pour chicken broth and lemon juice around chicken in cooker. Top with jalapeño chile slices.

2. Cover slow cooker; cook on low-heat setting for 5 to 6 hours or on high-heat setting for 2½ to 3 hours.

3. Transfer chicken and jalapeño chile slices to a serving platter, reserving cooking liquid. Cover chicken with aluminum foil to keep warm.

4. If necessary, raise temperature to high-heat setting. For sauce, in small bowl, combine cornstarch and the cold water; stir into cooking liquid in slow cooker. Add cream cheese, whisking until combined. Cover slow cooker; cook about 15 minutes longer or until thickened. If desired, sprinkle chicken with bacon. Serve sauce with chicken.

- -

Per serving: 307 cal., 15 g total fat (9 g sat. fat), 127 mg chol., 334 mg sodium, 4 g carbo., 1 g fiber, 37 g pro.

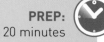

PREP:
20 minutes

COOKER SIZE:
4½- to 6-quart

COOK:
5 to 6 hours on low-heat or 2½ to 3 hours on high-heat setting, plus 15 minutes on high-heat setting

MAKES:
6 servings

MAKE IT A MEAL:
Rice Pilaf with Oranges and Nuts (see recipe, page 260)

Southern Corn Bread Mini Muffins (see recipe, page 268)

Purchased mixed berry pie served with vanilla ice cream

PREP:
20 minutes

COOKER SIZE:
3½- or 4-quart

COOK:
4 to 5 hours on low-heat or 2 to 2½ hours on high-heat setting

MAKES:
6 servings

KIDS' FAVORITE!

FREEZE WITH EASE

MAKE IT A MEAL:
Fruit and Broccoli Salad (see recipe, page 248)

Jalapeño-flavor kettle chips

Dill pickle spears

Purchased double chocolate cookies

To cut the cook time, brown the chicken in hot oil in a skillet—you'll need to do two batches. Then use the shorter side of the cooking time range.

Easy Chicken Rarebit

1¾ pounds boneless, skinless chicken breast halves
1 jar (14 to 16 ounces) Cheddar cheese pasta sauce
1 tablespoon Worcestershire sauce
1 large onion, halved crosswise and thinly sliced
6 pumpernickel or rye buns, split and toasted, or 6 slices pumpernickel or rye bread, toasted and halved diagonally
4 strips bacon, crisp-cooked, drained and crumbled (optional)
1 tomato, chopped (optional)

1. Cut chicken diagonally into ½-inch-thick slices; set aside. In 3½- or 4-quart slow cooker, stir together pasta sauce and Worcestershire sauce. Add onion and chicken.

2. Cover slow cooker; cook on low-heat setting for 4 to 5 hours or on high-heat setting for 2 to 2½ hours.

3. To serve, spoon chicken and sauce mixture over bun bottoms or bread slices. If desired, sprinkle with crumbled bacon and tomato. If using buns, add bun tops.

Per serving: 340 cal., 12 g total fat (4 g sat. fat), 102 mg chol., 823 mg sodium, 21 g carbo., 3 g fiber, 36 g pro.

PREP:
20 minutes

COOKER SIZE:
3½- or 4-quart

COOK:
6 to 7 hours on low-heat or 3 to 3½ hours on high-heat setting

MAKES:
6 to 8 servings

KIDS' FAVORITE!

MAKE IT A MEAL:
Refrigerated soft breadsticks, baked

Lemon-Spice Cupcakes (see recipe, page 271)

Chicken and cream of mushroom soup with roasted garlic give a new spin to stroganoff.

Chicken Stroganoff

2 pounds boneless, skinless chicken breast halves and/or thighs, cut into 1-inch pieces
1 cup chopped onions
1 can (4 ounces) sliced mushrooms, drained
2 cans (10¾ ounces each) condensed cream of mushroom soup with roasted garlic
⅓ cup water
1 carton (8 ounces) sour cream
  Hot cooked wide egg noodles
  Freshly ground black pepper (optional)
  Fresh thyme sprigs (optional)

1. In 3½- or 4-quart slow cooker, combine chicken pieces, onions and mushrooms. In medium-size bowl, stir together cream of mushroom soup and the water. Pour over chicken and vegetables.

2. Cover slow cooker; cook on low-heat setting for 6 to 7 hours or on high-heat setting for 3 to 3½ hours.

3. Just before serving, stir sour cream into mixture in slow cooker. Serve over hot cooked noodles. If desired, sprinkle with pepper and garnish with thyme.

Per serving: 539 cal., 14 g total fat (6 g sat. fat), 156 mg chol., 850 mg sodium, 55 g carbo., 3 g fiber, 57 g pro.

Just a dash of saffron, the usual seasoning for this Spanish dish, adds an appealing yellow color and a slightly pungent flavor note.

Fix-and-Forget Paella

PREP:
30 minutes

COOKER SIZE:
3½- to 5-quart

COOK:
8 to 9 hours on low-heat or 4 to 4½ hours on high-heat setting, plus 20 minutes on high-heat setting

STAND:
10 minutes

MAKES:
6 servings

2 medium-size carrots, cut into ½-inch pieces
1 large onion, coarsely chopped
1 bay leaf
3 pounds bone-in chicken thighs and drumsticks, skin removed
1 cup cubed cooked ham
1 can (14½ ounces) stewed tomatoes, cut up
½ can (6 ounces) tomato paste (⅓ cup)
2 teaspoons instant chicken bouillon granules
2 cloves garlic, chopped
¼ teaspoon black pepper
1 pound shrimp in shells, shelled and deveined
1 cup loose-pack frozen peas
2 cups water
1 cup long grain rice
¼ teaspoon salt
  Dash ground saffron or ⅛ teaspoon ground turmeric

1. In 3½- to 5-quart slow cooker, combine carrots, onion and bay leaf. Top with chicken pieces and ham. In medium-size bowl, combine tomatoes with their juices, tomato paste, bouillon granules, garlic and pepper; pour over mixture in slow cooker.

2. Cover slow cooker; cook on low-heat setting for 8 to 9 hours or on high-heat setting for 4 to 4½ hours.

3. If necessary, raise temperature to high-heat setting. Stir shrimp and peas into mixture in cooker. Cover slow cooker; cook about 20 minutes longer or until shrimp turn pink.

4. Meanwhile, in medium-size saucepan, combine the water, uncooked rice, salt and saffron or turmeric. Bring to a boil; reduce heat. Cover and simmer for 15 minutes. Remove from heat. Let stand, covered, for 10 minutes. Fluff rice with a fork.

5. To serve, remove and discard bay leaf. Using a slotted spoon, transfer chicken mixture to serving platter, reserving cooking liquid in slow cooker. Serve chicken mixture with rice. Drizzle with reserved cooking liquid to moisten.

· ·

Per serving: 445 cal., 9 g total fat (2 g sat. fat), 202 mg chol., 1,056 mg sodium, 42 g carbo., 4 g fiber, 47 g pro.

MAKE IT A MEAL:
Crusty Italian bread slices served with garlic-flavor olive oil

Mixed fresh berries topped with whipped cream

PREP:
30 minutes

COOKER SIZE:
5- to 6-quart

COOK:
7 to 8 hours on low-heat or 3 to 3½ hours on high-heat setting, plus 15 minutes on high-heat setting

MAKES:
6 servings

FREEZE WITH EASE

MAKE IT A MEAL:

Crusty rolls or bread

Mixed greens with creamy Parmesan dressing

Raspberry sorbet

Similar to the familiar Italian classic, this meal-in-a-pot is brimming with onions, mushrooms and tomatoes.

Cacciatore-Style Chicken

2 cups fresh mushrooms, halved or quartered
2 ribs celery, sliced
2 medium-size carrots, chopped
2 medium-size onions, cut into wedges
4 cloves garlic, chopped
3 tablespoons quick-cooking tapioca, crushed
2 bay leaves
1 tablespoon chopped fresh oregano or 1 teaspoon dried oregano
1 teaspoon sugar
½ teaspoon salt
¼ teaspoon black pepper
12 chicken drumsticks (about 3 pounds total), skin removed
½ cup chicken broth
¼ cup dry white wine or chicken broth
1 medium-size green or sweet red pepper, seeded and cut into strips
1 can (14½ ounces) diced tomatoes
⅓ to ½ cup tomato paste
 Shredded Parmesan cheese (optional)
 Chopped fresh oregano (optional)

1. In 5- to 6-quart slow cooker, combine mushrooms, celery, carrots, onions and garlic. Sprinkle with tapioca, bay leaves, the 1 tablespoon chopped fresh oregano or the dried oregano, sugar, salt and black pepper. Place chicken drumsticks on vegetables. Pour broth and wine over mixture in slow cooker.

2. Cover slow cooker; cook on low-heat setting for 7 to 8 hours or on high-heat setting for 3 to 3½ hours.

3. If necessary, raise temperature to high-heat setting. Stir in green pepper, tomatoes with their juices and tomato paste. Cover slow cooker; cook for 15 minutes longer. Remove and discard bay leaves. If desired, garnish with Parmesan cheese and additional chopped fresh oregano.

Per serving: 345 cal., 8 g total fat (2 g sat. fat), 157 mg chol., 568 mg sodium, 20 g carbo., 3 g fiber, 46 g pro.

PREP:
35 minutes

COOKER SIZE:
5- or 5½-quart

COOK:
4½ hours on low-heat or 3½ hours on high-heat setting, plus 10 minutes on high-heat setting

MAKES:
24 tacos

KIDS' FAVORITE!

FREEZE WITH EASE

MAKE IT A MEAL:
Mexican-Style Rice (see recipe, page 258)

Vanilla ice cream served with caramel sauce and toasted pecans

Another time, use the zesty shredded chicken mixture to top quesadillas.

Tex-Mex Chicken Tacos

  1 can (14½ ounces) diced tomatoes with jalapeño chiles, drained
1¼ cups salsa verde
  1 tablespoon ground cumin
  3 cloves garlic, chopped
  ½ teaspoon salt
  ½ teaspoon black pepper
  3 pounds boneless, skinless chicken thighs (10 to 12 thighs), fat removed
  1 large sweet red pepper, seeded and sliced
  1 large sweet yellow pepper, seeded and sliced
  1 medium-size onion, sliced
  1 can (14½ ounces) black beans, drained, rinsed and coarsely mashed
  1 can (14½ ounces) corn, drained
Tacos:
 24 hard taco shells
1½ cups shredded Monterey Jack cheese (6 ounces)
  2 avocados, halved, pitted, peeled and thinly sliced

1. In 5- or 5½-quart slow cooker, combine tomatoes, ¾ cup of the salsa verde, the cumin, garlic, salt and black pepper. Add chicken, sweet peppers and onion; stir to coat. Cover slow cooker; cook on low-heat setting for 4½ hours or on high-heat setting for 3½ hours.

2. Remove chicken from slow cooker to a cutting board and let cool slightly.

3. Strain vegetable mixture over large bowl or measuring cup; set liquid aside. If necessary, raise temperature to high-heat setting. Return vegetable mixture to slow cooker; stir in black beans and corn. Cover slow cooker; cook for 10 minutes.

4. Meanwhile, using two forks, pull chicken apart into shreds. Stir shredded chicken into vegetable mixture in slow cooker. Stir in the remaining ½ cup salsa verde and 1 cup of the reserved liquid (or more if desired).

5. Tacos: Heat shells following package directions. Divide mixture evenly among shells; top each with 1 tablespoon of the cheese and 1 or 2 avocado slices.

Per taco: 217 cal., 9 g total fat (3 g sat. fat), 53 mg chol., 418 mg sodium, 18 g carbo., 3 g fiber, 16 g pro.

Deep-colored hoisin sauce imparts a sweet yet spicy flavor to the chicken. Look for it in the Asian food section of the supermarket.

Plum-Sauced Chicken in Tortillas

1 can (30 ounces) whole unpitted purple plums, drained
1 cup hot-style vegetable juice
¼ cup hoisin sauce
4½ teaspoons quick-cooking tapioca
2 teaspoons finely chopped fresh ginger
½ teaspoon five-spice powder
¼ teaspoon salt
⅛ to ¼ teaspoon cayenne pepper
1¼ pounds boneless, skinless chicken thighs, cut into bite-size strips
6 (7- to 8-inch) flour tortillas, warmed*
2 cups packaged broccoli slaw or packaged coleslaw mix

1. Remove pits from drained plums. Place plums in blender or food processor. Cover and blend or process until smooth. Transfer plums to 3½- or 4-quart slow cooker. Stir in vegetable juice, hoisin sauce, tapioca, ginger, five-spice powder, salt and cayenne pepper. Stir chicken strips into plum mixture in slow cooker.

2. Cover slow cooker; cook on low-heat setting for 4 to 5 hours or on high-heat setting for 2 to 2½ hours. Remove chicken from slow cooker, reserving cooking liquid. Spoon about ⅓ cup of the chicken mixture onto each warmed tortilla, placing mixture just below the center. Drizzle chicken mixture with some of the reserved cooking liquid. Top each with ⅓ cup of the broccoli slaw. Roll up tortillas. Serve immediately.

Per serving: 331 cal., 4 g total fat (1 g sat. fat), 55 mg chol., 575 mg sodium, 47 g carbo., 3 g fiber, 26 g pro.

*Note: To warm the tortillas, heat oven to 350°. Stack the tortillas and wrap tightly in aluminum foil. Heat at 350° about 10 minutes or until heated through.

PREP:
25 minutes

COOKER SIZE:
3½- or 4-quart

COOK:
4 to 5 hours on low-heat or 2 to 2½ hours on high-heat setting

MAKES:
6 servings

KIDS' FAVORITE!

FREEZE WITH EASE

MAKE IT A MEAL:
Purchased corn salsa

Steamed fresh sugar snap peas

Prepared chocolate pudding served with oatmeal cookies

PREP:
20 minutes

COOKER SIZE:
5½- or 6-quart

COOK:
7 to 8 hours on low-heat or 3½ to 4 hours on high-heat setting

MAKES:
4 servings

KIDS' FAVORITE!

FREEZE WITH EASE

MAKE IT A MEAL:

Hot cooked rice

Refrigerated soft breadsticks, baked

Purchased apple pie

Frozen pearl onions are a nifty way to add lots of onion flavor to dishes of all kinds.

Chicken and Vegetables with Herbs

½ pound fresh mushrooms, halved
1 cup loose-pack frozen pearl onions
½ cup chicken broth
¼ cup dry red wine
2 tablespoons tomato paste
½ teaspoon garlic salt
½ teaspoon dried rosemary
½ teaspoon dried thyme
¼ teaspoon black pepper
1 bay leaf
4 small chicken legs (drumstick-thigh portion) (2 to 2½ pounds total), skin removed
Chicken broth (optional)
¼ cup chicken broth
2 tablespoons all-purpose flour
Fresh parsley sprigs (optional)

1. In 5½- or 6-quart slow cooker, combine mushrooms and pearl onions. Stir in the ½ cup chicken broth, the wine, tomato paste, garlic salt, rosemary, thyme, pepper and bay leaf. Add chicken legs to slow cooker.

2. Cover slow cooker; cook on low-heat setting for 7 to 8 hours or on high-heat setting for 3½ to 4 hours.

3. Using a slotted spoon, transfer chicken and vegetables to a serving platter. Remove and discard bay leaf. Cover chicken and vegetables and keep warm.

4. For sauce, skim fat from cooking liquid. Measure 2 cups of the cooking liquid, adding additional chicken broth, if necessary, to equal 2 cups total liquid. Transfer liquid to medium-size saucepan. In small bowl, stir the ¼ cup broth into the flour; stir into liquid in saucepan. Cook and stir until thickened and bubbly; cook and stir for 1 minute longer. Spoon some of the sauce over chicken. Pass remaining sauce. If desired, garnish with parsley.

Per serving: 304 cal., 9 g total fat (2 g sat. fat), 159 mg chol., 548 mg sodium, 9 g carbo., 1 g fiber, 43 g pro.

PREP:
20 minutes

COOKER SIZE:
4- to 5-quart

COOK:
5 to 6 hours on low-heat or 2½ to 3 hours on high-heat setting

MAKES:
6 servings

MAKE IT A MEAL:
Lemon-Almond Broccoli (see recipe, page 256)

Purchased chocolate-champagne truffles

Figs, balsamic vinegar, orange zest and polenta turn slow-cooked chicken thighs into a tender bistro-style dish.

Chicken with Figs And Blue Cheese

> 1 cup chicken broth
> ¼ cup balsamic vinegar
> 1 tablespoon grated orange zest
> 1 teaspoon salt
> ½ teaspoon black pepper
> ¼ teaspoon ground ginger
> 1 package (9 ounces) dried mission figs, stems removed
> 1 large onion, thinly sliced
> 2½ pounds boneless, skinless chicken thighs
> 1 tube (16 ounces) heat-and-serve polenta
> ⅔ cup crumbled blue cheese

1. In small bowl, stir together chicken broth, balsamic vinegar, orange zest, salt, pepper and ginger; set aside. Coarsely chop figs. In 4- to 5-quart slow cooker, combine figs and onion. Place chicken on mixture in cooker. Add broth mixture.

2. Cover slow cooker; cook on low-heat setting for 5 to 6 hours or on high-heat setting for 2½ to 3 hours.

3. Meanwhile, prepare polenta following package directions for polenta mush. Using tongs, remove chicken from cooker. Transfer fig mixture to a serving bowl. If necessary, skim fat from fig mixture. Serve chicken thighs and the fig mixture with polenta mush. Sprinkle each serving with blue cheese.

Per serving: 481 cal., 12 g total fat (5 g sat. fat), 162 mg chol., 1,174 mg sodium, 47 g carbo., 7 g fiber, 45 g pro.

This classic dish is updated with green beans and mushrooms, a dash of sherry and a sprinkling of parsley.

Chicken Tetrazzini

PREP:
20 minutes

COOKER SIZE:
5- or 5½-quart

COOK:
9 to 10 hours on low-heat or 4 to 5 hours on high-heat setting, plus 15 to 20 minutes on high-heat setting

MAKES:
6 servings

1 medium-size onion, finely chopped
½ pound green beans, trimmed and cut into 1-inch pieces
1 package (8 ounces) sliced fresh mushrooms
6 boneless, skinless chicken thighs (about 1½ pounds total)
1 teaspoon salt
1 teaspoon dried thyme
1 teaspoon black pepper
1 can (14 ounces) chicken broth
½ cup cold water
¼ cup all-purpose flour
½ cup heavy cream
1 jar (4 ounces) chopped pimientos, drained
3 tablespoons dry sherry
¼ cup grated Parmesan cheese
  Hot cooked spaghetti
1 tablespoon chopped parsley (optional)

1. In 5- or 5½-quart slow cooker, layer chopped onion, green beans and mushrooms. Arrange chicken thighs on top. Sprinkle with salt, thyme and pepper. Pour chicken broth over mixture in slow cooker.

2. Cover slow cooker; cook on low-heat setting for 9 to 10 hours or on high-heat setting for 4 to 5 hours or until the chicken and green beans are tender. If necessary, raise temperature to high-heat setting.

3. In small bowl, combine the cold water and flour, stirring until smooth. Add 1 cup of the cooking liquid from slow cooker to flour mixture, stirring until smooth. Stir into mixture in cooker. Cover slow cooker; cook for 10 to 15 minutes or until thickened. Stir in heavy cream, pimientos and sherry. Cover slow cooker; cook for 5 minutes longer. Stir in Parmesan cheese.

4. Serve chicken mixture over hot cooked spaghetti. If desired, sprinkle with chopped parsley.

KIDS' FAVORITE!

MAKE IT A MEAL:
Tossed green salad

Cookie dough ice cream

- -

Per serving: 505 cal., 15 g total fat (7 g sat. fat), 125 mg chol., 818 mg sodium, 55 g carbo., 5 g fiber, 35 g pro.

PREP:
25 minutes

COOKER SIZE:
6-quart

COOK:
8 hours on low-heat
or 5 hours on high-
heat setting

MAKES:
8 servings

MAKE IT A MEAL:

Hot cooked couscous

**Purchased hard
breadsticks**

Cinnamon ice cream

A tagine is a Morrocan-inspired stew such as
this one that stars chicken, vegetables, dried
fruit, and an exotic mix of spices.

Tagine-Style Chicken

8 boneless, skinless chicken thighs (about 1¾ pounds total), cut into 1-inch
   pieces
2 large onions, halved and thinly sliced
4 large carrots, thinly sliced
½ cup raisins
½ cup dried apricots, coarsely chopped
2 cups chicken broth
2 tablespoons all-purpose flour
2 tablespoons tomato paste
2 tablespoons lemon juice
2 teaspoons garlic salt
1½ teaspoons ground cumin
1½ teaspoons ground ginger
1 teaspoon ground cinnamon
¾ teaspoon black pepper
   Hot cooked couscous
   Toasted pine nuts (optional)

1. In 6-quart slow cooker, layer chicken, onions, carrots, raisins and apricots.

2. In medium-size bowl, whisk together chicken broth, flour, tomato paste,
lemon juice, garlic salt, cumin, ginger, cinnamon and black pepper. Pour over
chicken and vegetables.

3. Cover slow cooker; cook on low-heat setting for 8 hours or on high-heat setting for
5 hours.

4. Serve chicken mixture over hot cooked couscous. If desired, garnish with toasted
pine nuts.

· ·

Per serving: 415 cal., 7 g total fat (2 g sat. fat), 98 mg chol., 794 mg sodium, 61 g carbo.,
5 g fiber, 28 g pro.

Curry powder, ginger and cayenne pepper give this saucy chicken and vegetable dish a pleasantly spicy flavor.

Chicken Curry Noodles

1 large onion, sliced
2 pounds boneless, skinless chicken thighs (about 6 large), cut into 1-inch pieces
4 cups 1-inch cauliflower flowerets (about ½ of a large head)
1 sweet red pepper, seeded and sliced into ¼-inch-wide strips
1 sweet yellow pepper, seeded and sliced into ¼-inch-wide strips
1 sweet orange pepper, seeded and sliced into ¼-inch-wide strips
1 can (14 ounces) chicken broth
1 can (14 ounces) unsweetened coconut milk
2 teaspoons curry powder
1½ teaspoons salt
1½ teaspoons paprika
¾ teaspoon ground ginger
¼ teaspoon cayenne pepper
1 can (15½ ounces) chickpeas, drained and rinsed
1 box (8 ounces) rice noodles
1 cup fresh basil leaves, rinsed and patted dry (optional)

1. In 5- or 5½-quart slow cooker, layer onion, chicken, cauliflower and sweet pepper strips.

2. In medium-size bowl, whisk together chicken broth, coconut milk, curry powder, salt, paprika, ginger and cayenne pepper. Pour over the chicken and vegetables in slow cooker. Spread chickpeas evenly over top.

3. Cover slow cooker; cook on high-heat setting for 5 hours and 20 minutes.

4. At end of 5 hours of cooking time, in large bowl, soak rice noodles in warm water for 10 minutes. Drain.

5. At end of 5 hours and 20 minutes cooking time, add noodles to slow cooker. Cover slow cooker; cook for 10 minutes longer. To serve, if desired, stir basil leaves into curry.

· ·

Per serving: 443 cal., 16 g total fat (11 g sat. fat), 95 mg chol., 972 mg sodium, 46 g carbo., 6 g fiber, 29 g pro.

PREP:
30 minutes

COOKER SIZE:
5- or 5½-quart

COOK:
5½ hours on high-heat setting

MAKES:
8 servings

MAKE IT A MEAL:
Purchased naan (Indian flatbread)

Pineapple sorbet

PREP:
15 minutes

COOKER SIZE:
3½- or 4-quart

COOK:
5 to 6 hours on low-heat or 2½ to 3 hours on high-heat setting

STAND:
5 minutes

MAKES:
6 servings

FREEZE WITH EASE

MAKE IT A MEAL:
Steamed fresh broccoli

Shortbread Brownies (see recipe, page 270)

Blending the sweet licorice flavor of anise seeds with the fruitiness of plums and oranges adds a hint of wonderfully exotic Asian flavor.

Chicken with Orange Couscous

¾ cup plum sauce
⅓ cup orange juice
¼ cup orange marmalade
2 tablespoons quick-cooking tapioca
¼ teaspoon anise seeds, crushed
2½ to 2¾ pounds boneless, skinless chicken thighs
2¼ cups water
1 tablespoon orange marmalade
1 package (10 ounces) quick-cooking couscous
¼ teaspoon salt
Orange slices, halved (optional)
Orange peel strips (optional)

1. For sauce, in small bowl, combine plum sauce, orange juice, the ¼ cup orange marmalade, the tapioca and anise seeds. Place chicken in a 3½- or 4-quart slow cooker. Pour sauce over chicken.

2. Cover slow cooker; cook on low-heat setting for 5 to 6 hours or on high-heat setting for 2½ to 3 hours. Remove chicken; keep warm. Skim fat from sauce.

3. In medium-size saucepan, combine the water and the 1 tablespoon orange marmalade; bring to a boil. Remove from heat. Stir in couscous and salt. Cover; let stand for 5 minutes. Fluff couscous with a fork just before serving. If desired, serve couscous on orange slices. Serve chicken and sauce with couscous. If desired, garnish with orange peel strips.

Per serving: 538 cal., 8 g total fat (2 g sat. fat), 157 mg chol., 404 mg sodium, 70 g carbo., 3 g fiber, 44 g pro.

PREP:
20 minutes

COOKER SIZE:
3½- or 4-quart

COOK:
5 to 6 hours on low-heat or 2½ to 3 hours on high-heat setting

MAKES:
6 servings

FREEZE WITH EASE

MAKE IT A MEAL:
Steamed fresh asparagus spears

Purchased carrot cake

A bed of colorful pasta makes the ideal backdrop for showing off this luscious creamy chicken and vegetable entrée.

Pesto-Sauced Chicken

2 **pounds boneless, skinless chicken thighs, cut into 1-inch pieces**
1½ **cups purchased Alfredo pasta sauce**
¼ **cup purchased basil pesto**
1 **package (16 ounces) frozen sweet peppers and onion stir-fry vegetables**
  Hot cooked spinach linguine
  Fresh basil leaves (optional)

1. Coat an unheated large nonstick skillet with nonstick cooking spray. Heat over medium heat. Add chicken, half at a time; cook until browned. In 3½- or 4-quart slow cooker, combine chicken, Alfredo sauce and pesto. Stir in frozen vegetables.

2. Cover slow cooker; cook on low-heat setting for 5 to 6 hours or on high-heat setting for 2½ to 3 hours. Serve over hot cooked linguine. If desired, top each serving with a fresh basil leaf.

Per serving: 470 cal., 20 g total fat (6 g sat. fat), 160 mg chol., 600 mg sodium, 27 g carbo., 2 g fiber, 43 g pro.

Here are two secrets to great dumplings: First, be sure the stew is bubbling hot before dropping in the dough; second, don't peek during cooking.

Chicken and Dumplings

Stew:
- 2 **cups chopped carrots**
- 2 **cups chopped potatoes**
- 1½ **cups chopped parsnips**
- 1 **clove garlic, chopped**
- 2 **bay leaves**
- 1 **teaspoon dried sage**
- ½ **teaspoon salt**
- ¼ **teaspoon black pepper**
- 2 **pounds boneless, skinless chicken thighs, cut into 1-inch pieces**
- 1 **can (14 ounces) chicken broth**
- 1 **can (10¾ ounces) condensed cream of chicken soup**
- 2 **tablespoons cold water**
- 1 **tablespoon cornstarch**

Dumplings:
- ½ **cup all-purpose flour**
- ½ **cup shredded Cheddar cheese (2 ounces)**
- ⅓ **cup cornmeal**
- 1 **teaspoon baking powder**
- ¼ **teaspoon salt**
- 1 **egg, beaten**
- 2 **tablespoons milk**
- 2 **tablespoons butter, melted**

1. **Stew:** In 4- to 5-quart slow cooker, combine carrots, potatoes, parsnips, garlic, bay leaves, sage, the ½ teaspoon salt and the pepper. Place chicken on top of the vegetables. In medium-size bowl, gradually whisk chicken broth into cream of chicken soup. Pour broth mixture over chicken.

2. Cover slow cooker; cook on low-heat setting for 8 to 10 hours or on high-heat setting for 4 to 5 hours.

3. If necessary, raise temperature to high-heat setting. Using a wooden spoon, stir stew. Remove and discard bay leaves. In small bowl, combine the water and cornstarch; stir into stew until combined.

4. **Dumplings:** In medium-size bowl, combine flour, cheese, cornmeal, baking powder and the ¼ teaspoon salt. In small bowl, combine egg, milk and melted butter. Add egg mixture to flour mixture. Stir with a fork until moistened. Using two spoons, drop dough into eight mounds directly on top of stew.

5. Cover slow cooker; cook for 25 to 30 minutes longer or until a toothpick inserted into a dumpling comes out clean. (Do not lift cover during cooking.)

Per serving: 361 cal., 14 g total fat (6 g sat. fat), 140 mg chol., 948 mg sodium, 29 g carbo., 4 g fiber, 29 g pro.

PREP:
30 minutes

COOKER SIZE:
4- to 5-quart

COOK:
8 to 10 hours on low-heat or 4 to 5 hours on high-heat setting, plus 25 to 30 minutes on high-heat setting

MAKES:
8 servings

KIDS' FAVORITE!

MAKE IT A MEAL:
Tossed salad

Purchased sugar cookies

POULTRY AND FISH

95

PREP:
15 minutes

COOKER SIZE:
3½- or 4-quart

COOK:
5 to 6 hours on low-heat or 2½ to 3 hours on high-heat setting

MAKES:
6 servings

For a change of pace, prepare your favorite recipe for rice pilaf and substitute it for the plain hot cooked rice.

Cranberry Chicken

2½ to 3 pounds bone-in chicken thighs and/or drumsticks, skin removed
1 can (16 ounces) whole cranberry sauce
2 tablespoons dry onion soup mix
2 tablespoons quick-cooking tapioca
Hot cooked rice

1. Place chicken pieces in 3½- or 4-quart slow cooker. In small bowl, stir together cranberry sauce, dry soup mix and tapioca. Pour over chicken pieces.

2. Cover slow cooker; cook on low-heat setting for 5 to 6 hours or on high-heat setting for 2½ to 3 hours. Serve chicken and sauce over hot cooked rice.

. . . .

Per serving: 357 cal., 4 g total fat (1 g sat. fat), 89 mg chol., 268 mg sodium, 55 g carbo., 1 g fiber, 23 g pro.

KIDS' FAVORITE!

FREEZE WITH EASE

MAKE IT A MEAL:
Steamed fresh Brussels sprouts

Frozen whole wheat bread, baked

Purchased chocolate cheesecake

PREP:
25 minutes

COOKER SIZE:
3½- or 4-quart

COOK:
10 to 12 hours on low-heat or 5 to 6 hours on high-heat setting

MAKES:
4 or 5 servings

KIDS' FAVORITE!

MAKE IT A MEAL:
Melon wedges

Vanilla ice cream with purchased hot fudge sauce

Chicken thighs and drumsticks generally are a meat-department bargain. Cooked in a robust sauce, they're as tasty as they are economical.

Barbecue-Style Chicken

2 medium-size potatoes, cut into ½-inch pieces
1 large green pepper, seeded and cut into strips
1 medium-size onion, sliced
1 tablespoon quick-cooking tapioca
2 pounds bone-in chicken thighs or drumsticks, skin and fat removed
1 can (8 ounces) tomato sauce
2 tablespoons brown sugar
1 tablespoon yellow mustard
1 tablespoon Worcestershire sauce
1 clove garlic, chopped
¼ teaspoon salt

1. In 3½- or 4-quart slow cooker, combine potatoes, green pepper and onion. Sprinkle tapioca over potato mixture. Place chicken on top of vegetables. For sauce, in small bowl, stir together tomato sauce, brown sugar, mustard, Worcestershire sauce, garlic and salt. Pour sauce over chicken.

2. Cover slow cooker; cook on low-heat setting for 10 to 12 hours or on high-heat setting for 5 to 6 hours.

3. Transfer chicken and vegetables to large serving bowl. Skim fat from sauce. Spoon sauce over chicken and vegetables.

Per serving: 267 cal., 4 g total fat (1 g sat. fat), 98 mg chol., 594 mg sodium, 27 g carbo., 2 g fiber, 29 g pro.

Lemonade concentrate takes the edge off
the mustard in this chicken-and-potato duo.

Tangy Chicken And New Potatoes

1½ pounds tiny new potatoes, quartered
 1 small onion, cut into wedges
 1 tablespoon quick-cooking tapioca
 3 pounds meaty chicken pieces (breast halves, thighs
     and drumsticks), skinned
 ½ teaspoon salt
 ¼ teaspoon black pepper
 ¼ cup frozen lemonade concentrate, thawed
 3 tablespoons Dijon-style mustard
 1 teaspoon finely shredded lemon zest
 1 jar (6 ounces) marinated artichoke hearts

1. In a 6- to 7-quart slow cooker, combine potatoes and onion; sprinkle with tapioca.

2. Arrange chicken over vegetables. Sprinkle with salt and pepper. In a small bowl, combine lemonade concentrate, mustard and lemon zest; pour over chicken.

3. Cover and cook on low-heat setting for 7 to 8 hours or on high-heat setting for 3½ to 4 hours.

4. Divide chicken among four to six shallow bowls. Stir undrained artichoke hearts into vegetable mixture in slow cooker. Spoon vegetable mixture over chicken.

· ·

Per serving: 509 cal., 14 g total fat (3 g sat. fat), 138 mg chol., 829 mg sodium, 47 g carbo., 3 g fiber, 51 g pro.

PREP:
20 minutes

COOKER SIZE:
6- to 7-quart

COOK:
7 to 8 hours on low-heat or 3½ to 4 hours on high-heat setting

MAKES:
4 to 6 servings

MAKE IT A MEAL:
Purchased coleslaw
Purchased macaroons

PREP:
20 minutes

COOKER SIZE:
3½- or 4-quart

COOK:
4½ to 5 hours on low-heat or 2½ hours on high-heat setting

MAKES:
4 or 5 servings

KIDS' FAVORITE!

MAKE IT A MEAL:
Fruit and Broccoli Salad (see recipe, page 248)

Sliced whole wheat bread served with butter

Purchased banana cream pie

This homey dish uses frozen hash browns for the traditional potatoes and substitutes ground chicken or turkey for leftover cooked meat.

Cheesy Chicken Hash

- 6 **cups loose-pack frozen diced hash brown potatoes, thawed**
- 1 **pound uncooked ground chicken or turkey**
- 1 **large onion, finely chopped**
- ½ **cup chopped fresh parsley**
- 1 **can (12 ounces) evaporated milk**
- 2 **tablespoons Worcestershire-style marinade for chicken**
- 1 **tablespoon yellow mustard**
- ¾ **teaspoon salt**
- ¼ **teaspoon black pepper**
- ½ **cup shredded Swiss cheese (2 ounces)**

1. Lightly coat 3½- or 4-quart slow cooker with nonstick cooking spray. In prepared slow cooker, stir together potatoes, ground chicken, onion and parsley. In medium-size bowl, whisk together evaporated milk, Worcestershire-style marinade for chicken, mustard, salt and pepper; stir into potato mixture.

2. Cover slow cooker; cook on low-heat setting for 4½ to 5 hours or on high-heat setting for 2½ hours.

3. Spoon off fat. Sprinkle chicken mixture with cheese.

. . . .

Per serving: 617 cal., 22 g total fat (7 g sat. fat), 38 mg chol., 845 mg sodium, 72 g carbo., 5 g fiber, 37 g pro.

A hint of curry adds spice to winter vegetables and tender turkey breast for a hearty, wholesome meal with attitude!

Curried Turkey And Vegetables

PREP:
25 minutes

COOKER SIZE:
6-quart

COOK:
8 hours on low-heat setting or 4½ hours on high-heat setting, plus 10 minutes on high-heat setting

STAND:
10 minutes

MAKES:
6 servings

- 1 **tablespoon curry powder**
- 2 **teaspoons ground ginger**
- ½ **teaspoon salt**
- ¼ **teaspoon black pepper**
- 1 **cup chicken broth**
- 1 **tablespoon sugar**
- 8 **large cauliflower pieces (from a 2-pound head)**
- 1 **can (15 ounces) chickpeas, drained and rinsed**
- ½ **cup dried apricots, coarsely chopped**
- ½ **cup golden raisins**
- 1 **cinnamon stick**
- 1 **bone-in turkey breast half (2½ to 3 pounds), skin removed**
- 1 **box (10 ounces) frozen cut green beans, thawed**
- 2 **tablespoons cornstarch mixed with 2 tablespoons cold water**
- 1 **jar (12 ounces) mango chutney (optional)**

1. In small bowl, stir together curry powder, ginger, salt and pepper. In medium-size bowl, stir 2 teaspoons of the spice mixture into broth along with the sugar.

2. In 6-quart slow cooker, combine cauliflower, chickpeas, apricots and golden raisins. Tuck in cinnamon stick. Rub remaining spice mixture onto turkey breast. Place turkey on top of vegetables. Pour broth mixture around turkey.

3. Cover slow cooker; cook on low-heat setting for 8 hours or on high-heat setting for 4½ hours.

4. Remove turkey to a cutting board; cover loosely with aluminum foil and let stand for 10 minutes. If necessary, raise temperature to high-heat setting. Stir green beans and cornstarch-water mixture into slow cooker. Cover slow cooker; cook about 10 minutes longer or until green beans are tender.

5. Cut turkey into ¼-inch-thick slices. Pour a little of the cooking liquid on top of turkey; serve with vegetables and, if desired, mango chutney.

Per serving: 423 cal., 4 g total fat (1 g sat. fat), 130 mg chol., 621 mg sodium, 44 g carbo., 7 g fiber, 54 g pro.

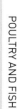

MAKE IT A MEAL:
Mango sorbet topped with toasted coconut

POULTRY AND FISH

PREP:
30 minutes

COOKER SIZE:
3½- or 4-quart

COOK:
6 to 7 hours on low-heat or 3 to 3½ hours on high-heat setting

STAND:
5 minutes

MAKES:
12 servings

FREEZE WITH EASE

MAKE IT A MEAL:
Kettle-cooked potato chips

Purchased angel food cake topped with raspberries

If you're not feeding a crowd, refrigerate or freeze the leftover turkey to reheat for another meal.

Sesame-Ginger Turkey Wraps

> 3 turkey thighs (3½ to 4 pounds total), skin removed
> 1 cup bottled sesame-ginger stir-fry sauce
> ¼ cup water
> 1 bag (1 pound) broccoli slaw
> 12 (8-inch) flour tortillas, warmed*
> ¾ cup sliced scallions

1. Lightly coat 3½- or 4-quart slow cooker with nonstick cooking spray. Place turkey thighs in prepared slow cooker. In small bowl, stir together stir-fry sauce and the water. Pour over turkey in slow cooker.

2. Cover slow cooker; cook on low-heat setting for 6 to 7 hours or on high-heat setting for 3 to 3½ hours.

3. Remove turkey from slow cooker; cool slightly. Using two forks, remove turkey from bones and pull meat apart into bite-size pieces; discard bones. Return turkey to mixture in slow cooker. Stir broccoli slaw into mixture in slow cooker. Cover slow cooker and let stand for 5 minutes. Using a slotted spoon, remove turkey-broccoli mixture from slow cooker.

4. Spoon turkey-broccoli mixture onto warmed tortillas. Top turkey mixture with scallions. If desired, spoon some of the sauce from slow cooker on top of scallions. Roll up and serve immediately.

Per serving: 207 cal., 5 g total fat (1 g sat. fat), 67 mg chol., 422 mg sodium, 20 g carbo., 2 g fiber, 20 g pro.

*Note: To warm tortillas, heat oven to 350°. Stack tortillas and wrap tightly in aluminum foil. Heat at 350° about 10 minutes or until heated through.

A creamy Alfredo sauce cooks with turkey breast tenderloin, mushrooms and shredded carrots to top angel hair pasta.

Mushroom-Sauced Turkey

PREP:
30 minutes

COOKER SIZE:
4- to 5-quart

COOK:
4 to 5 hours on low-heat setting

MAKES:
12 servings

1 **can (10¾ ounces) condensed cream of chicken soup**
½ **tub (8 ounces) cream cheese with chives and onion**
1 **package (1¼ ounces) Alfredo pasta sauce mix**
1 **can (5 ounces) evaporated milk**
½ **cup water**
2 **pounds turkey breast tenderloins, cut into ¾-inch pieces**
2 **cans (8 ounces each) sliced mushrooms, drained**
2 **cups shredded carrots**
1 **cup finely chopped onions**
   Hot cooked angel hair pasta

1. In 4- to 5-quart slow cooker, combine cream of chicken soup, cream cheese and dry pasta sauce mix, stirring until mixed. Gradually stir in evaporated milk and the water. Add turkey pieces, mushrooms, carrots and onions to mixture in slow cooker.

2. Cover slow cooker; cook on low-heat setting for 4 to 5 hours.

3. Serve turkey mixture over hot cooked pasta.

Per serving: 340 cal., 9 g total fat (4 g sat. fat), 61 mg chol., 542 mg sodium, 38 g carbo., 3 g fiber, 26 g pro.

MAKE IT A MEAL:
Steamed fresh broccoli

Cookie dough ice cream served in waffle cones

PREP:
20 minutes

COOKER SIZE:
4½- to 6-quart

COOK:
4 to 5 hours on low-heat or 2 to 2½ hours on high-heat setting

MAKES:
8 servings

KIDS' FAVORITE!

FREEZE WITH EASE

MAKE IT A MEAL:
Buttermilk Angel Biscuits (see recipe, page 267)

Purchased apple pie served with vanilla ice cream

A sprinkling of Parmesan cheese brings a tantalizingly sharp note to this creamy blend of turkey, pasta and vegetables.

Turkey and Pasta Primavera

2 pounds turkey breast tenderloins or boneless, skinless chicken breast halves, cut into 1-inch pieces
1 package (16 ounces) loose-pack frozen stir-fry vegetables (sugar snap peas, carrots, onions and mushrooms)
2 teaspoons dried basil, oregano or Italian seasoning
1 jar (16 ounces) Alfredo pasta sauce
¾ pound linguine or spaghetti, broken
  Shredded Parmesan cheese (optional)

1. In 4½- to 6-quart slow cooker, combine turkey and frozen vegetables. Sprinkle with dried herb. Stir in Alfredo sauce.

2. Cover slow cooker; cook on low-heat setting for 4 to 5 hours or on high-heat setting for 2 to 2½ hours.

3. Meanwhile, cook pasta following package directions; drain. Stir cooked pasta into mixture in slow cooker. If desired, sprinkle each serving with Parmesan cheese.

Per serving: 488 cal., 19 g total fat (0 g sat. fat), 99 mg chol., 267 mg sodium, 39 g carbo., 3 g fiber, 37 g pro.

PREP:
25 minutes

COOKER SIZE:
4- to 5-quart

COOK:
3 to 4 hours on low-heat setting

MAKES:
8 to 10 servings

KIDS' FAVORITE!

MAKE IT A MEAL:
Super Simple B.L.T. Salad (see recipe, page 252)

Sliced fresh peaches

Purchased sugar cookies

Savory sage flavors a mixture of turkey, a Swiss-American cheese sauce and bowtie pasta. Choose tricolor bowties for more color.

Creamy Turkey Bowties and Cheese

4 **cups chopped cooked turkey**
2 **cups chopped onions**
2 **cups heavy cream**
8 **ounces American cheese, cubed (2 cups)**
8 **ounces process Swiss cheese, torn (2 cups)**
1 **teaspoon dried sage**
½ **teaspoon black pepper**
1 **pound bowtie pasta**

1. In 4- to 5-quart slow cooker, combine turkey, onions, heavy cream, American cheese, Swiss cheese, sage and pepper.

2. Cover slow cooker; cook on low-heat setting for 3 to 4 hours.

3. Meanwhile, cook pasta following package directions; drain. Stir cheese mixture in cooker. Stir cooked pasta into the cheese mixture. Serve immediately.

Per serving: 754 cal., 43 g total fat (25 g sat. fat), 186 mg chol., 886 mg sodium, 49 g carbo., 3 g fiber, 43 g pro.

Love sausage and olives on pizza? Here's the same great combo in a pasta sauce.

Turkey Pasta Sauce With Mixed Olives

PREP:
30 minutes

COOKER SIZE:
6- to 7-quart

COOK:
7 to 8 hours on low-heat or 3½ to 4 hours on high-heat setting

MAKES:
12 servings

3   **pounds bulk Italian turkey sausage**
3   **cans (14½ ounces each) no-salt-added diced tomatoes**
2   **cans (6 ounces each) tomato paste**
1   **cup finely chopped onions**
1   **jar (5 ounces) sliced pimiento-stuffed green olives, drained**
1   **can (3.8 ounces) sliced, pitted ripe olives, drained**
1   **jar (3½ ounces) capers, drained**
8   **cloves garlic, chopped**
4   **teaspoons dried Italian seasoning**
     Hot cooked cut ziti or penne pasta
     Finely shredded or grated Parmesan cheese (optional)

1. Lightly coat 6- to 7-quart slow cooker with nonstick cooking spray. In very large skillet, cook sausage, half at a time, over medium heat until cooked through, stirring to break into bite-size pieces. Drain off fat. Transfer sausage to very large bowl. Stir tomatoes with their juices, tomato paste, onions, olives, capers, garlic and Italian seasoning into sausage. Transfer to prepared slow cooker.

2. Cover slow cooker; cook on low-heat setting for 7 to 8 hours or on high-heat setting for 3½ to 4 hours.

3. Serve sauce over hot cooked pasta. If desired, sprinkle each serving with Parmesan cheese.

Per serving: 663 cal., 41 g total fat (12 g sat. fat), 69 mg chol., 1,482 mg sodium, 56 g carbo., 6 g fiber, 26 g pro.

FREEZE WITH EASE

MAKE IT A MEAL:
Italian bread slices served with olive oil

Lemon-Spice Cupcakes (see recipe, page 271)

PREP:
35 minutes

COOKER SIZE:
5- to 6-quart

COOK:
7 hours on low-heat or 3½ hours on high-heat setting, plus 30 to 45 minutes on high-heat setting

MAKES:
12 servings

MAKE IT A MEAL:
Steamed fresh broccoli and cauliflower

Purchased hard breadsticks

Fruity Waffle Bowls (see recipe, page 277)

Because this sensational soup serves a crowd, it's ideal for toting to potlucks, church suppers or family get-togethers.

Dilled Fish Chowder

2 pounds potatoes, peeled and chopped
3 large onions, chopped
¾ cup chopped celery
2 tablespoons butter or margarine
3 bay leaves
1 tablespoon salt
¾ teaspoon dried dill
¾ teaspoon black pepper
3 cups water
¾ cup dry vermouth, dry white wine or water
3 pounds fish fillets (such as cod, haddock or orange roughy), cut into 2-inch pieces
3 cups heavy cream, half-and-half or light cream
⅓ cup chopped fresh parsley

1. In 5- to 6-quart slow cooker, combine potatoes, onions, celery, butter, bay leaves, salt, dill and pepper. Stir in the water and vermouth.

2. Cover slow cooker; cook on low-heat setting for 7 hours or on high-heat setting for 3½ hours.

3. If necessary, raise temperature to high-heat setting. Place fish on top of the vegetable mixture. Cover slow cooker; cook for 30 to 45 minutes longer or until fish flakes easily when tested with fork. Remove and discard bay leaves. Using a fork, break fish into bite-size pieces. Stir in heavy cream and parsley.

· ·

Per serving: 396 cal., 25 g total fat (15 g sat. fat), 136 mg chol., 680 mg sodium, 17 g carbo., 2 g fiber, 23 g pro.

Easy is right! The dry scalloped potato mix makes this wonderful dill-infused salmon chowder as simple as can be.

Easy Potato and Salmon Chowder

    2 cans (14 ounces each) chicken broth
  1½ cups loose-pack frozen whole kernel corn
    3 medium-size carrots, thinly sliced
  1½ cups water
    1 medium-size onion, chopped
    1 package (4.9 ounces) scalloped potato mix
    2 teaspoons dried dill
    2 cups half-and-half or light cream
    ½ cup all-purpose flour
    2 cans (6 ounces each) skinless, boneless salmon, drained

1. In 3½- or 4-quart slow cooker, combine chicken broth, corn, carrots, the water, onion, dry potato mix with seasoning packet and the dill. Cover slow cooker; cook on low-heat setting for 6 to 8 hours or on high-heat setting for 3 to 4 hours.

2. If necessary, raise temperature to high-heat setting. In medium-size bowl, whisk together half-and-half and flour. Gradually stir half-and-half mixture into vegetable mixture in slow cooker. Gently stir in salmon. Cover slow cooker; cook for 20 to 30 minutes longer or until thickened.

Per serving: 269 cal., 10 g total fat (5 g sat. fat), 45 mg chol., 827 mg sodium, 32 g carbo., 2 g fiber, 14 g pro.

PREP:
20 minutes

COOKER SIZE:
3½- or 4-quart

COOK:
6 to 8 hours on low-heat or 3 to 4 hours on high-heat setting, plus 20 to 30 minutes on high-heat setting

MAKES:
8 servings

MAKE IT A MEAL:
Greens and Berry Salad (see recipe, page 247)

Frozen whole wheat rolls, baked

Purchased ice cream sandwiches

PREP:
25 minutes

COOKER SIZE:
3½- or 4-quart

COOK:
6 to 7 hours on low-heat or 3 to 3½ hours on high-heat setting, plus 1 hour on high-heat setting

MAKES:
6 servings

MAKE IT A MEAL:
Fruit and Broccoli Salad (see recipe, page 248)

Frozen whole wheat rolls, baked

Purchased pumpkin pie served with sweetened whipped cream

Thick and chunky, this fish soup measures up to the finest chowders anywhere. If you prefer halibut or haddock, substitute either for the cod.

Hearty Fish Chowder

2 medium-size potatoes, chopped
1 cup chopped onions
1 can (10¾ ounces) condensed cream of celery soup
1 package (10 ounces) frozen whole kernel corn
1 package (10 ounces) frozen baby lima beans or 2 cups loose-pack frozen baby lima beans
1½ cups chicken broth
⅓ cup dry white wine or chicken broth
2 cloves garlic, chopped
1 teaspoon lemon-pepper seasoning
1 pound cod or other whitefish fillets
1 can (14½ ounces) stewed tomatoes
⅓ cup nonfat dry milk powder

1. In 3½- or 4-quart slow cooker, combine potatoes, onions, cream of celery soup, corn, lima beans, chicken broth, white wine, garlic and lemon-pepper seasoning.

2. Cover slow cooker; cook on low-heat setting for 6 to 7 hours or on high-heat setting for 3 to 3½ hours.

3. If necessary, raise temperature to high-heat setting. Place fish on the mixture in the cooker. Cover slow cooker; cook for 1 hour longer.

4. Add tomatoes with their juices and nonfat dry milk powder to cooker, stirring gently to break up the fish.

Per serving: 310 cal., 4 g total fat (1 g sat. fat), 39 mg chol., 1,013 mg sodium, 45 g carbo., 6 g fiber, 23 g pro.

PREP:
25 minutes

COOKER SIZE:
3½- or 4-quart

COOK:
6 to 7 hours on low-heat or 3 to 4 hours on high-heat setting, plus 30 minutes on high-heat setting

MAKES:
6 servings

This creamy clam soup with half-and-half and bacon is extra rich and slightly smoky.

Potato-Clam Chowder

3 strips bacon, cut up, or ¼ pound salt pork, diced
2 cans (6½ ounces each) minced clams
3 medium-size potatoes (1 pound), peeled and cut into bite-size pieces (3 cups)
1 cup chopped onions
1 cup coarsely shredded carrots
1 can (10¾ ounces) condensed cream of mushroom soup
¼ teaspoon black pepper
3 cups half-and-half or light cream

1. In skillet, cook bacon or salt pork until crisp; drain off fat. Drain clams, reserving liquid; add enough water to clam liquid to measure 1¾ cups total liquid. Cover clams; chill.

2. In 3½- or 4-quart slow cooker, combine reserved clam liquid, potatoes, onions and carrots. Stir in cream of mushroom soup and pepper. Add bacon or salt pork.

3. Cover slow cooker; cook on low-heat setting for 6 to 7 hours or on high-heat setting for 3 to 4 hours.

4. If necessary, raise temperature to high-heat setting. Stir in clams and half-and-half. Cover slow cooker; cook for 30 minutes longer.

· ·

Per serving: 339 cal., 19 g total fat (10 g sat. fat), 76 mg chol., 558 mg sodium, 26 g carbo., 2 g fiber, 17 g pro.

MAKE IT A MEAL:
Oyster crackers

Sliced green and/or red apples served with purchased caramel dip

Old Bay is a seafood seasoning that originated in the Chesapeake Bay area. Look for it with the herbs and spices at the supermarket.

Bacon-Topped Shrimp Bisque

PREP:
35 minutes

COOKER SIZE:
3½- or 4-quart

COOK:
6 to 8 hours on low-heat or 3 to 4 hours on high-heat setting, plus 45 minutes on high-heat setting

MAKES:
6 servings

- 3 **medium-size carrots, chopped**
- 1 **large potato, peeled and chopped**
- 2 **ribs celery, chopped**
- 1 **large onion, chopped**
- 2 **tablespoons tomato paste**
- 1 **teaspoon dried thyme**
- ½ **teaspoon Old Bay seasoning**
- ¼ **teaspoon salt**
- 2 **cans (14 ounces each) chicken broth**
- 1 **can (14½ ounces) diced tomatoes**
- ¾ **pound medium-size shrimp, shelled, deveined and halved lengthwise**
- ⅔ **cup half-and-half or light cream**
  Crisp-cooked bacon, crumbled

1. In 3½- or 4-quart slow cooker, combine carrots, potato, celery, onion, tomato paste, thyme, Old Bay seasoning and salt. Stir in chicken broth and tomatoes with their juices.

2. Cover slow cooker; cook on low-heat setting for 6 to 8 hours or on high-heat setting for 3 to 4 hours. Cool slightly.

3. Transfer one-quarter of the soup mixture to blender or food processor. Cover and blend or process until smooth. Repeat with the remaining soup mixture, one-quarter at a time, until all of the soup is blended.

4. If necessary, raise temperature to high-heat setting. Return pureed soup to slow cooker. Stir in shrimp and half-and-half. Cover slow cooker; cook about 45 minutes or until shrimp turn pink. Sprinkle each serving with bacon.

Per serving: 185 cal., 6 g total fat (3 g sat. fat), 80 mg chol., 988 mg sodium, 18 g carbo., 2 g fiber, 13 g pro.

MAKE IT A MEAL:
Mixed greens and Mandarin orange salad served with balsamic vinaigrette

Oyster crackers

Purchased frozen crème brûlée, baked

PREP:
15 minutes

COOKER SIZE:
3½- or 4-quart

COOK:
5 to 6 hours on low-heat or 3 to 3½ hours on high-heat setting, plus 15 minutes on high-heat setting

MAKES:
6 servings

Right after you put the shrimp in the slow cooker to heat through, bake the corn bread twists to serve with the kicked-up dish.

Cajun Shrimp And Rice

1 can (28 ounces) tomatoes, cut up
1 can (14 ounces) chicken broth
1 cup chopped onions
1 cup chopped green peppers
1 package (6 to 6¼ ounces) long-grain and wild rice mix
¼ cup water
2 cloves garlic, chopped
½ teaspoon Cajun seasoning
1 pound cooked, shelled and deveined shrimp with tails
  Hot-pepper sauce (optional)

1. In 3½- or 4-quart slow cooker, combine tomatoes with their juices, chicken broth, onions, green peppers, rice mix with seasoning packet, the water, garlic and Cajun seasoning.

2. Cover slow cooker; cook on low-heat setting for 5 to 6 hours or on high-heat setting for 3 to 3½ hours.

3. If necessary, raise temperature to high-heat setting. Stir shrimp into rice mixture. Cover slow cooker; cook for 15 minutes longer. If desired, pass hot-pepper sauce.

· ·

Per serving: 223 cal., 2 g total fat (0 g sat. fat), 147 mg chol., 1,063 mg sodium, 32 g carbo., 3 g fiber, 21 g pro.

MAKE IT A MEAL:
Fruit and Broccoli Salad (see recipe, page 248)

Refrigerated corn bread twists, baked

Purchased apple pie served with vanilla ice cream

PREP:
30 minutes

COOKER SIZE:
5- or 5½-quart

COOK:
5 hours on high-heat setting

MAKES:
8 servings

MAKE IT A MEAL:
Crusty Italian bread slices served with olive oil

Strawberry ice cream served with pirouette cookies

When you want to liven up a weeknight meal, you can't go wrong with this Cajun-inspired stew!

Seafood and Chorizo Jambalaya

1 large onion, chopped
2 ribs celery, sliced
1 green pepper, seeded and chopped
1 sweet red pepper, seeded and chopped
3 cloves garlic, chopped
1 package (10 ounces) frozen corn kernels, thawed
½ pound chorizo, cut into ½-inch pieces
1 can (6½ ounces) chopped clams, drained
1 can (15½ ounces) red kidney beans, drained
1 can (14½ ounces) stewed tomatoes
1 cup vegetable broth
1 can (8 ounces) tomato sauce
1½ teaspoons Cajun seasoning
½ teaspoon salt
1½ cups instant brown rice
½ pound cooked, shelled and deveined small shrimp with tails
3 scallions, trimmed and thinly sliced

1. In 5- or 5½-quart slow cooker, layer onion, celery, peppers, garlic, corn, chorizo, clams and kidney beans.

2. In large bowl, combine tomatoes with their juices, vegetable broth, tomato sauce, Cajun seasoning and salt. Pour into slow cooker.

3. Cover slow cooker; cook on high-heat setting for 5 hours. Before last 10 minutes of cooking, stir in instant brown rice and shrimp.

4. To serve, sprinkle with scallions.

Per serving: 360 cal., 13 g total fat (4 g sat. fat), 70 mg chol., 980 mg sodium, 43 g carbo., 8 g fiber, 21 g pro.

Meatless Dishes

120 Pasta with Eggplant Sauce

Vegetarian Chili 132

142 Sweet-and-Sour Cabbage Rolls

Smashed Potato Soup 143

Whether you eat meatless full time or just are looking to add some vegetarian fare to your repertoire, these recipes offer something for you. Full-flavor soups, pastas, casseroles and stews offer bold flavors and vibrant veggies, beans and lentils.

COOKER SIZE:
3½- or 4-quart

COOK:
7 to 9 hours on low-heat or 3½ to 4½ hours on high-heat setting

MAKES:
6 to 8 servings

FREEZE WITH EASE

MAKE IT A MEAL:
Fresh spinach leaves served with poppy seed dressing

Hot cooked pasta

Purchased cheesecake topped with cherry pie filling

There's no missing the meat when you have this thick and rich mixture mixed with pasta!

Pesto Beans and Pasta

2 cans (19 ounces each) white cannellini beans, drained and rinsed
1 can (14½ ounces) Italian-style stewed tomatoes
1 medium-size green pepper, seeded and chopped
1 medium-size sweet red pepper, seeded and chopped
1 medium-size onion, cut into thin wedges
2 teaspoons dried Italian seasoning
½ teaspoon cracked black pepper
4 cloves garlic, chopped
½ cup vegetable broth
½ cup dry white wine or vegetable broth
1 container (7 ounces) basil pesto
¾ pound penne pasta
½ cup finely shredded Parmesan cheese or Romano cheese

1. In 3½- or 4-quart slow cooker, combine beans, tomatoes with their juices, green pepper, sweet red pepper, onion, Italian seasoning, black pepper and garlic. Pour vegetable broth and wine over all.

2. Cover slow cooker; cook on low-heat setting for 7 to 9 hours or on high-heat setting for 3½ to 4½ hours. Using a slotted spoon, transfer bean mixture to a very large serving bowl, reserving cooking liquid. Stir pesto into bean mixture.

3. Meanwhile, cook pasta following package directions; drain well. Add pasta to bean mixture; toss gently to combine, adding enough of the reserved cooking liquid to make desired consistency. Sprinkle each serving with Parmesan cheese.

Per serving: 580 cal., 20 g total fat (2 g sat. fat), 10 mg chol., 843 mg sodium, 80 g carbo., 11 g fiber, 25 g pro.

PREP:
25 minutes

COOKER SIZE:
3½- to 5-quart

COOK:
7 to 8 hours on low-heat or 3½ to 4 hours on high-heat setting

MAKES:
6 servings

MAKE IT A MEAL:
Purchased hard breadsticks

Praline ice cream topped with crushed pecan sandies

Chunks of eggplant cook in a traditional spaghetti sauce, making a tasty alternative to ground beef or sausage.

Pasta with Eggplant Sauce

  1 **medium-size eggplant**
  ½ **cup chopped onion**
  2 **cans (14½ ounces each) diced tomatoes**
  1 **can (6 ounces) Italian-style tomato paste**
  1 **can (4 ounces) sliced mushrooms, drained**
  ¼ **cup dry red wine**
  ¼ **cup water**
  2 **cloves garlic, chopped**
1½ **teaspoons dried oregano**
  ⅓ **cup pitted kalamata olives or pitted ripe olives, sliced**
  2 **tablespoons chopped fresh parsley**
    Black pepper
    Hot cooked penne
  3 **tablespoons grated or shredded Parmesan cheese**

1. Peel eggplant, if desired; cut eggplant into 1-inch cubes. In 3½- to 5-quart slow cooker, combine eggplant, onion, tomatoes with their juices, tomato paste, mushrooms, wine, the water, garlic and oregano.

2. Cover slow cooker; cook on low-heat setting for 7 to 8 hours or on high-heat setting for 3½ to 4 hours.

3. Stir in olives and parsley. Season to taste with pepper. Serve over hot cooked pasta. Top each serving with Parmesan cheese.

Per serving:
346 cal., 4 g total fat (1 g sat. fat), 2 mg chol., 739 mg sodium, 65 g carbo., 9 g fiber, 13 g pro.

This easy-does-it recipe allows you to serve delicious homemade pasta sauce with fix-it-and-forget-it convenience.

Marinara Sauce With Pasta

1 can (28 ounces) whole Italian-style tomatoes, cut up
2 large carrots, coarsely chopped
3 ribs celery, sliced
1 large onion, chopped
1 large green pepper, seeded and chopped
1 can (6 ounces) tomato paste
½ cup water
3 cloves garlic, chopped
2 teaspoons sugar
2 teaspoons dried Italian seasoning
1 teaspoon salt
¼ teaspoon black pepper
1 bay leaf
¾ pound spaghetti or other favorite pasta
  Shredded Parmesan cheese
  Fresh herb sprigs (optional)

1. In 3½- or 4-quart slow cooker, combine tomatoes with their juices, carrots, celery, onion, green pepper, tomato paste, the water, garlic, sugar, Italian seasoning, salt, black pepper and bay leaf.

2. Cover slow cooker; cook on low-heat setting for 8 to 10 hours or on high-heat setting for 4 to 5 hours.

3. Remove and discard bay leaf. Cook pasta following package directions; drain well. Toss sauce with hot cooked pasta. Sprinkle mixture with Parmesan cheese. If desired, garnish with fresh herb sprigs.

Per serving: 308 cal., 1 g total fat (0 g sat. fat), 0 mg chol., 636 mg sodium, 64 g carbo., 6 g fiber, 11 g pro.

PREP:
25 minutes

COOKER SIZE:
3½- or 4-quart

COOK:
8 to 10 hours on low-heat or 4 to 5 hours on high-heat setting

MAKES:
6 servings

KIDS' FAVORITE!

FREEZE WITH EASE

MAKE IT A MEAL:
Iceberg lettuce served with ranch dressing and seasoned croutons

Crusty Italian bread slices served with herbed butter

Purchased biscotti

PREP:
20 minutes

COOKER SIZE:
3½- or 4-quart

COOK:
5 to 6 hours plus
1 hour on low-heat or
2½ to 3 hours plus
45 minutes on high-heat setting

MAKES:
4 servings

MAKE IT A MEAL:
Grilled provolone cheese sandwiches

Brownie and Walnut Pie (see recipe, page 274)

White sauce mix and dried tortellini make this soup extra easy; stirring in the spinach at the last minute gives it fresh flavor.

Creamy Tortellini Soup

1 envelope (1.8 ounces) white sauce mix
4 cups water
1 can (14 ounces) vegetable broth
1½ cups sliced fresh mushrooms
½ cup chopped onion
3 cloves garlic, chopped
½ teaspoon dried basil
¼ teaspoon salt
¼ teaspoon dried oregano
⅛ teaspoon cayenne pepper
1 package (7 to 8 ounces) dried cheese tortellini (about 2 cups)
1 can (12 ounces) evaporated milk
6 cups fresh baby spinach leaves or torn spinach
   Black pepper (optional)
   Finely shredded Parmesan cheese (optional)

1. Place dry white sauce mix in 3½- or 4-quart slow cooker. Gradually add the water to the white sauce mix, stirring until smooth. Stir in vegetable broth, mushrooms, onion, garlic, basil, salt, oregano and cayenne pepper.

2. Cover slow cooker; cook on low-heat setting for 5 to 6 hours or on high-heat setting for 2½ to 3 hours.

3. Stir in dried tortellini. Cover slow cooker; cook on low-heat setting for 1 hour longer or on high-heat setting for 45 minutes longer.

4. Stir in evaporated milk; stir in spinach. If desired, sprinkle each serving with black pepper and/or Parmesan cheese.

. . . .

Per serving: 450 cal., 18 g total fat (7 g sat. fat), 34 mg chol., 1,710 mg sodium, 53 g carbo., 2 g fiber, 22 g pro.

PREP:
15 minutes

COOKER SIZE:
3½- or 4-quart

COOK:
6 to 8 hours on low-heat or 3 to 4 hours on high-heat setting

STAND:
5 minutes

MAKES:
6 servings

Herb-infused tomatoes tango with garlic, artichokes and cream—a dance that renders pasta sauce with Mediterranean flair.

Garlic-Artichoke Pasta

3 cans (14½ ounces each) diced tomatoes with basil, oregano and garlic
2 cans (14 ounces each) artichoke hearts, drained and quartered
6 cloves garlic, chopped
½ cup heavy cream
  Hot cooked linguine, fettuccine or other favorite pasta
  Sliced pimiento-stuffed green olives and/or sliced pitted ripe olives (optional)
  Crumbled feta cheese or finely shredded Parmesan cheese (optional)

1. Coat 3½- or 4-quart slow cooker with nonstick cooking spray. Drain two of the cans of diced tomatoes (do not drain remaining can). In the prepared cooker, combine drained and undrained tomatoes, artichoke hearts and garlic.

2. Cover slow cooker; cook on low-heat setting for 6 to 8 hours or on high-heat setting for 3 to 4 hours. Stir in heavy cream; cover slow cooker and let stand about 5 minutes to heat through.

3. Serve sauce over hot cooked pasta. If desired, top with olives and/or cheese.

Per serving: 403 cal., 8 g total fat (5 g sat. fat), 27 mg chol., 1,513 mg sodium, 68 g carbo., 7 g fiber, 13 g pro.

MAKE IT A MEAL:
Mixed greens served with French dressing

Home Run Garlic Rolls (see recipe, page 263)

Purchased crepes, warmed and served with butter and cinnamon sugar

MEATLESS DISHES

Cream of mushroom soup and parma rosa pasta sauce mix give this dish creaminess and lots of flavor.

Tomato-Broccoli Sauced Pasta

2 **cans (14½ ounces each) diced tomatoes with basil, oregano and garlic**
2 **cans (10¾ ounces each) condensed cream of mushroom soup**
1 **cup water**
1 **envelope (1.3 ounces) parma rosa pasta sauce mix**
1 **package (16 ounces) frozen cut broccoli**
1 **pound penne or mostaccioli pasta**

1. Coat 3½- or 4-quart slow cooker with nonstick cooking spray. In large bowl, combine tomatoes with their juices, cream of mushroom soup, the water and dry sauce mix. Pour into prepared slow cooker.

2. Cover slow cooker; cook on low-heat setting for 6 to 8 hours or on high-heat setting for 3 to 4 hours.

3. If necessary, raise temperature to high-heat setting. Stir in broccoli. Cover slow cooker; cook on high-heat setting about 15 minutes longer or until broccoli is crisp-tender.

4. Meanwhile, cook pasta following package directions; drain well. Toss pasta with broccoli mixture.

- -

Per serving: 365 cal., 7 g total fat (2 g sat. fat), 1 mg chol., 1,270 mg sodium, 62 g carbo., 4 g fiber, 12 g pro.

PREP:
15 minutes

COOKER SIZE:
3½- or 4-quart

COOK:
6 to 8 hours on low-heat or 3 to 4 hours on high-heat setting, plus 15 minutes on high-heat setting

MAKES:
8 to 10 servings

KIDS' FAVORITE!

MAKE IT A MEAL:
Mixed greens with creamy garlic dressing

Parmesan Dinner Rolls (see recipe, page 264)

Chocolate mint sandwich cookies

PREP:
20 minutes

COOKER SIZE:
4½- to 5½-quart

COOK:
7 to 9 hours on low-heat or 3½ to 4½ hours on high-heat setting, plus 15 minutes on high-heat setting

MAKES:
6 servings

KIDS' FAVORITE!

MAKE IT A MEAL:
Broccoli-Cheddar Salad (see recipe, page 251)

Refrigerated garlic herb breadsticks, baked

Purchased pineapple upside-down cake

This isn't your ordinary vegetable soup! Chickpeas and potatoes make it hefty and satisfying.

Cream of Vegetable Soup

    1 package (16 ounces) loose-pack frozen small whole onions
    2 cups cubed potatoes
    2 cups sliced carrots
    1 can (15 ounces) chickpeas or navy beans, drained and rinsed
    1 package (10 ounces) frozen whole kernel corn
    1 cup sliced celery
    ½ teaspoon salt
    ½ teaspoon paprika
    ½ teaspoon black pepper
    2 cans (14 ounces each) vegetable broth or chicken broth
  1½ cups half-and-half or light cream
    ¼ cup all-purpose flour
       Salt
       Black pepper

1. In 4½- to 5½-quart slow cooker, combine onions, potatoes, carrots, chickpeas, frozen corn, celery, the ½ teaspoon salt, the paprika and the ½ teaspoon pepper. Pour vegetable broth over all.

2. Cover slow cooker; cook on low-heat setting for 7 to 9 hours or on high-heat setting for 3½ to 4½ hours. If necessary, raise temperature to high-heat setting.

3. In medium-size bowl, stir half-and-half into flour. Stir into vegetable mixture in cooker. Cover slow cooker; cook for 15 minutes longer. Season to taste with additional salt and pepper.

· ·

Per serving: 282 cal., 9 g total fat (4 g sat. fat), 22 mg chol., 1,079 mg sodium, 48 g carbo., 8 g fiber, 9 g pro.

With its combo of Cajun seasoning, black beans, tomatoes and okra, this zesty gumbo is sure to be a hit on any menu.

Cajun-Seasoned Vegetarian Gumbo

- 2 **cans (15 ounces each) black beans, drained and rinsed**
- 1 **can (28 ounces) diced tomatoes**
- 1 **package (16 ounces) frozen sweet peppers and onion stir-fry vegetables**
- 2 **cups loose-pack frozen cut okra**
- 2 **to 3 teaspoons Cajun seasoning**
  Hot cooked white rice or brown rice (optional)

1. In 3½- to 4½-quart slow cooker, combine black beans, tomatoes with their juices, frozen stir-fry vegetables, frozen okra and Cajun seasoning.

2. Cover slow cooker; cook on low-heat setting for 6 to 8 hours or on high-heat setting for 3 to 4 hours. If desired, serve over hot cooked rice.

Per serving: 153 cal., 0 g total fat (0 g sat. fat), 0 mg chol., 639 mg sodium, 31 g carbo., 10 g fiber, 12 g pro.

PREP:
10 minutes

COOKER SIZE:
3½- to 4½-quart

COOK:
6 to 8 hours on low-heat or 3 to 4 hours on high-heat setting

MAKES:
6 servings

FREEZE WITH EASE

MAKE IT A MEAL:
Grilled Swiss cheese and tomato sandwiches

Easy Apple-Cherry Crisp (see recipe, page 280)

PREP:
25 minutes

COOKER SIZE:
3½- to 5-quart

COOK:
7 to 9 hours on low-heat or 3½ to 4½ hours on high-heat setting

STAND:
5 minutes

MAKES:
4 servings

MAKE IT A MEAL:
Toasted pita bread wedges

Lemon sorbet topped with crushed amaretti cookies

Vary the flavor by the type of curry powder you use. Since each brand is different, try a few kinds to find the one you like best.

Vegetable Curry Over Rice

- 4 **medium-size carrots, sliced**
- 2 **medium-size potatoes, cut into ½-inch cubes**
- 1 **can (15 ounces) chickpeas, drained and rinsed**
- ½ **pound fresh green beans, cut into 1-inch pieces**
- 1 **cup coarsely chopped onion**
- 3 **cloves garlic, chopped**
- 2 **tablespoons quick-cooking tapioca**
- 2 **teaspoons curry powder**
- 1 **teaspoon ground coriander**
- ¼ **to ½ teaspoon crushed red pepper**
- ¼ **teaspoon salt**
- ⅛ **teaspoon ground cinnamon**
- 1 **can (14 ounces) vegetable broth or chicken broth**
- 1 **can (14½ ounces) diced tomatoes**
  Hot cooked rice

1. In 3½- to 5-quart slow cooker, combine carrots, potatoes, chickpeas, green beans, onion, garlic, tapioca, curry powder, coriander, crushed red pepper, salt and cinnamon. Pour vegetable broth over all.

2. Cover slow cooker; cook on low-heat setting for 7 to 9 hours or on high-heat setting for 3½ to 4½ hours.

3. Stir in tomatoes with their juices. Cover slow cooker; let stand for 5 minutes. Serve over hot cooked rice.

Per serving: 407 cal., 3 g total fat (0 g sat. fat), 0 mg chol., 1,068 mg sodium, 87 g carbo., 12 g fiber, 13 g pro.

PREP:
20 minutes

COOKER SIZE:
3½- or 4-quart

COOK:
6 to 8 hours on low-heat or 3 to 4 hours on high-heat setting

MAKES:
8 servings

KIDS' FAVORITE!

FREEZE WITH EASE

MAKE IT A MEAL:

Purchased fruit salad

Mexican-Style Rice
(see recipe, page 258)

Purchased Key
lime pie

Take your choice of kidney beans or black beans for these flavorful bundles. Or better yet, use a combo of both kinds of beans.

Bean and Corn Burritos

- 3 cans (15 ounces each) red kidney and/or black beans, drained and rinsed
- 1 can (14½ ounces) diced tomatoes
- 1½ cups bottled salsa or picante sauce
- 1 can (11 ounces) whole kernel corn with sweet peppers, drained
- 1 fresh jalapeño chile, seeded and finely chopped* (optional)
- 2 teaspoons chili powder
- 2 cloves garlic, chopped
- 16 (8- to 10-inch) flour tortillas, warmed**
- 2 cups shredded lettuce
- 1 cup shredded taco cheese or Cheddar cheese (4 ounces)
  Sliced scallions and/or sour cream (optional)

1. In 3½- or 4-quart slow cooker, combine beans, tomatoes with their juices, salsa or picante sauce, corn, jalapeño chile (if desired), chili powder and garlic.

2. Cover slow cooker; cook on low-heat setting for 6 to 8 hours or on high-heat setting for 3 to 4 hours.

3. To serve, spoon bean mixture just below centers of tortillas. Top with lettuce and cheese. If desired, top with scallions and/or sour cream. Fold bottom edge of each tortilla up and over filling. Fold in opposite sides; roll up from bottom.

- -

Per serving: 417 cal., 5 g total fat (4 g sat. fat), 14 mg chol., 1,126 mg sodium, 69 g carbo., 12 g fiber, 17 g pro.

*Note: Because chiles contain volatile oils that can burn your skin and eyes, avoid direct contact with them as much as possible. When working with chiles, wear plastic or rubber gloves. If your bare hands do touch the chiles, wash your hands and nails well with soap and warm water.

**Note: To warm tortillas, heat oven to 350°. Stack tortillas and wrap tightly in aluminum foil. Warm at 350° about 10 minutes or until heated through.

Salsa adds zip to this soup which features a multitude of chunky vegetables.

Mexican Minestrone

2 cans (15 ounces each) black beans, drained and rinsed
2 cans (14½ ounces each) Mexican-style stewed tomatoes
2 cans (14 ounces) vegetable broth
1 can (15¼ ounces) whole kernel corn, drained and rinsed
1 can (15 ounces) chickpeas, drained and rinsed
2 cups diced red-skin potatoes
2 cups loose-pack frozen cut green beans
1 cup bottled salsa
   Sour cream (optional)

1. In 5- to 6-quart slow cooker, combine black beans, tomatoes with their juices, vegetable broth, corn, chickpeas, potatoes, frozen green beans and salsa.

2. Cover slow cooker; cook on low-heat setting for 9 to 11 hours or on high-heat setting for 4½ to 5½ hours. If desired, serve with sour cream.

Per serving: 199 cal., 4 g total fat (2 g sat. fat), 5 mg chol., 1,051 mg sodium, 37 g carbo., 7 g fiber, 10 g pro.

PREP:
15 minutes

COOKER SIZE:
5- to 6-quart

COOK:
9 to 11 hours on low-heat or 4½ to 5½ hours on high-heat setting

MAKES:
12 servings

KIDS' FAVORITE!

FREEZE WITH EASE

MAKE IT A MEAL:
Tortilla chips

Sliced apples and pears

Rocky Road Malts (see recipe, page 278)

MEATLESS DISHES

131

PREP:
20 minutes

COOKER SIZE:
1½-quart

COOK:
6 to 8 hours on low-heat or 3 to 4 hours on high-heat setting

MAKES:
2 servings

KIDS' FAVORITE!

FREEZE WITH EASE

MAKE IT A MEAL:
Saltine crackers

Baby carrots and celery sticks

Purchased white chocolate macadamia nut cookies

This hearty chili for two is so full of flavor that you'll never miss the meat.

Vegetarian Chili

 1 can (15 ounces) black beans, drained and rinsed
1½ cups low-sodium tomato juice
 1 cup loose-pack frozen whole kernel corn
 ¾ cup coarsely chopped zucchini or yellow summer squash
 ⅓ cup coarsely chopped sweet red or yellow pepper
 ¼ cup chopped onion
 1 teaspoon chili powder
 ¼ teaspoon dried oregano
 ⅛ teaspoon salt
 1 clove garlic, chopped

1. In 1½-quart slow cooker, combine drained beans, tomato juice, corn, zucchini, sweet pepper, onion, chili powder, oregano, salt and garlic.

2. Cover slow cooker; cook on low-heat setting for 6 to 8 hours or on high-heat setting for 3 to 4 hours. If no heat setting is available, cook for 5 to 6 hours.

Per serving: 271 cal., 2 g total fat (0 g sat. fat), 0 mg chol., 790 mg sodium, 59 g carbo., 14 g fiber, 19 g pro.

PREP:
20 minutes

COOKER SIZE:
3½- or 4-quart

COOK:
5 to 7 hours on low-heat or 2½ to 3½ hours on high-heat setting

MAKES:
6 servings

MAKE IT A MEAL:
Toasted pita bread wedges with purchased tapenade

Strawberry frozen yogurt topped with sliced fresh strawberries

Converted rice is just right for this dish; instant or long-grain rice would lose its shape during the long cooking time.

Savory Bean and Spinach Soup

3 cans (14 ounces each) vegetable broth
1 can (15 ounces) tomato puree
1 can (15 ounces) small white beans or Great Northern beans, drained and rinsed
½ cup converted rice
½ cup finely chopped onion
1 teaspoon dried basil
¼ teaspoon salt
¼ teaspoon black pepper
2 cloves garlic, chopped
8 cups coarsely chopped fresh spinach or kale leaves
Finely shredded Parmesan cheese

1. In 3½- or 4-quart slow cooker, combine vegetable broth, tomato puree, white beans, uncooked rice, onion, basil, salt, pepper and garlic.

2. Cover slow cooker; cook on low-heat setting for 5 to 7 hours or on high-heat setting for 2½ to 3½ hours.

3. Just before serving, stir in spinach. Sprinkle each serving with Parmesan cheese.

· ·

Per serving: 150 cal., 3 g total fat (1 g sat. fat), 4 mg chol., 1,137 mg sodium, 31 g carbo., 8 g fiber, 9 g pro.

Enjoy these Greek-seasoned lentils on flatbread wedges with sprinkles of sliced scallions, chopped tomatoes and a little sour cream.

Greek-Seasoned Lentils

2 cups dry brown lentils, rinsed and drained
2 cups shredded carrots
1 cup chopped onions
3 cans (14 ounces each) vegetable broth
2 teaspoons Greek seasoning

1. Lightly coat 3½- to 5-quart slow cooker with nonstick cooking spray. In the prepared cooker, combine brown lentils, carrots, onions, vegetable broth and Greek seasoning.

2. Cover slow cooker; cook on low-heat setting for 6 to 7 hours or on high-heat setting for 3 to 3½ hours. Serve lentils with a slotted spoon.

• •

Per serving: 260 cal., 2 g total fat (0 g sat. fat), 0 mg chol., 874 mg sodium, 45 g carbo., 21 g fiber, 20 g pro.

PREP:
20 minutes

COOKER SIZE:
3½- to 5-quart

COOK:
6 to 7 hours on low-heat or 3 to 3½ hours on high-heat setting

MAKES:
6 servings

MAKE IT A MEAL:
Flatbread wedges

Steamed cauliflower

Mixed berries

Rocky Road Malts
(see recipe, page 278)

PREP:
30 minutes

COOKER SIZE:
1½-quart

COOK:
4½ to 5 hours on low-heat or 2 to 2½ hours on high-heat setting

BROIL:
30 seconds

MAKES:
2 servings

MAKE IT A MEAL:

Fresh broccoli flowerets with dill-flavor sour cream dip

Fresh blueberries topped with sweetened whipped cream

This slow-cooked version of the French classic ratatouille has the typical vegetables—eggplant, peppers, tomatoes, onions and squash.

Ratatouille with Parmesan Toast

Ratatouille:
- 1½ cups cubed, peeled (if desired) eggplant
- ½ cup coarsely chopped yellow summer squash or zucchini
- ½ cup coarsely chopped tomato
- ½ of a can (8 ounces) no-salt-added tomato sauce
- ⅓ cup coarsely chopped sweet red or green pepper
- ¼ cup finely chopped onion
- ¼ teaspoon salt
- ⅛ teaspoon black pepper
- 1 clove garlic, chopped
- 1 tablespoon chopped fresh basil

Parmesan Toast:
- 4 ½-inch-thick slices baguette-style French bread
- 1 teaspoon olive oil
- 3 tablespoons finely shredded Parmesan cheese

1. **Ratatouille:** In 1½-quart slow cooker, combine eggplant, squash, chopped tomato, tomato sauce, sweet pepper, onion, salt, black pepper and garlic.

2. Cover slow cooker; cook on low-heat setting for 4½ to 5 hours or on high-heat setting for 2 to 2½ hours. If no heat setting is available, cook for 4 to 4½ hours.

3. **Parmesan Toast:** Heat broiler. Brush one side of each bread slice with olive oil. Place bread slices, oiled sides up, on a baking sheet. Broil 3 to 4 inches from heat about 15 seconds or until toasted (watch carefully to avoid burning). Sprinkle bread slices with 1 tablespoon of the Parmesan cheese. Broil about 15 seconds longer or until cheese is melted.

4. Stir basil into mixture in cooker. Serve in shallow bowls with Parmesan Toast. Sprinkle with the remaining 2 tablespoons Parmesan cheese.

Per serving: 248 cal., 6 g total fat (2 g sat. fat), 5 mg chol., 739 mg sodium, 39 g carbo., 6 g fiber, 10 g pro.

PREP:
15 minutes

COOKER SIZE:
3½- or 4-quart

COOK:
3½ to 4½ hours on low-heat setting

MAKES:
4 servings

KIDS' FAVORITE!

FREEZE WITH EASE

MAKE IT A MEAL:
Greens and Berry Salad (see recipe, page 247)

Frozen whole wheat rolls, baked

Bake some rolls and toss the salad to go with this cheesy chickpea-and-veggie combo, and dinner is ready.

Vegetable-Rice Casserole

1 package (16 ounces) loose-pack frozen cauliflower, broccoli and carrots
1 can (15 ounces) chickpeas, drained and rinsed
1 can (10¾ ounces) condensed cream of celery soup
   or cream of mushroom soup
1 cup instant white rice
½ of a jar (15 ounces) process cheese dip (about 1 cup)
1 cup water

1. In 3½- or 4-quart slow cooker, combine frozen vegetables and chickpeas. In medium-size bowl, stir together cream of celery soup, uncooked rice, cheese dip and the water; pour over mixture in cooker.

2. Cover slow cooker; cook on low-heat setting for 3½ to 4½ hours or until vegetables and rice are tender. Stir well before serving.

Per serving: 436 cal., 17 g total fat (10 g sat. fat), 34 mg chol., 1,923 mg sodium, 52 g carbo., 9 g fiber, 17 g pro.

Barley adds a hearty texture and slightly nutty flavor to this homey soup. Look for it in the grains section of your supermarket.

Vegetable-Barley Soup

PREP:
15 minutes

COOKER SIZE:
3½- or 4-quart

COOK:
8 to 10 hours on low-heat or 4 to 5 hours on high-heat setting

MAKES:
3 servings

3½ cups water
1 can (14½ ounces) diced tomatoes
1½ cups sliced zucchini
1 package (10 ounces) frozen mixed vegetables
1 can (8 ounces) tomato sauce
1 cup chopped celery
½ cup regular barley (not quick-cooking)
½ cup chopped onion
2 large vegetable bouillon cubes (each cube makes 2 cups broth)
1½ teaspoons dried Italian seasoning

1. In 3½- or 4-quart slow cooker, combine the water, tomatoes with their juices, zucchini, frozen mixed vegetables, tomato sauce, celery, barley, onion, bouillon cubes and Italian seasoning.

2. Cover slow cooker; cook on low-heat setting for 8 to 10 hours or on high-heat setting for 4 to 5 hours.

• •

Per serving: 254 cal., 2 g total fat (0 g sat. fat), 0 mg chol., 1,430 mg sodium, 54 g carbo., 12 g fiber, 10 g pro.

KIDS' FAVORITE!

FREEZE WITH EASE

MAKE IT A MEAL:
Grilled Cheddar cheese sandwiches

Vanilla milkshakes

MEATLESS DISHES

PREP:
30 minutes

COOKER SIZE:
3½- or 4-quart

COOK:
8 to 10 hours on low-heat or 4 to 5 hours on high-heat setting, plus 50 minutes on high-heat setting

MAKES:
6 servings

KIDS' FAVORITE!

MAKE IT A MEAL:
Seedless red or green grapes

Fudge Cookies in Chocolate Cream (see recipe, page 276)

The hint of Parmesan cheese in the cornmeal dumplings makes them a fine match for this garlic-seasoned stew.

Vegetable Stew with Cornmeal Dumplings

Stew:
- 3 cups peeled butternut or acorn squash cut into ½-inch cubes
- 2 cups sliced fresh mushrooms
- 2 cans (14½ ounces each) diced tomatoes
- 1 can (15 ounces) Great Northern beans, drained and rinsed
- 1 cup water
- 4 cloves garlic, chopped
- 1 teaspoon dried Italian seasoning
- ¼ teaspoon black pepper
- 1 package (9 ounces) frozen Italian-style green beans or frozen cut green beans

Dumplings:
- ½ cup all-purpose flour
- ⅓ cup cornmeal
- 2 tablespoons grated Parmesan cheese
- 1 tablespoon chopped fresh parsley
- 1 teaspoon baking powder
- ¼ teaspoon salt
- 1 egg
- 2 tablespoons milk
- 2 tablespoons vegetable oil
  Paprika

1. Stew: In 3½- or 4-quart slow cooker, combine squash, mushrooms, tomatoes with their juices, Great Northern beans, the water, garlic, Italian seasoning and pepper.

2. Cover slow cooker; cook on low-heat setting for 8 to 10 hours or on high-heat setting for 4 to 5 hours.

3. Dumplings: In medium-size bowl, stir together flour, cornmeal, Parmesan cheese, parsley, baking powder and salt. In small bowl, whisk together egg, milk and oil. Add to the flour mixture; stir with a fork just until combined.

4. If necessary, raise temperature to high-heat setting. Stir frozen green beans into stew. Drop the dumpling dough into six mounds on top of the stew. Sprinkle with paprika. Cover slow cooker; cook for 50 minutes longer. (Do not lift lid while dumplings are cooking.)

- -

Per serving: 288 cal., 7 g total fat (2 g sat. fat), 37 mg chol., 442 mg sodium, 45 g carbo., 7 g fiber, 12 g pro.

PREP:
45 minutes

COOKER SIZE:
5- to 6-quart

COOK:
6 to 7 hours on low-heat or 3 to 3½ hours on high-heat setting

MAKES:
4 servings

MAKE IT A MEAL:
Buttermilk Angel Biscuits (see recipe, page 267)

Purchased carrot cake

Raisins add a touch of sweetness and a splash of lemon juice adds a bit of tartness to the sauce for these plump cabbage rolls.

Sweet-and-Sour Cabbage Rolls

 1 large head green cabbage
3½ cups purchased marinara sauce or meatless spaghetti sauce
 1 can (15 ounces) black beans or red kidney beans, drained and rinsed
 1 cup cooked brown rice
 ½ cup chopped carrot
 ½ cup chopped celery
 ½ cup chopped onion
 1 clove garlic, chopped
 ⅓ cup raisins
 3 tablespoons lemon juice
 1 tablespoon brown sugar

1. Remove eight large outer leaves from cabbage. In Dutch oven, cook cabbage leaves in boiling water for 4 to 5 minutes or just until limp; drain well. Trim the heavy vein from each cabbage leaf; set leaves aside. Shred 4 cups of the remaining cabbage; place shredded cabbage in 5- to 6-quart slow cooker.

2. In medium-size bowl, combine ½ cup of the marinara sauce, the drained beans, cooked rice, carrot, celery, onion and garlic. Spoon about ⅓ cup of the bean mixture onto each cabbage leaf. Fold in sides; roll up each leaf.

3. In another medium-size bowl, combine the remaining 3 cups marinara sauce, the raisins, lemon juice and brown sugar. Stir about half of the sauce mixture into shredded cabbage in slow cooker. Place cabbage rolls on top of shredded cabbage. Spoon the remaining sauce mixture over all.

4. Cover slow cooker; cook on low-heat setting for 6 to 7 hours or on high-heat setting for 3 to 3½ hours. Carefully remove cabbage rolls and serve with the shredded cabbage mixture.

Per serving: 387 cal., 6 g total fat (1 g sat. fat), 0 mg chol., 1,368 mg sodium, 76 g carbo., 11 g fiber, 15 g pro.

Potatoes blend with Cheddar cheese, cream and roasted garlic in this good-to-the-last-spoonful chunky soup.

Smashed Potato Soup

3½ pounds potatoes, peeled and cut into ¾-inch cubes
½ cup chopped sweet yellow and/or red pepper
1½ teaspoons bottled roasted garlic
½ teaspoon black pepper
4½ cups vegetable broth or chicken broth
1 cup shredded Cheddar cheese (4 ounces)
½ cup heavy cream, half-and-half or light cream
½ cup thinly sliced scallions
  Sliced scallions (optional)

1. In 4- to 6-quart slow cooker, combine potatoes, sweet pepper, roasted garlic and black pepper. Pour vegetable broth over all.

2. Cover slow cooker; cook on low-heat setting for 8 to 10 hours or on high-heat setting for 4 to 5 hours.

3. Using potato masher, mash potatoes slightly. Stir in Cheddar cheese, heavy cream and the ½ cup thinly sliced scallions. If desired, top each serving with additional sliced scallions.

Per serving: 238 cal., 10 g total fat (6 g sat. fat), 35 mg chol., 633 mg sodium, 30 g carbo., 3 g fiber, 7 g pro.

PREP:
25 minutes

COOKER SIZE:
4- to 6-quart

COOK:
8 to 10 hours on low-heat or 4 to 5 hours on high-heat setting

MAKES:
8 servings

KIDS' FAVORITE!

MAKE IT A MEAL:
Egg salad sandwiches on marble rye bread

Purchased mixed berry pie

PREP:
20 minutes

COOKER SIZE:
3½- or 4-quart

COOK:
7 to 8 hours on low-heat or 3½ to 4 hours on high-heat setting

MAKES:
6 servings

MAKE IT A MEAL:
Refrigerated Southern-style biscuits, baked

Root Beer Float Cake (see recipe, page 272)

Look for tubes of refrigerated polenta in the produce section of the supermarket.

Sweet Beans and Lentils over Polenta

1 can (14 ounces) vegetable broth
1 package (12 ounces) frozen sweet soybeans (edamame)
1 cup dry brown lentils, rinsed and drained
1 medium-size sweet red pepper, seeded and chopped
½ cup water
1 teaspoon dried oregano
2 cloves garlic, chopped
½ teaspoon salt
1 package (16 ounces) heat-and-serve refrigerated polenta
2 medium-size tomatoes, chopped

1. In 3½- or 4-quart slow cooker, combine vegetable broth, soybeans, lentils, sweet pepper, the water, oregano, garlic and salt.

2. Cover slow cooker; cook on low-heat setting for 7 to 8 hours or on high-heat setting for 3½ to 4 hours.

3. Prepare polenta following package directions. Stir tomatoes into lentil mixture; serve over polenta.

Per serving: 280 cal., 5 g total fat (1 g sat. fat), 0 mg chol., 794 mg sodium, 43 g carbo., 15 g fiber, 19 g pro.

Soups and Stews

150   Italian Wedding Soup

Asian-Style Beef Stew   165

182   Confetti Chicken Chili

Zesty Minestrone Soup   211

Creamy chowders, meaty stews, brothy soups and spicy chilis—these are the heart and soul of the slow cooker for many cooks. The variety of soups and stews in this chapter offers something for every taste and every occasion.

PREP:
20 minutes

COOKER SIZE:
3½- or 4-quart

COOK:
8 to 10 hours on low-heat or 4 to 5 hours on high-heat setting

MAKES:
4 servings

KIDS' FAVORITE!

MAKE IT A MEAL:
Crusty rolls

Chocolate mint ice cream with hot fudge sauce

Start this quick-to-assemble recipe before you head out, and supper will be ready and waiting when you return.

Busy-Day Beef-Vegetable Soup

1 pound boneless beef chuck roast, trimmed and cut into bite-size pieces
3 medium-size carrots, cut into ½-inch-thick slices
2 small potatoes, peeled if desired and cut into ½-inch cubes
1 medium-size onion, chopped
½ teaspoon salt
½ teaspoon dried thyme
1 bay leaf
2 cans (14½ ounces each) diced tomatoes
1 cup water
½ cup loose-pack frozen peas
   Fresh parsley sprigs (optional)

1. In 3½- or 4-quart slow cooker, combine beef, carrots, potatoes and onion. Sprinkle with salt and thyme. Add bay leaf. Pour tomatoes with their juices and the water over mixture in slow cooker.

2. Cover slow cooker; cook on low-heat setting for 8 to 10 hours or on high-heat setting for 4 to 5 hours. Remove and discard bay leaf. Stir in frozen peas. If desired, garnish with parsley.

· ·

Per serving: 269 cal., 4 g total fat (1 g sat. fat), 67 mg chol., 746 mg sodium, 29 g carbo., 4 g fiber, 28 g pro.

PREP:
25 minutes

COOKER SIZE:
3½- or 4-quart

COOK:
10 to 12 hours on low-heat or 5 to 6 hours on high-heat setting

MAKES:
4 servings

Look for ground chipotle chiles in the spice section of a large supermarket or use chili powder to season the beef.

Zesty Beef and Vegetable Soup

2 tablespoons all-purpose flour
1 teaspoon ground chipotle chiles or chili powder
1 pound beef stew meat cubes
2 tablespoons vegetable oil
1 cup sliced fresh mushrooms
½ cup chopped carrot
½ cup chopped onion
1 cup loose-pack frozen succotash
1 teaspoon dried oregano
2 cans (14 ounces each) beef broth

1. In plastic food-storage bag, combine flour and ground chipotle chiles or chili powder. Add beef cubes; shake until beef is coated. In large skillet, brown beef, half at a time, in hot oil.

2. In 3½- or 4-quart slow cooker, layer mushrooms, carrot, onion and succotash. Add browned beef and oregano. Pour beef broth over mixture in slow cooker.

3. Cover slow cooker; cook on low-heat setting for 10 to 12 hours or on high-heat setting for 5 to 6 hours.

· ·

Per serving: 312 cal., 15 g total fat (3 g sat. fat), 54 mg chol., 884 mg sodium, 15 g carbo., 3 g fiber, 30 g pro.

FREEZE WITH EASE

MAKE IT A MEAL:
Purchased corn bread muffins

Purchased fudge brownies with cream cheese frosting

Instant coffee crystals and a trio of spices—cumin, ginger and allspice—lend rich, brown color and piquant flavor to this meaty soup.

Zesty Tomato-Beef Soup

PREP:
30 minutes

COOKER SIZE:
3½- or 4-quart

COOK:
8 to 10 hours on low-heat or 4 to 5 hours on high-heat setting

MAKES:
6 servings

- 2 tablespoons all-purpose flour
- 1 pound beef stew meat cubes
- 2 tablespoons vegetable oil
- ¾ pound tiny new potatoes, halved or quartered
- 4 medium-size carrots, cut into ½-inch pieces
- 1 large onion, chopped
- 1 can (14½ ounces) diced tomatoes with chili spices
- 1 can (14 ounces) beef broth
- 2 tablespoons brown sugar
- 1 tablespoon Worcestershire sauce
- 1 tablespoon apple cider vinegar
- 1½ teaspoons instant coffee crystals
- 1 teaspoon ground cumin
- ½ teaspoon ground ginger
- ¼ teaspoon ground allspice

1. Place flour in a large resealable plastic food-storage bag. Add beef; shake until beef is coated. In large skillet, brown half of the beef in 1 tablespoon of the oil, turning to brown evenly. Remove beef from skillet. Brown the remaining beef in the remaining 1 tablespoon oil. Drain off fat.

2. In 3½- or 4-quart slow cooker, combine potatoes, carrots and onion. Add beef.

3. In large bowl, stir together tomatoes with their juices, beef broth, brown sugar, Worcestershire sauce, vinegar, coffee crystals, cumin, ginger and allspice. Pour over mixture in slow cooker.

4. Cover slow cooker; cook on low-heat setting for 8 to 10 hours or on high-heat setting for 4 to 5 hours.

Per serving: 257 cal., 8 g total fat (2 g sat. fat), 45 mg chol., 663 mg sodium, 27 g carbo., 3 g fiber, 19 g pro.

MAKE IT A MEAL:
Purchased sourdough rolls served with butter

Rocky Road Malts (see recipe, page 278)

PREP:
30 minutes

COOKER SIZE:
4½- to 5½-quart

COOK:
8 to 10 hours on low-heat or 4 to 5 hours on high-heat setting, plus 15 minutes on high-heat setting

MAKES:
6 servings

KIDS' FAVORITE!

FREEZE WITH EASE

MAKE IT A MEAL:

Refrigerated Parmesan garlic breadsticks, baked

Purchased tiramisu

Reportedly Italian wedding soup derived its name from the marriage of beef and greens.

Italian Wedding Soup

1 **large onion**
1 **egg, lightly beaten**
¼ **cup packaged plain dry bread crumbs**
3 **oil-pack dried tomatoes, finely chopped**
2 **teaspoons dried Italian seasoning**
1 **pound lean ground beef (93% lean)**
2 **teaspoons extra-virgin olive oil**
1 **large fennel bulb**
4 **cans (14 ounces each) chicken broth**
6 **cloves garlic, thinly sliced**
½ **teaspoon freshly ground white pepper**
1 **cup orzo pasta**
5 **cups shredded fresh spinach**

1. Finely chop one-third of the onion; thinly slice the remaining onion. In medium-size bowl, combine the chopped onion, egg, bread crumbs, dried tomatoes and 1 teaspoon of the Italian seasoning. Add ground beef; mix well. Shape into 12 meatballs. In large skillet, brown meatballs in hot oil. Drain off fat. Place meatballs and the sliced onion in 4½- to 5½-quart slow cooker.

2. Cut off and discard upper stalks of fennel. If desired, save some of the feathery leaves for a garnish. Remove any wilted outer layers; cut off a thin slice from fennel base. Cut fennel into thin wedges. Add fennel, chicken broth, garlic, white pepper and the remaining 1 teaspoon Italian seasoning to slow cooker.

3. Cover slow cooker; cook on low-heat setting for 8 to 10 hours or on high-heat setting for 4 to 5 hours.

4. If necessary, raise temperature to high-heat setting. Gently stir uncooked orzo into mixture in slow cooker. Cover slow cooker; cook for 15 minutes longer. Stir in spinach. If desired, garnish soup with reserved fennel leaves.

Per serving: 318 cal., 9 g total fat (3 g sat. fat), 76 mg chol., 868 mg sodium, 34 g carbo., 4 g fiber, 26 g pro.

PREP:
20 minutes

COOKER SIZE:
3½- or 4-quart

COOK:
7 to 8 hours on low-heat or 3½ to 4 hours on high-heat setting

MAKES:
4 or 5 servings

FREEZE WITH EASE

MAKE IT A MEAL:
Frozen whole wheat bread, baked

Steamed fresh sugar snap peas

Purchased pound cake topped with mixed berries

Lentils make this dish extra easy because they don't require presoaking or precooking; just rinse and add them with the other ingredients.

Beef and Lentil Soup

¾	pound lean boneless beef or lamb, trimmed and cut into ½-inch cubes
1	tablespoon vegetable oil
1	cup thinly sliced celery
1	cup coarsely chopped carrots
1	cup dry lentils, rinsed and drained
1	can (10½ ounces) condensed French onion soup
1½	teaspoons dried thyme
½	teaspoon salt
½	teaspoon black pepper
3¼	cups water

1. In large skillet, brown beef in hot oil. In 3½- or 4-quart slow cooker, combine celery, carrots and lentils. Top with browned beef. Stir in French onion soup, thyme, salt and pepper. Gradually stir in the water.

2. Cover slow cooker; cook on low-heat setting for 7 to 8 hours or on high-heat setting for 3½ to 4 hours.

Per serving: 365 cal., 10 g total fat (2 g sat. fat), 38 mg chol., 918 mg sodium, 37 g carbo., 17 g fiber, 32 g pro.

The robust Italian flavors of this soup call for a hearty bread to go along with it. Try wedges of focaccia or thick slices of crusty bread.

Beef and Tortellini Soup

1 tablespoon all-purpose flour
½ teaspoon salt
½ teaspoon black pepper
½ pound 1-inch-thick boneless beef round steak, trimmed and cut into 1-inch pieces
½ cup chopped onion
1 tablespoon butter or margarine
1 can (14 ounces) beef broth
1 jar (14 ounces) roasted garlic pasta sauce
1 cup sliced carrot
½ cup water
½ teaspoon dried Italian seasoning
1 medium-size zucchini, cut in thin bite-size strips (1¼ cups)
1 package (9 ounces) refrigerated cheese-filled tortellini

1. In large plastic food-storage bag, combine flour, salt and pepper. Add steak pieces, a few at a time, shaking to coat. In large skillet, cook steak and onion in hot butter over medium heat until steak is brown and onion is tender. Drain off fat. Transfer steak mixture to 3½- or 4-quart slow cooker. Stir in beef broth, pasta sauce, carrot, the water and Italian seasoning.

2. Cover slow cooker; cook on low-heat setting for 7 to 8 hours or on high-heat setting for 3½ to 4 hours.

3. If necessary, raise temperature to high-heat setting. Stir zucchini and tortellini into slow cooker. Cover slow cooker; cook for 30 minutes longer.

. . . .

Per serving: 383 cal., 11 g total fat (4 g sat. fat), 71 mg chol., 1,252 mg sodium, 45 g carbo., 3 g fiber, 26 g pro.

PREP:
20 minutes

COOKER SIZE:
3½- or 4-quart

COOK:
7 to 8 hours on low-heat or 3½ to 4 hours on high-heat setting, plus 30 minutes on high-heat setting

MAKES:
4 servings

KIDS' FAVORITE!

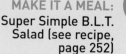

MAKE IT A MEAL:
Super Simple B.L.T. Salad (see recipe, page 252)

Purchased focaccia wedges served with olive oil

Chocolate ice cream sprinkled with crushed biscotti

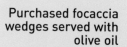

PREP:
25 minutes

COOKER SIZE:
5½- or 6-quart

COOK:
10 to 12 hours on low-heat or 5 to 6 hours on high-heat setting

MAKES:
10 to 12 servings

FREEZE WITH EASE

MAKE IT A MEAL:
Refrigerated corn bread twists, baked

Shortbread Brownies (see recipe, page 270)

It's easy to feed a crowd with this great-tasting beef-and-bean combo. Come serving time, set out your favorite toppers and a stack of bowls.

Spicy Game-Day Chili

2 pounds boneless beef round steak or boneless pork shoulder, trimmed and cut into ½-inch cubes
2 large onions, chopped
2 large sweet yellow, red and/or green peppers, seeded and coarsely chopped
2 cans (15 ounces each) chili beans with chili gravy
2 cans (14½ ounces each) Mexican-style stewed tomatoes, cut up
1 can (15 ounces) kidney beans or pinto beans, drained and rinsed
1 cup beer or beef broth
1 to 2 tablespoons chopped canned chipotle chiles in adobo sauce*
2 teaspoons garlic salt
2 teaspoons ground cumin
1 teaspoon dried oregano
   Assorted toppings (such as sour cream, chopped avocado, shredded Cheddar cheese, bottled salsa, chopped fresh cilantro, seeded and chopped sweet red or green peppers and/or crumbled tortilla chips) (optional)
   Lime slices, halved (optional)

1. In 5½- or 6-quart slow cooker, combine beef, onions, coarsely chopped sweet peppers, chili beans with chili gravy, tomatoes with their juices, kidney or pinto beans, beer or beef broth, chipotle chiles, garlic salt, cumin and oregano.

2. Cover slow cooker; cook on low-heat setting for 10 to 12 hours or on high-heat setting for 5 to 6 hours. Spoon off fat. If desired, serve with assorted toppings and lime slices.

- -

Per serving: 294 cal., 5 g total fat (1 g sat. fat), 52 mg chol., 823 mg sodium, 32 g carbo., 8 g fiber, 29 g pro.

*Note: Because chiles contain volatile oils that can burn your skin and eyes, avoid direct contact with them as much as possible. When working with chiles, wear plastic or rubber gloves. If your bare hands do touch the chiles, wash your hands and nails well with soap and warm water.

PREP:
25 minutes

COOKER SIZE:
3½- or 4-quart

COOK:
10 to 12 hours on low-heat or 5 to 6 hours on high-heat setting

STAND:
1 hour

MAKES:
8 servings

FREEZE WITH EASE

MAKE IT A MEAL:
Assorted Crackers

Fruity Waffle Bowls
(see recipe, page 277)

If you usually make chili with hamburger, give this recipe a go for something different. You'll love the chunky pieces of succulent pot roast.

Beef and Red Bean Chili

1 cup dry red beans or dry kidney beans
2 pounds boneless beef chuck pot roast, trimmed and cut into 1-inch pieces
1 cup coarsely chopped onions
1 tablespoon extra-virgin olive oil
1 can (15 ounces) tomato sauce
1 can (14½ ounces) diced tomatoes with mild chiles
1 can (14 ounces) beef broth
1 or 2 chipotle chiles in adobo sauce, finely chopped* plus 2 teaspoons adobo sauce
2 teaspoons dried oregano
1 teaspoon ground cumin
¾ cup chopped sweet red pepper
¼ cup chopped fresh cilantro

1. Rinse beans. Place beans in large saucepan or Dutch oven; add enough water to cover by 2 inches. Bring to a boil; reduce heat. Simmer, uncovered, for 10 minutes. Remove from heat. Cover; let stand for 1 hour.

2. Meanwhile, in large skillet, cook half of the pot roast pieces and the onion in hot oil over medium-high heat until beef is brown. Using a slotted spoon, transfer to 3½- or 4-quart slow cooker. Repeat with remaining pot roast pieces. Add tomato sauce, tomatoes with their juices, beef broth, chipotle chiles and adobo sauce, oregano and cumin to mixture in cooker; stir to combine. Drain and rinse beans; stir into mixture in slow cooker.

3. Cover slow cooker; cook on low-heat setting for 10 to 12 hours or on high-heat setting for 5 to 6 hours. Top each serving with sweet pepper and cilantro.

Per serving: 269 cal., 6 g total fat (2 g sat. fat), 67 mg chol., 550 mg sodium, 21 g carbo., 8 g fiber, 32 g pro.

*Note: Because chiles contain volatile oils that can burn your skin and eyes, avoid direct contact with them as much as possible. When working with chiles, wear plastic or rubber gloves. If your bare hands do touch the chiles, wash your hands and nails well with soap and warm water.

Three kinds of beans add a variety of color and texture to this sure-to-please chili.

Three Bean and Beef Chili

1 pound ground beef
1 cup chopped onions
2 cloves garlic, finely chopped
1 can (14½ ounces) stewed tomatoes, cut up
1 cup ketchup
⅓ cup packed brown sugar
¼ cup chili powder
¼ cup molasses
¼ cup Worcestershire sauce
1 tablespoon ground cumin
1 tablespoon dry mustard
2 cans (15 to 16 ounces each) dark-red kidney beans, drained and rinsed
2 cans (15 to 16 ounces each) pinto beans, drained and rinsed
1 can (15 ounces) white cannellini beans, drained and rinsed
  Roasted sweet red and/or yellow pepper strips (optional)
  Sliced fresh jalapeño chile (optional)

1. In large skillet, cook ground beef, onions and garlic over medium-high heat until ground beef is cooked through, stirring to break into bite-size pieces. Drain off fat. Transfer to 5- to 6-quart slow cooker.

2. Add tomatoes with their juices, ketchup, brown sugar, chili powder, molasses, Worcestershire sauce, cumin and mustard to mixture in slow cooker; stir to combine. Stir in kidney, pinto and cannellini beans. Cover slow cooker; cook on low-heat setting for 8 to 10 hours or on high-heat setting for 4 to 5 hours.

3. To serve, ladle chili into bowls. If desired, top each serving with roasted pepper strips and/or jalapeño slices.

Per serving: 381 cal., 6 g total fat (2 g sat. fat), 24 mg chol., 1,172 mg sodium, 62 g carbo., 13 g fiber, 23 g pro.

PREP:
25 minutes

COOKER SIZE:
5- to 6-quart

COOK:
8 to 10 hours on low-heat or 4 to 5 hours on high-heat setting

MAKES:
10 to 12 servings

KIDS' FAVORITE!

FREEZE WITH EASE

MAKE IT A MEAL:
Purchased corn bread muffins served with whipped honey

Purchased angel food cake with whipped cream and sliced strawberries

PREP:
25 minutes

COOKER SIZE:
4- to 5½-quart

COOK:
12 to 14 hours on low-heat or 6 to 7 hours on high-heat setting

MAKES:
6 servings

FREEZE WITH EASE

MAKE IT A MEAL:
Mexican-Style Rice (see recipe, page 258)

Corn chips

Raspberry sorbet topped with crumbled snickerdoodle cookies

Chipotle chiles in adobo sauce pack considerable heat. Look for them in the Mexican food section of the supermarket.

New Mexico Beef Stew

2 cups fresh corn kernels or one package (10 ounces) frozen whole kernel corn, thawed
1 can (15 ounces) chickpeas, drained
2 cups chopped peeled celery root or 1 cup sliced celery
1 cup chopped onions
3 cloves garlic, chopped
2 to 3 canned chipotle chiles in adobo sauce, chopped*
1½ pounds boneless beef chuck, trimmed and cut into ¾-inch pieces
1 teaspoon salt
1 teaspoon dried thyme
½ teaspoon black pepper
1 can (28 ounces) whole tomatoes, cut up
  Lime slices, quartered (optional)
  Fresh cilantro sprigs (optional)

1. In 4- to 5½-quart slow cooker, combine corn, chickpeas, celery root or celery, onions, garlic and chipotle chiles. Add meat. Sprinkle with salt, thyme and black pepper. Pour tomatoes with their juices over mixture in slow cooker.

2. Cover slow cooker; cook on low-heat setting for 12 to 14 hours or on high-heat setting for 6 to 7 hours. Stir before serving. Season to taste with additional salt and black pepper. If desired, garnish with quartered lime slices and cilantro sprigs.

Per serving: 367 cal., 8 g total fat (2 g sat. fat), 54 mg chol., 1,078 mg sodium, 42 g carbo., 7 g fiber, 33 g pro.

*Note: Because chiles contain volatile oils that can burn your skin and eyes, avoid direct contact with them as much as possible. When working with chiles, wear plastic or rubber gloves. If your bare hands do touch the chiles, wash your hands well with soap and water.

PREP:
35 minutes

COOKER SIZE:
4- to 5½-quart

COOK:
8 to 10 hours on low-heat or 4 to 5 hours on high-heat setting

MAKES:
4 servings

FREEZE WITH EASE

MAKE IT A MEAL:
Home Run Garlic Rolls (see recipe, page 263)

Purchased peanut butter chocolate fudge

If too many beef stew recipes have left you wanting more flavor, this is your winner. It's hearty and toothsome, colorful, rich and herby.

Herbed Beef-Chickpea Stew

1½ pounds beef stew meat cubes
 2 tablespoons extra-virgin olive oil
1½ cups chopped onions
1½ cups sliced carrots
1½ cups sliced celery
 1 can (15 ounces) chickpeas, drained and rinsed
 1 can (14 ounces) beef broth
 ½ cup dry white wine
 2 tablespoons quick-cooking tapioca, crushed
 6 cloves garlic, chopped
 ½ teaspoon salt
 ½ teaspoon dried basil
 ½ teaspoon dried thyme
 ½ teaspoon dried rosemary
 ¼ teaspoon dried sage
 ¼ teaspoon black pepper
     Finely shredded Parmesan cheese (optional)

1. In large skillet, brown beef, half at a time, in hot oil over medium heat. Drain off fat. In 4- to 5½-quart slow cooker, combine onions, carrots, celery and chickpeas. Top vegetable mixture with beef. In medium-size bowl, combine beef broth, wine, tapioca, garlic, salt, basil, thyme, rosemary, sage and pepper; pour over mixture in cooker.

2. Cover slow cooker; cook on low-heat setting for 8 to 10 hours or on high-heat setting for 4 to 5 hours.

3. If desired, top each serving with Parmesan cheese.

. . . .

Per serving: 693 cal., 38 g total fat (13 g sat. fat), 112 mg chol., 1,141 mg sodium, 43 g carbo., 8 g fiber, 40 g pro.

This creamy dish will make you see stew in a new light. Thanks to some cream and a dose of thyme, it's smooth with an herbal accent.

Creamy Beef and Potato Stew

¾ pound boneless beef chuck, trimmed and cut into ¾-inch pieces
1 package (16 ounces) loose-pack frozen cut green beans
1 package (5 to 5½ ounces) dry au gratin potato mix
½ teaspoon dried thyme
3 cups water
1½ cups half-and-half or light cream
  Finely shredded Parmesan cheese (optional)

1. In 3½- or 4-quart slow cooker, combine beef, frozen green beans, dry potato mix (including contents of sauce packet) and thyme. Pour the water over mixture in slow cooker.

2. Cover slow cooker; cook on low-heat setting for 7 to 8 hours or on high-heat setting for 3½ to 4 hours.

3. If necessary, lower temperature to low-heat setting. Stir in half-and-half. Cover slow cooker; cook about 15 minutes longer or until heated through. If desired, sprinkle each serving with Parmesan cheese.

· ·

Per serving: 373 cal., 15 g total fat (8 g sat. fat), 84 mg chol., 845 mg sodium, 39 g carbo., 5 g fiber, 26 g pro.

PREP:
15 minutes

COOKER SIZE:
3½- or 4-quart

COOK:
7 to 8 hours on low-heat or 3½ to 4 hours on high-heat setting, plus 15 minutes on low-heat setting

MAKES:
4 servings

KIDS' FAVORITE!

MAKE IT A MEAL:
Greens and Berry Salad (see recipe, page 247)

Crusty Italian bread slices served with butter

Purchased rice pudding

PREP:
30 minutes

COOKER SIZE:
3½- to 4½-quart

COOK:
10 to 12 hours on low-heat or 5 to 6 hours on high-heat setting, plus 15 minutes on high-heat setting

MAKES:
6 servings

Chunks of butternut squash impart just a hint of sweetness to this homey stew. A dash of allspice adds an intriguing "just what is that?" flavor.

Beef Stew with Butternut Squash

2 tablespoons all-purpose flour
1 pound boneless beef chuck roast, trimmed and cut into 1-inch pieces
2 tablespoons vegetable oil
1 pound tiny new potatoes, quartered
1 pound butternut squash, peeled, seeded and cut into 1-inch pieces (about 2½ cups)
2 small onions, cut in wedges
2 cloves garlic, chopped
1 can (14 ounces) beef broth
1 cup vegetable juice
2 tablespoons Worcestershire sauce
1 tablespoon lemon juice
½ teaspoon sugar
½ teaspoon paprika
¼ teaspoon black pepper
⅛ teaspoon ground allspice
1 package (9 ounces) frozen Italian-style green beans or 2 cups loose-pack frozen peas

1. Place flour in a large plastic food-storage bag. Add beef pieces, a few at time, shaking to coat. In large skillet, brown beef in hot oil; drain off fat. In 3½- to 4½-quart slow cooker, combine beef, potatoes, squash, onions and garlic. In large bowl, combine beef broth, vegetable juice, Worcestershire sauce, lemon juice, sugar, paprika, pepper and allspice. Pour over mixture in slow cooker.

2. Cover slow cooker; cook on low-heat setting for 10 to 12 hours or on high-heat setting for 5 to 6 hours.

3. If necessary, raise temperature to high-heat setting. Add green beans or peas to slow cooker. Cover slow cooker; cook for 15 minutes longer.

Per serving: 304 cal., 13 g total fat (4 g sat. fat), 48 mg chol., 456 mg sodium, 30 g carbo., 4 g fiber, 19 g pro.

MAKE IT A MEAL:
Tossed green salad

Purchased soft breadsticks, baked

Purchased coconut cream pie

PREP:
20 minutes

COOKER SIZE:
5- or 5½-quart

COOK:
9 to 10 hours on low-heat or 6 hours on high-heat setting

MAKES:
6 servings

Be sure to use regular, and not quick-cooking, barley in this hearty stew. Mop up bowls with pieces of crusty bread.

Beef, Bean and Barley Stew

4 medium-size all-purpose potatoes (about 1 pound), peeled and quartered
2 cloves garlic, chopped
1 large onion, coarsely chopped
1½ pounds beef chuck stew meat cubes
⅓ cup regular barley (not quick-cooking)
2 cans (15½ ounces each) white cannellini beans, drained and rinsed
1 can (14½ ounces) beef broth
½ cup water
¼ cup ketchup
2 tablespoons sweet Hungarian paprika or regular paprika
1 teaspoon salt
¼ teaspoon black pepper

1. Place the quartered potatoes in an even layer in 5- or 5½-quart slow cooker. On top of the potatoes, layer garlic, onion, beef cubes, barley and cannellini beans.

2. In small bowl, stir together beef broth, the water, ketchup, paprika, salt and black pepper. Pour ketchup mixture over beef mixture in slow cooker.

3. Cover slow cooker; cook on low-heat setting for 9 to 10 hours or on high-heat setting for 6 hours or until the stew meat, potatoes and barley are tender and the stew liquid is nicely thickened.

Per serving: 385 cal., 10 g total fat (4 g sat. fat), 82 mg chol., 935 mg sodium, 41 g carbo., 8 g fiber, 32 g pro.

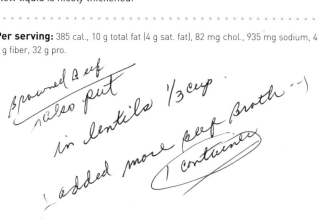

Browned Beef
also put
in lentils ⅓ cup
I added more Beef Broth :-)
1 container

MAKE IT A MEAL:
Refrigerated crescent rolls, baked

Shortbread Brownies (see recipe, page 270)

SOUPS AND STEWS

164

When you're craving Asian food but want the convenience of slow cooking, this recipe offers the best of both worlds.

Asian-Style Beef Stew

2 large onions, sliced
2 pounds beef round steak, sliced for stir-fry
2 ribs celery, cut into ¼-inch-thick slices
1 cup packaged peeled baby carrots
1 cup plus 2 tablespoons beef broth
1 cup orange juice
3 tablespoons soy sauce
2 tablespoons hoisin sauce
1½ teaspoons Chinese five-spice powder
1 teaspoon Asian chili paste
3 tablespoons cornstarch
1 package (10 ounces) frozen peas, thawed
Hot cooked rice

1. In 5- or 5½-quart slow cooker, layer onions, beef, celery and carrots.

2. In medium-size bowl, whisk together 1 cup broth, the orange juice, soy sauce, hoisin sauce, five-spice powder and chili paste. Pour into slow cooker.

3. Cover slow cooker; cook on high-heat setting for 5 hours.

4. In small bowl, stir together the remaining 2 tablespoons broth and the cornstarch. Stir into mixture in slow cooker. Cover slow cooker; cook for 30 minutes longer.

5. Stir in peas; cook about 5 minutes longer or until heated through. Serve with hot cooked rice.

Per serving: 365 cal., 5 g total fat (2 g sat. fat), 65 mg chol., 728 mg sodium, 45 g carbo., 4 g fiber, 32 g pro.

PREP:
20 minutes

COOKER SIZE:
5- or 5½-quart

COOK:
5 hours plus 35 minutes on high-heat setting

MAKES:
8 servings

FREEZE WITH EASE

MAKE IT A MEAL:
Lemon-Spice Cupcakes (see recipe, page 271)

PREP:
25 minutes

COOKER SIZE:
4- to 5-quart

COOK:
8 to 10 hours on low-heat or 4 to 5 hours on high-heat setting

MAKES:
6 to 8 servings

MAKE IT A MEAL:
Home Run Garlic Rolls (see recipe, page 263)

Caramel swirl ice cream served with shortbread cookies

Fennel and parsnips are an appealing change of pace from celery and carrots in this boldly flavored beef stew.

Country Italian Beef Stew

½ pound tiny new potatoes, halved or quartered
2 medium-size carrots or parsnips, peeled and cut into 1- to 2-inch pieces
1 cup chopped onion
1 medium-size fennel bulb, trimmed and cut into ½-inch-thick wedges
2 pounds boneless beef chuck pot roast, trimmed and cut into 2-inch pieces
1 teaspoon dried rosemary
1 can (14 ounces) beef broth
1 cup dry red wine or beef broth
1 can (6 ounces) tomato paste
2 tablespoons quick-cooking tapioca
½ teaspoon black pepper
4 cloves garlic, chopped
1 to 2 cups fresh basil leaves, spinach leaves or torn fresh escarole

1. In 4- to 5-quart slow cooker, combine potatoes, carrots or parsnips, onion and fennel. Add beef to slow cooker; sprinkle beef with rosemary. In medium-size bowl, whisk together beef broth, wine, tomato paste, tapioca, pepper and garlic. Pour over meat mixture in cooker.

2. Cover slow cooker; cook on low-heat setting for 8 to 10 hours or on high-heat setting for 4 to 5 hours. Just before serving, stir in basil, spinach or escarole.

Per serving: 319 cal., 6 g total fat (2 g sat. fat), 89 mg chol., 596 mg sodium, 23 g carbo., 4 g fiber, 36 g pro.

PREP:
25 minutes

COOKER SIZE:
3½- or 4-quart

COOK:
7 to 8 hours on low-heat or 3½ to 4 hours on high-heat setting

MAKES:
4 servings

If you haven't thought of using parsnips lately, it's time to give this nutty-tasting root a try.

Autumn Harvest Stew

    2 cups coarsely chopped, peeled sweet potatoes
1¾ cups sliced, peeled parsnips
1¾ cups sliced apples
    ½ cup chopped onion
    1 pound boneless pork shoulder roast, trimmed and cut into 1-inch cubes
    ¾ teaspoon dried thyme
    ½ teaspoon dried rosemary
    ½ teaspoon salt
    ¼ teaspoon black pepper
    1 cup chicken broth or beef broth
    1 cup apple cider or apple juice

1. In 3½- or 4-quart slow cooker, combine sweet potatoes, parsnips, apples and onion. Add roast to slow cooker. Sprinkle with thyme, rosemary, salt and pepper. Pour broth and apple cider over mixture in slow cooker.

2. Cover slow cooker; cook on low-heat setting for 7 to 8 hours or on high-heat setting for 3½ to 4 hours.

Per serving: 336 cal., 8 g total fat (3 g sat. fat), 76 mg chol., 660 mg sodium, 40 g carbo., 7 g fiber, 25 g pro.

MAKE IT A MEAL:
Baguette-style French bread served with butter

Steamed fresh broccoli

Purchased pumpkin bars with cream cheese frosting

SOUPS AND STEWS

168

Two kinds of pork make this hearty stew extra flavorful. Mop up the wine-flavored gravy with dinner rolls.

Italian Sausage And Pork Stew

      2 cups dry Great Northern beans
      6 cups cold water
     ½ pound Italian sausage (remove casings, if present)
      1 pound lean boneless pork, trimmed and cut into ½-inch pieces
   1½ cups coarsely chopped onions
      3 medium-size carrots, cut into ½-inch pieces
      3 cloves garlic, chopped
      3 cups water
      1 teaspoon instant beef bouillon granules
     ½ teaspoon dried thyme
     ½ teaspoon dried oregano
     ¼ cup dry red wine or water
     ⅓ cup (½ of a 6-ounce can) tomato paste
     ¼ cup chopped fresh parsley

1. Rinse beans; drain. In large saucepan, combine beans and the 6 cups water. Bring to a boil; reduce heat. Simmer, uncovered, for 10 minutes. Remove from heat. Cover and let stand for 1 hour. Drain and rinse beans. Transfer beans to 4- to 5-quart slow cooker.

2. In large skillet, cook sausage over medium heat until cooked through, stirring to break sausage into bite-size pieces. Using a slotted spoon, transfer sausage to slow cooker, reserving drippings in skillet. In the same skillet, cook pork, half at a time, until browned. Drain off fat. Transfer to slow cooker. Add onions, carrots and garlic to slow cooker. Stir in the 3 cups water, bouillon granules, thyme and oregano.

3. Cover slow cooker; cook on low-heat setting for 7 to 8 hours or on high-heat setting for 3½ to 4 hours.

4. If necessary, raise temperature to high-heat setting. In small bowl, stir wine into tomato paste; add to mixture in slow cooker along with parsley. Cover slow cooker; cook for 15 minutes longer.

Per serving: 473 cal., 13 g total fat (5 g sat. fat), 73 mg chol., 566 mg sodium, 49 g carbo., 15 g fiber, 37 g pro.

PREP:
35 minutes

STAND:
1 hour

COOKER SIZE:
4- to 5-quart

COOK:
7 to 8 hours on low-heat or 3½ to 4 hours on high-heat setting, plus 15 minutes on high-heat setting

MAKES:
6 servings

FREEZE WITH EASE

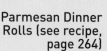

MAKE IT A MEAL:
Spinach salad with poppy seed dressing

Parmesan Dinner Rolls (see recipe, page 264)

Purchased lemon bars

Beef Stew with Red Wine Gravy

PREP:
30 minutes

COOKER SIZE:
4½- to 6-quart

COOK:
12 to 14 hours on low-heat or 6 to 7 hours on high-heat setting

MAKES:
6 servings

¼ cup all-purpose flour
2 teaspoons dried Italian seasoning
1 teaspoon salt
½ teaspoon freshly ground black pepper
2 pounds boneless beef chuck roast, trimmed and cut into 1-inch cubes
2 tablespoons extra-virgin olive oil
2 large onions, cut into thin wedges
½ pound parsnips, peeled, quartered lengthwise and halved
½ pound carrots, quartered lengthwise and halved
½ pound Jerusalem artichokes (sunchokes), peeled and coarsely chopped
1 cup Cabernet Sauvignon or beef broth
½ cup beef broth
¼ cup tomato paste
 Chopped plum tomatoes, golden raisins and/or red wine vinegar or balsamic vinegar

1. In large plastic food-storage bag, combine flour, Italian seasoning, salt and pepper. Add beef cubes to bag; seal. Shake to coat beef cubes with flour mixture. In 12-inch skillet, brown beef cubes, half at a time, in hot olive oil (add more oil, if necessary).

2. In 4½- to 6-quart slow cooker, layer onions, parsnips, carrots and Jerusalem artichokes; top with browned beef cubes. In small bowl, combine wine and beef broth; pour over beef cubes.

3. Cover slow cooker; cook on low-heat setting for 12 to 14 hours or on high-heat setting for 6 to 7 hours. Stir in tomato paste. Top each serving with tomatoes, raisins and/or vinegar.

Per serving: 356 cal., 9 g total fat (2 g sat. fat), 90 mg chol., 601 mg sodium, 26 g carbo., 4 g fiber, 35 g pro.

MAKE IT A MEAL:

Broccoli-Cheddar Salad (see recipe, page 251)

French bread slices

Peppermint ice cream sprinkled with crushed chocolate wafer cookies

PREP:
20 minutes

COOKER SIZE:
4- to 5-quart

COOK:
6 to 7 hours on low-heat or 3 to 3½ hours on high-heat setting, plus 10 minutes on high-heat setting

MAKES:
8 servings

FREEZE WITH EASE

MAKE IT A MEAL:
Fruit and Broccoli Salad (see recipe, page 248)

Crackers

Purchased chocolate cake

Take the chill off a cold, blustery day with this creamy golden chowder accented with bits of sweet red pepper and bacon.

Corn and Clam Chowder

2 cans (6½ ounces each) chopped clams
1 bottle (8 ounces) clam juice
2 cups water
2 cans (15 ounces each) cream-style corn
1 can (10¾ ounces) condensed cream of onion soup or cream of celery soup
1 package (10 ounces) frozen whole kernel corn
1 medium-size onion, chopped
½ cup chopped sweet red pepper
1 small fresh jalapeño chile, seeded and finely chopped*
½ cup half-and-half or light cream
2 slices bacon, crisp-cooked, drained and crumbled

1. Drain clams, reserving juice. Cover and chill clams. In 4- to 5-quart slow cooker, combine the reserved clam juice, the bottled clam juice, the water, cream-style corn, cream of onion soup, frozen corn, onion, sweet pepper and chile.

2. Cover slow cooker; cook on low-heat setting for 6 to 7 hours or on high-heat setting for 3 to 3½ hours.

3. If necessary, raise temperature to high-heat setting. Stir in clams, half-and-half and bacon. Cover slow cooker; cook for 10 minutes longer.

. . . .

Per serving: 234 cal., 6 g total fat (2 g sat. fat), 37 mg chol., 706 mg sodium, 35 g carbo., 3 g fiber, 15 g pro.

*Note: Because chiles contain volatile oils that can burn your skin and eyes, avoid direct contact with them as much as possible. When working with chiles, wear plastic or rubber gloves. If your bare hands do touch the chiles, wash your hands and nails well with soap and warm water.

Andouille sausage is a smoked sausage used in Cajun cooking. In this dish, it combines with Cajun seasoning to provide plenty of zing.

Cajun Shrimp Soup

½ pound andouille sausage or other cooked smoked sausage, halved lengthwise and cut into ½-inch-thick slices
2 cans (14½ ounces each) diced tomatoes
1 medium-size sweet red pepper, seeded and chopped
1 medium-size onion, finely chopped
1 rib celery, sliced
1 teaspoon Cajun seasoning
2 cloves garlic, minced
¼ teaspoon hot-pepper sauce
1 bay leaf
2 cans (14 ounces each) chicken broth
¾ pound medium-size shrimp, shelled and deveined
¾ cup instant white rice
1 tablespoon chopped fresh parsley

1. In 3½- or 4-quart slow cooker, combine sausage, tomatoes with their juices, sweet pepper, onion, celery, Cajun seasoning, garlic, hot-pepper sauce and bay leaf. Pour chicken broth over mixture in slow cooker.

2. Cover slow cooker; cook on low-heat setting for 6 to 8 hours or on high-heat setting for 3 to 4 hours.

3. If necessary, raise temperature to high-heat setting. Stir shrimp and uncooked rice into mixture in slow cooker. Cover slow cooker; cook for 5 to 10 minutes longer or until shrimp turns pink. Remove and discard bay leaf. Stir in parsley.

Per serving: 294 cal., 4 g total fat (1 g sat. fat), 146 mg chol., 1,698 mg sodium, 33 g carbo., 2 g fiber, 28 g pro.

PREP:
30 minutes

COOKER SIZE:
3½- or 4-quart

COOK:
6 to 8 hours on low-heat or 3 to 4 hours on high-heat setting, plus 5 to 10 minutes on high-heat setting

MAKES:
4 servings

MAKE IT A MEAL:
Southern Corn Bread Mini Muffins (see recipe, page 268)

Apple slices served with purchased caramel dip

SOUPS AND STEWS

173

PREP:
30 minutes

COOKER SIZE:
4½- to 6-quart

COOK:
8 to 10 hours on low-heat or 4 to 5 hours on high-heat setting, plus 20 minutes on high-heat setting

MAKES:
8 servings

FREEZE WITH EASE

MAKE IT A MEAL:
Purchased antipasto platter

Purchased hard breadsticks

Fruity Waffle Bowls (see recipe, page 277)

This zesty stick-to-the-ribs soup boasts six seasonings plus Italian sausage. Vary the spiciness by choosing either sweet or hot sausage.

Italian Sausage Soup

1 pound Italian sausage (remove casings, if present)
1 large onion, chopped
1 clove garlic, chopped
2 medium-size carrots, chopped
1 rib celery, chopped
1 can (14½ ounces) diced tomatoes
1 can (8 ounces) tomato sauce
1 teaspoon dried oregano
½ teaspoon dried rosemary
½ teaspoon dried basil
¼ teaspoon dried thyme
¼ teaspoon fennel seeds
1 bay leaf
3 cans (14 ounces each) reduced-sodium chicken broth
½ cup orzo pasta or finely broken capellini pasta
    Finely shredded Parmesan cheese (optional)

1. In large skillet, combine Italian sausage, onion and garlic. Cook over medium heat until sausage is cooked through, stirring to break into bite-size pieces. Drain fat.

2. In 4½- to 6-quart slow cooker, combine carrots and celery. Place sausage mixture on top of vegetables. In medium-size bowl, combine tomatoes with their juices, tomato sauce, oregano, rosemary, basil, thyme, fennel seeds and bay leaf. Pour over sausage mixture. Pour chicken broth over mixture in slow cooker.

3. Cover slow cooker; cook on low-heat setting for 8 to 10 hours or on high-heat setting for 4 to 5 hours.

4. If necessary, raise temperature to high-heat setting. Stir in uncooked pasta. Cover slow cooker; cook for 20 minutes longer. Remove and discard bay leaf. If desired, serve with Parmesan cheese.

Per serving: 250 cal., 13 g total fat (5 g sat. fat), 38 mg chol., 923 mg sodium, 17 g carbo., 2 g fiber, 12 g pro.

PREP:
30 minutes

COOKER SIZE:
3½- or 4-quart

COOK:
8 to 10 hours on low-heat or 4 to 5 hours on high-heat setting

MAKES:
6 servings

MAKE IT A MEAL:
Tortilla chips served with purchased guacamole dip

Cinnamon ice cream topped with crushed gingerbread cookies

Cinnamon, garlic, chili powder, oregano and fresh cilantro blend delightfully in this hearty meal.

Pork, Potato and Chile Stew

1½ pounds boneless pork shoulder roast, trimmed and cut into 1-inch pieces
1 tablespoon vegetable oil
1 pound tiny new potatoes (10 to 12), quartered
1 large onion, chopped
2 fresh poblano chiles, seeded and cut into 1-inch pieces*
1 fresh jalapeño chile, seeded and finely chopped*
4 cloves garlic, chopped
2 inches stick cinnamon
3 cups chicken broth
1 can (14½ ounces) diced tomatoes
1 tablespoon chili powder
1 teaspoon dried oregano
¼ teaspoon black pepper
¼ cup chopped fresh cilantro or parsley
   Hot cooked rice (optional)
   Fresh chives (optional)

1. In large skillet, brown pork in hot oil over medium-high heat. Drain off fat. Set pork aside.

2. In 3½- or 4-quart slow cooker, combine potatoes, onion, poblano chiles, jalapeño chile, garlic and cinnamon. Add pork. Stir in chicken broth, tomatoes with their juices, chili powder, oregano and black pepper.

3. Cover slow cooker; cook on low-heat setting for 8 to 10 hours or on high-heat setting for 4 to 5 hours. Remove and discard cinnamon.

4. Before serving, stir in cilantro. If desired, serve with rice and garnish each serving with fresh chives.

Per serving: 290 cal., 10 g total fat (3 g sat. fat), 75 mg chol., 731 mg sodium, 24 g carbo., 4 g fiber, 26 g pro.

*Note: Because chiles contain volatile oils that can burn your skin and eyes, avoid direct contact with them as much as possible. When working with chiles, wear plastic or rubber gloves. If your bare hands do touch the chiles, wash your hands well with soap and water.

Spooned over hot polenta and given a dusting of shredded Parmesan, this stew is a standout.

Pork Stew with Polenta

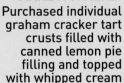

PREP:
25 minutes

COOKER SIZE:
3½- or 4-quart

COOK:
7 to 8 hours on low-heat or 3½ to 4 hours on high-heat setting

MAKES:
4 servings

1½ pounds boneless pork country-style ribs, trimmed and cut into 1½-inch pieces
1 large onion, chopped
1 large sweet green, yellow and/or red pepper, chopped
1 can (14½ ounces) diced tomatoes with basil and oregano
1 can (14 ounces) beef broth
¼ cup dry red wine
3 tablespoons quick-cooking tapioca, crushed
1 teaspoon dried Italian seasoning
¼ teaspoon salt
2 cloves garlic, chopped
1 package (16 ounces) heat-and-serve polenta
2 cups torn fresh baby spinach (optional)
Shredded Parmesan cheese (optional)

1. In 3½- or 4-quart slow cooker, combine pork, onion and sweet pepper. Stir tomatoes with their juices, beef broth, red wine, tapioca, Italian seasoning, salt and garlic into mixture in slow cooker.

2. Cover slow cooker; cook on low-heat setting for 7 to 8 hours or on high-heat setting for 3½ to 4 hours.

3. Meanwhile, prepare polenta following package directions.

4. Just before serving, if desired, stir spinach into stew. Serve stew with polenta. If desired, sprinkle each serving with Parmesan cheese.

FREEZE WITH EASE

Per serving: 450 cal., 17 g total fat (5 g sat. fat), 116 mg chol., 1,342 mg sodium, 32 g carbo., 2 g fiber, 39 g pro.

MAKE IT A MEAL:
Purchased individual graham cracker tart crusts filled with canned lemon pie filling and topped with whipped cream

PREP:
10 minutes

COOKER SIZE:
3½- or 4-quart

COOK:
6 to 8 hours on low-heat or 3 to 4 hours on high-heat setting

MAKES:
4 servings

KIDS' FAVORITE!

MAKE IT A MEAL:
Fruit and Broccoli Salad (see recipe, page 248)

Hard breadsticks

Purchased butterscotch pudding

Because the meatballs are cooked before they're frozen, you can add them straight from the package.

Meatball-Vegetable Stew

1 package (16 or 18 ounces) frozen cooked meatballs
1 package (16 ounces) loose-pack frozen mixed vegetables
1 can (14½ ounces) diced tomatoes with onion and garlic or stewed tomatoes
1 jar (12 ounces) mushroom gravy
⅓ cup water
1½ teaspoons dried basil

1. In 3½- or 4-quart slow cooker, combine cooked meatballs and mixed vegetables. In medium-size bowl, stir together tomatoes with their juices, gravy, the water and basil. Pour over meatballs and vegetables.

2. Cover slow cooker; cook on low-heat setting for 6 to 8 hours or on high-heat setting for 3 to 4 hours.

Per serving: 472 cal., 32 g total fat (14 g sat. fat), 87 mg chol., 1,833 mg sodium, 26 g carbo., 6 g fiber, 21 g pro.

PREP:
35 minutes

COOKER SIZE:
4- to 5½-quart

COOK:
8 to 9 hours on low-heat or 4 to 4½ hours on high-heat setting, plus 30 minutes on high-heat setting

MAKES:
6 servings

MAKE IT A MEAL:

Hot cooked polenta slices

Chocolate frozen yogurt served with chocolate cream-filled wafer cookies

Tender veggies and chunks of pork taste terrific in this lightly spiced, flavorful stew.

Spiced Pork Stew With Green Beans

- 3 **tablespoons all-purpose flour**
- 1 **teaspoon ground cumin**
- 2 **to 2½ pounds boneless pork shoulder, trimmed and cut into 1-inch pieces**
- 1 **medium-size onion, chopped**
- 2 **tablespoons vegetable oil**
- 4 **cups coarsely chopped red-skin potatoes and/or peeled and coarsely chopped sweet potatoes (about 4 medium)**
- 2 **medium-size carrots, chopped**
- 2 **cans (14½ ounces each) diced tomatoes**
- ⅓ **cup water**
- 1 **teaspoon salt**
- 1 **teaspoon ground ginger**
- 1 **teaspoon ground cinnamon**
- ½ **teaspoon sugar**
- ½ **teaspoon black pepper**
- 2 **cups loose-pack frozen cut green beans, thawed**
- 2 **tablespoons chopped fresh cilantro or parsley (optional)**

1. In resealable plastic food-storage bag, combine flour and cumin. Add pork pieces to plastic bag; shake to coat pork. In large skillet, cook pork and onion, half at a time, in hot oil over medium heat until pork is browned and onion is tender.

2. In 4- to 5½-quart slow cooker, combine pork mixture, potatoes and carrots. Stir tomatoes with their juices, the water, salt, ginger, cinnamon, sugar and pepper into mixture in slow cooker.

3. Cover slow cooker; cook on low-heat setting for 8 to 9 hours or on high-heat setting for 4 to 4½ hours.

4. If necessary, raise temperature to high-heat setting. Stir in green beans. Cover slow cooker; cook about 30 minutes longer or until beans are tender. If desired, top each serving with cilantro.

Per serving: 314 cal., 11 g total fat (3 g sat. fat), 62 mg chol., 751 mg sodium, 31 g carbo., 6 g fiber, 22 g pro.

Serve this pork-filled chili at an after-the-game open-house or for a bowl-watching party.

Hearty Bean and Pork Chili

1½ pounds boneless pork shoulder roast, trimmed and cut into 1-inch cubes
 2 cans (15 ounces each) black beans, kidney beans and/or chickpeas, drained and rinsed
 2 cans (14½ ounces each) diced tomatoes with onions and garlic
 1 can (10 ounces) chopped tomatoes and green chiles
1½ cups chopped celery
 1 cup chopped green pepper
 3 cloves garlic, chopped
 1 tablespoon chili powder
 1 teaspoon ground cumin
 1 teaspoon dried oregano
 2 cups vegetable juice or tomato juice
   Toppers (such as shredded Mexican-blend cheese or Cheddar cheese, sour cream, thinly sliced scallions, chopped fresh cilantro, thinly sliced jalapeño chiles* and/or sliced pitted ripe olives) (optional)

1. In 5- to 6-quart slow cooker, combine pork, beans or chickpeas, tomatoes with their juices, celery, green pepper, garlic, chili powder, cumin and oregano. Stir in vegetable juice.

2. Cover slow cooker; cook on low-heat setting for 8 to 10 hours or on high-heat setting for 4 to 5 hours. If desired, serve with toppers.

Per serving: 251 cal., 6 g total fat (2 g sat. fat), 55 mg chol., 1,126 mg sodium, 28 g carbo., 8 g fiber, 27 g pro.

*Note: Because chiles contain volatile oils that can burn your skin and eyes, avoid direct contact with them as much as possible. When working with chiles, wear plastic or rubber gloves. If your bare hands do touch the chiles, wash your hands and nails well with soap and warm water.

PREP:
25 minutes

COOKER SIZE:
5- to 6-quart

COOK:
8 to 10 hours on low-heat or 4 to 5 hours on high-heat setting

MAKES:
8 servings

KIDS' FAVORITE!

FREEZE WITH EASE

MAKE IT A MEAL:
Southern Corn Bread Mini Muffins (see recipe, page 268)

Sliced pears

Purchased Key lime pie

PREP:
25 minutes

COOKER SIZE:
3½- or 4-quart

COOK:
6 to 8 hours on low-heat or 3 to 4 hours on high-heat setting, plus 15 minutes on high-heat setting

MAKES:
6 to 8 servings

KIDS' FAVORITE!

FREEZE WITH EASE

MAKE IT A MEAL:
Bread bowls

Purchased oatmeal raisin cookies

Make bread bowls by slicing off the tops and hollowing out the centers of sourdough rolls that are about 4 inches in diameter.

Confetti Chicken Chili

    3 cans (15 ounces each) Great Northern, pinto and/or white cannellini beans
1½ cups chopped sweet red, green and/or yellow peppers
    1 cup coarsely shredded carrots
    ½ cup sliced scallions
    2 cloves garlic, chopped
    2 teaspoons dried oregano
    1 teaspoon ground cumin
    ½ teaspoon salt
    2 cans (14 ounces each) chicken broth
2½ cups shredded or chopped cooked chicken* or turkey
    Shredded Monterey Jack cheese (optional)

1. Drain and rinse two cans of the beans and place in 3½- or 4-quart slow cooker. Use a potato masher or fork to mash beans. Drain and rinse the remaining one can of beans (do not mash). Stir beans, sweet peppers, carrots, scallions, garlic, oregano, cumin and salt into mashed beans. Add chicken broth. Stir until well mixed.

2. Cover slow cooker; cook on low-heat setting for 6 to 8 hours or high-heat setting for 3 to 4 hours.

3. If necessary, raise temperature to high-heat setting. Stir chicken into chili. Cover slow cooker; cook about 15 minutes longer or until chicken is heated through.

4. If desired, sprinkle each serving with cheese.

Per serving: 397 cal., 7 g total fat (2 g sat. fat), 52 mg chol., 846 mg sodium, 51 g carbo., 12 g fiber, 35 g pro.

*Note: For the cooked chicken, poach 3 or 4 boneless, skinless chicken breast halves in boiling water or chicken broth, covered, about 12 minutes or until no longer pink. Drain, cool slightly, then chop.

PREP:
25 minutes

STAND:
1 hour

COOKER SIZE:
3½- to 5-quart

COOK:
8 to 10 hours on low-heat or 4 to 5 hours on high-heat setting, plus 30 minutes on high-heat setting

MAKES:
4 to 6 servings

KIDS' FAVORITE!

FREEZE WITH EASE

MAKE IT A MEAL:
Purchased croissants

Rocky Road Malts
(see recipe, page 278)

To save time on early morning preparation, precook the beans the night before, drain, rinse and store in the refrigerator.

Chicken and Vegetable Bean Soup

    1 cup dry Great Northern beans
    6 cups cold water
    1 cup chopped onion
    1 medium-size fennel bulb, trimmed and cut into ½-inch pieces
    2 medium-size carrots, chopped
    2 cloves garlic, chopped
    2 tablespoons chopped fresh parsley
    1 teaspoon dried rosemary
    ¼ teaspoon black pepper
  4½ cups chicken broth
  2½ cups shredded or chopped cooked chicken or turkey
    1 can (14½ ounces) diced tomatoes

1. Rinse beans; drain. In large saucepan, combine beans and the water. Bring to a boil; reduce heat. Simmer, uncovered, for 10 minutes. Remove from heat. Cover and let stand for 1 hour. Drain and rinse beans.

2. Meanwhile, in 3½- to 5-quart slow cooker, combine onion, fennel, carrots, garlic, parsley, rosemary and pepper. Place beans on vegetables. Pour broth over.

3. Cover slow cooker; cook on low-heat setting for 8 to 10 hours or on high-heat setting for 4 to 5 hours.

4. If necessary, raise temperature to high-heat setting. Stir in cooked chicken and tomatoes with their juices. Cover slow cooker; cook about 30 minutes longer or until heated through.

Per serving: 426 cal., 10 g total fat (3 g sat. fat), 78 mg chol., 1,454 mg sodium, 46 g carbo., 15 g fiber, 40 g pro.

During cooking, the split peas soften and begin to fall apart, which helps bring a pleasing consistency to the cozy soup.

Golden Turkey-Split Pea Soup

PREP:
20 minutes

COOKER SIZE:
4½- or 5-quart

COOK:
9 to 10 hours on low-heat or 4½ to 5 hours on high-heat setting

MAKES:
6 servings

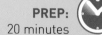

- 2 **cups dry yellow split peas**
- 2 **cans (14 ounces each) reduced-sodium chicken broth**
- 2 **cups water**
- 2 **cups loose-pack frozen whole kernel corn**
- 1½ **cups sliced carrots**
- 1 **can (10¾ ounces) condensed cream of chicken soup**
- ½ **pound cooked smoked turkey sausage, halved lengthwise and sliced**
- ½ **cup sliced scallions**
- ½ **cup chopped sweet red pepper**
- 2 **teaspoons dried thyme**

1. Rinse and drain split peas. In 4½- or 5-quart slow cooker, combine split peas, chicken broth, the water, frozen corn, carrots, cream of chicken soup, turkey sausage, scallions, sweet pepper and thyme.

2. Cover slow cooker; cook on low-heat setting for 9 to 10 hours or on high-heat setting for 4½ to 5 hours.

Per serving: 409 cal., 8 g total fat (2 g sat. fat), 30 mg chol., 1,076 mg sodium, 60 g carbo., 19 g fiber, 27 g pro.

FREEZE WITH EASE

MAKE IT A MEAL:
Purchased fruit salad

Refrigerated soft breadsticks, baked

Brownie and Walnut Pie (see recipe, page 274)

SOUPS AND STEWS

PREP:
15 minutes

COOKER SIZE:
3½- or 4-quart

COOK:
6 to 7 hours on low-heat or 3 to 3½ hours on high-heat setting

MAKES:
4 servings

KIDS' FAVORITE!

FREEZE WITH EASE

MAKE IT A MEAL:
Fresh fruit plate

Vanilla ice cream served with hot caramel sauce

There's no need to measure lots of herbs or spices for this soup. They're already in the seasoned chicken broth and Mexican-style tomatoes.

Chicken Tortilla Soup

2 cans (14 ounces each) chicken broth with roasted garlic
2 cups shredded cooked chicken
2 cups loose-pack frozen sweet peppers and onion stir-fry vegetables
1 can (14½ ounces) Mexican-style stewed tomatoes
1 cup broken tortilla chips
  Sliced fresh jalapeño chiles* (optional)

1. In 3½- or 4-quart slow cooker, combine chicken broth, chicken, frozen vegetables and tomatoes with their juices.

2. Cover slow cooker; cook on low-heat setting for 6 to 7 hours or on high-heat setting for 3 to 3½ hours.

3. To serve, ladle soup into warm soup bowls and top with tortilla chips. If desired, top with chiles.

• •

Per serving: 181 cal., 4 g total fat (1 g sat. fat), 36 mg chol., 1,383 mg sodium, 19 g carbo., 1 g fiber, 18 g pro.

*Note: Because chiles contain volatile oils that can burn your skin and eyes, avoid direct contact with them as much as possible. When working with chiles, wear plastic or rubber gloves. If your bare hands do touch the chiles, wash your hands and nails well with soap and warm water.

PREP:
15 minutes

COOKER SIZE:
3½- or 4-quart

COOK:
7 to 8 hours on low-heat or 3½ to 4 hours on high-heat setting

MAKES:
6 servings

FREEZE WITH EASE

MAKE IT A MEAL:
Whole wheat crackers served with purchased hummus

Mixed greens served with citrus vinaigrette

Easy Apple-Cherry Crisp (see recipe, page 280)

To make sure the spinach stays bright green, stir it in just before serving.

Spinach, Chicken And Wild Rice Soup

3 cups water
1 can (14 ounces) chicken broth
1 can (10¾ ounces) condensed cream of chicken soup
⅔ cup wild rice, rinsed and drained
½ teaspoon dried thyme
¼ teaspoon salt
¼ teaspoon black pepper
3 cups cubed cooked chicken or turkey
2 cups shredded fresh spinach

1. In 3½- or 4-quart slow cooker, combine the water, chicken broth, cream of chicken soup, wild rice, thyme, salt and pepper.

2. Cover slow cooker; cook on low-heat setting for 7 to 8 hours or on high-heat setting for 3½ to 4 hours. To serve, stir chicken and spinach into mixture in slow cooker.

Per serving: 263 cal., 9 g total fat (3 g sat. fat), 66 mg chol., 741 mg sodium, 19 g carbo., 2 g fiber, 25 g pro.

Cream of chicken soup, cooked chicken and chicken broth triple the poultry flavor of this no-fuss, hearty soup.

Wild Rice and Chicken Soup

2½ **cups chopped cooked chicken**
2 **cups sliced fresh mushrooms**
2 **medium-size carrots, coarsely shredded**
2 **ribs celery, sliced**
1 **can (10¾ ounces) condensed cream of chicken soup or cream of mushroom soup**
1 **package (6 ounces) long grain and wild rice mix**
5 **cups chicken broth**
5 **cups water**

1. In 5- to 6-quart slow cooker, combine cooked chicken, mushrooms, carrots, celery, cream of chicken soup, rice and the contents of the rice seasoning packet. Gradually stir in chicken broth and the water.

2. Cover slow cooker; cook on low-heat setting for 6 to 8 hours or on high-heat setting for 3 to 4 hours.

Per serving: 221 cal., 7 g total fat (2 g sat. fat), 44 mg chol., 1,251 mg sodium, 23 g carbo., 2 g fiber, 18 g pro.

PREP:
20 minutes

COOKER SIZE:
5- to 6-quart

COOK:
6 to 8 hours on low-heat or 3 to 4 hours on high-heat setting

MAKES:
8 to 10 servings

FREEZE WITH EASE

MAKE IT A MEAL:
Purchased crusty rolls

Purchased frosted sugar cookies

SOUPS AND STEWS

189

PREP:
10 minutes

COOKER SIZE:
4- to 5-quart

COOK:
8 to 10 hours on low-heat or 4 to 5 hours on high-heat setting, plus 15 minutes on high-heat setting

MAKES:
6 servings

KIDS' FAVORITE!

MAKE IT A MEAL:
Fresh baby carrots and celery sticks with ranch-flavor sour cream dip

Cheese French Bread (see recipe, page 266)

Purchased custard pie

For a traditional Italian trattoria presentation, purchase a wedge of Parmesan cheese and use a vegetable peeler to cut wide shavings.

Sausage and Tortellini Soup

2 cans (14½ ounces each) Italian-style stewed tomatoes
3 cups water
2 cups loose-pack frozen whole green beans or Italian-style green beans
1 can (10½ ounces) condensed French onion soup
½ pound fully cooked smoked turkey sausage, halved lengthwise and cut into ½-inch-thick slices
2 cups packaged coleslaw mix
1 package (9 ounces) refrigerated cheese-filled tortellini
Shredded or shaved Parmesan cheese

1. In 4- to 5-quart slow cooker, combine tomatoes with their juices, the water, frozen green beans, French onion soup and turkey sausage.

2. Cover slow cooker; cook on low-heat setting for 8 to 10 hours or on high-heat setting for 4 to 5 hours.

3. If necessary, raise temperature to high-heat setting. Stir coleslaw mix and tortellini into mixture in slow cooker. Cover slow cooker; cook for 15 minutes longer. Top each serving with Parmesan cheese.

· ·

Per serving: 271 cal., 7 g total fat (3 g sat. fat), 51 mg chol., 1,207 mg sodium, 37 g carbo., 4 g fiber, 14 g pro.

PREP:
25 minutes

COOKER SIZE:
3½- or 4-quart

COOK:
6 to 7 hours on low-heat or 3 to 3½ hours on high-heat setting, plus 1 hour on high-heat setting

MAKES:
6 servings

KIDS' FAVORITE!

FREEZE WITH EASE

MAKE IT A MEAL:
Fruit and Broccoli Salad (see recipe, page 248)

Oyster crackers

Purchased apple pie served with cinnamon ice cream

Although chicken soup is touted as being comforting when you're under the weather, don't wait until then to enjoy this version.

Herbed Chicken-Noodle Soup

1 pound boneless, skinless chicken thighs, cut into 1-inch pieces
1 can (10¾ ounces) condensed cream of chicken soup
2 ribs celery, thinly sliced
2 medium-size carrots, thinly sliced
1 medium-size onion, chopped
1 can (4½ ounces) sliced mushrooms, drained
1 clove garlic, chopped
½ teaspoon dried sage
½ teaspoon dried thyme
¼ teaspoon dried rosemary
⅛ teaspoon black pepper
2 cans (14 ounces each) chicken broth
½ of a package (16 ounces) frozen homestyle egg noodles (about 3 cups)

1. In 3½- or 4-quart slow cooker, combine chicken, cream of chicken soup, celery, carrots, onion, drained mushrooms, garlic, sage, thyme, rosemary and pepper. Pour chicken broth over mixture in slow cooker.

2. Cover slow cooker; cook on low-heat setting for 6 to 7 hours or on high-heat setting for 3 to 3½ hours.

3. If necessary, raise temperature to high-heat setting. Stir in frozen noodles. Cover slow cooker; cook for 1 hour longer.

Per serving: 241 cal., 8 g total fat (2 g sat. fat), 103 mg chol., 1,115 mg sodium, 22 g carbo., 2 g fiber, 20 g pro.

Shelf-stable, fully cooked gnocchi are your ticket to no-prep dumplings in this flavorful stick-to-your-ribs stew.

Chicken Stew with Potato Dumplings

3 **pounds bone-in chicken thighs, skin removed**
2 **large carrots, peeled and cut into ½-inch-thick slices**
2 **ribs celery, cut into ½-inch pieces**
3 **medium-size parsnips, peeled and cut into ½-inch-thick slices**
1 **large sweet potato (about 1 pound), peeled and cut into 1-inch cubes**
4 **scallions, trimmed and sliced**
1 **quart (4 cups) chicken broth**
1 **cup water**
½ **teaspoon dried sage leaves**
¼ **teaspoon salt**
¼ **teaspoon black pepper**
1 **package (1.1 pounds) shelf-stable, fully cooked gnocchi (dumplings)**
2 **tablespoons cornstarch mixed with ¼ cup cold water**
Hot-pepper sauce

1. Place chicken in 6-quart slow cooker. Top with carrots, celery, parsnips, sweet potato and scallions. Pour chicken broth and the water over vegetables. Sprinkle with sage, salt and pepper.

2. Cover slow cooker; cook on low-heat setting for 6 hours or on high-heat setting for 4 hours.

3. Transfer chicken to a cutting board. If necessary, raise temperature to high-heat setting. Add gnocchi to mixture in slow cooker. Cover slow cooker; cook for 10 minutes. Meanwhile, let chicken cool slightly. Using two forks, remove chicken from bones and pull chicken apart into shreds; discard bones.

4. When gnocchi are cooked, return chicken to slow cooker. Stir cornstarch mixture into mixture in slow cooker. Cover slow cooker; cook for 10 to 20 minutes longer or until thickened slightly. Add hot-pepper sauce to taste before serving.

Per serving: 362 cal., 10 g total fat (3 g sat. fat), 72 mg chol., 881 mg sodium, 45 g carbo., 4 g fiber, 23 g pro.

PREP:
30 minutes

COOKER SIZE:
6-quart

COOK:
6 hours on low-heat or 4 hours on high-heat setting, plus 20 to 30 minutes on high-heat setting

MAKES:
8 servings

KIDS' FAVORITE!

MAKE IT A MEAL:
Mixed greens served with Italian dressing and shredded Parmesan cheese

Fudge Cookies in Chocolate Cream (see recipe, page 276)

PREP:
25 minutes

COOKER SIZE:
3½- or 4-quart

COOK:
5 to 6 hours on low-heat or 2½ to 3 hours on high-heat setting

MAKES:
4 servings

Beefy onion soup mix and red wine combine with chicken for a stew that's luscious and comforting on a cold night.

Chicken Stew With Wine

3 **pounds bone-in chicken thighs, skin removed**
1 **envelope (½ of a 2.2-ounce package) beefy onion soup mix**
2 **cups fresh mushrooms, quartered**
1½ **cups loose-pack frozen small whole onions**
½ **cup dry red wine**
   Chopped fresh parsley (optional)

1. Lightly coat an unheated large skillet with nonstick cooking spray. Preheat skillet over medium heat. Cook chicken thighs, several at a time, in the hot skillet until browned; drain off fat. Place chicken thighs in 3½- or 4-quart slow cooker.

2. Sprinkle chicken thighs with dry soup mix. Add mushrooms and onions. Pour wine over mixture in slow cooker.

3. Cover slow cooker; cook on low-heat setting for 5 to 6 hours or on high-heat setting for 2½ to 3 hours. Using a slotted spoon, remove chicken from slow cooker. Using two forks, remove chicken from bones and pull chicken apart into bite-size pieces; discard bones. Stir chicken into mixture in cooker. If desired, sprinkle each serving with parsley.

. . . .

Per serving: 305 cal., 8 g total fat (2 g sat. fat), 161 mg chol., 759 mg sodium, 12 g carbo., 2 g fiber, 41 g pro.

MAKE IT A MEAL:
Volcano Mashed Potatoes (see recipe, page 262)

French bread slices served with olive oil

Frozen crème brûlée, baked

PREP:
30 minutes

COOKER SIZE:
3½- or 4-quart

COOK:
6 to 7 hours on low-heat or 3 to 3½ hours on high-heat setting, plus 15 minutes on high-heat setting

MAKES:
6 servings

Look for canned coconut milk in the baking aisle of the supermarket.

Mulligatawny Soup

- 1 tablespoon extra-virgin olive oil
- 1 pound boneless, skinless chicken thighs, cut into 1-inch pieces
- 2 cups chopped potato
- 2 medium-size carrots, sliced
- 1 medium-size Granny Smith apple, peeled and coarsely chopped
- 1 large onion, chopped
- 1 teaspoon grated lime zest
- 1 tablespoon lime juice
- 1½ teaspoons curry powder
- ¼ teaspoon salt
- 2 cans (14 ounces each) chicken broth
- ½ cup purchased unsweetened coconut milk
- ½ cup instant white rice

1. In large skillet, heat olive oil over medium-high heat. Brown chicken, half at a time, in hot oil. Drain off fat.

2. In 3½- or 4-quart slow cooker, combine chicken, potato, carrots, apple, onion, lime zest, lime juice, curry powder and salt. Pour chicken broth over mixture in slow cooker.

3. Cover slow cooker; cook on low-heat setting for 6 to 7 hours or on high-heat setting for 3 to 3½ hours.

4. If necessary, raise temperature to high-heat setting. Stir in coconut milk and uncooked rice. Cover slow cooker; cook about 15 minutes longer or until rice is tender.

· ·

Per serving: 250 cal., 10 g total fat (4 g sat. fat), 62 mg chol., 701 mg sodium, 22 g carbo., 2 g fiber, 18 g pro.

MAKE IT A MEAL:

Purchased naan (Indian flatbread)

Passion fruit sorbet topped with crushed vanilla wafers

Serve this stew with extra hot-pepper sauce and/or red pepper flakes so diners can spice it up as much as they like.

Puttanesca Turkey Stew

2 pounds turkey drumsticks (about 1½ pounds), skin removed
1 can (28 ounces) plum tomatoes
1 can (8 ounces) tomato sauce
1 red onion, finely chopped
2 tablespoons tomato paste
¼ cup pitted green olives, halved
3 tablespoons drained capers
½ teaspoon dried Italian seasoning
¼ teaspoon salt
¼ teaspoon black pepper
¼ teaspoon red pepper flakes
   Dash hot-pepper sauce
¼ cup dry red wine
   Grated Parmesan cheese (optional)

1. In 5-quart slow cooker, combine drumsticks, tomatoes with their juices, tomato sauce, red onion, tomato paste, green olives, capers, Italian seasoning, salt, black pepper, red pepper flakes and hot-pepper sauce.

2. Cover slow cooker; cook on low-heat setting for 7½ hours. Uncover. Check temperature of drumsticks by inserting an instant-read thermometer into the thickest part of drumstick without touching bone. Thermometer should register 160° to 170°. If temperature is too low, cover cooker and continue cooking, rechecking temperature every 30 minutes. Once turkey reaches the proper temperature, remove turkey drumsticks to platter and let cool.

3. Stir red wine into mixture in slow cooker. Using the back of a large spoon, crush the tomatoes in the slow cooker. Raise temperature to high-heat setting. Cook, uncovered, for 20 minutes.

4. Once turkey has cooled slightly, remove meat from the bones; discard bones. Stir turkey into mixture in slow cooker. Cook, uncovered, for 5 to 10 minutes longer or until sauce has thickened slightly. If desired, sprinkle each serving with Parmesan cheese.

. . . .

Per serving: 238 cal., 8 g total fat (2 g sat. fat), 66 mg chol., 1,338 mg sodium, 18 g carbo., 2 g fiber, 26 g pro.

PREP:
25 minutes

COOKER SIZE:
5-quart

COOK:
7½ hours on low-heat setting, plus 25 to 35 minutes on high-heat setting

MAKES:
4 servings

FREEZE WITH EASE

MAKE IT A MEAL:
Mixed greens served with poppy seed dressing and sliced, toasted almonds

Purchased focaccia wedges served with olive oil

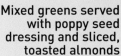

MAKE IT A MEAL:
Purchased corn bread muffins served with butter

Broccoli-Cheddar Salad (see recipe, page 251)

Purchased chocolate cream pie

This lively version of corn chowder uses the "three sisters" of Native American cooking: corn, beans and squash.

Corn-Chile Chowder

    3 large red-skin potatoes (about 1½ pounds), peeled if desired
        and cut into ½-inch cubes
 1½ cups loose-pack frozen whole kernel corn
    1 cup loose-pack frozen baby lima beans
    1 medium-size onion, chopped
    ½ cup chopped fresh Anaheim or poblano chiles* or green pepper
    1 can (4 ounces) diced green chiles, drained
    ½ cup chopped sweet red pepper
    3 cloves garlic, chopped
    ½ teaspoon salt
    2 cans (14 ounces each) vegetable broth
    1 can (14¾ ounces) cream-style corn
    1 small zucchini, halved lengthwise and sliced
    1 cup heavy cream

1. In 4- to 6-quart slow cooker, combine potatoes, frozen corn, frozen lima beans, onion, chiles, sweet red pepper, garlic and salt. Pour vegetable broth over mixture in slow cooker.

2. Cover slow cooker; cook on low-heat setting for 8 to 9 hours or on high-heat setting for 4 to 4½ hours.

3. If necessary, raise temperature to high-heat setting. Stir in cream-style corn and zucchini. Cover slow cooker; cook for 30 minutes longer. Stir in heavy cream.

· ·

Per serving: 383 cal., 17 g total fat (9 g sat. fat), 55 mg chol., 1,073 mg sodium, 54 g carbo., 6 g fiber, 10 g pro.

*Note: Because chiles contain volatile oils that can burn your skin and eyes, avoid direct contact with them as much as possible. When working with chiles, wear plastic or rubber gloves. If your bare hands do touch the chiles, wash your hands and nails well with soap and warm water.

PREP:
30 minutes

COOKER SIZE:
3½- or 4-quart

COOK:
7 to 8 hours on low-heat or 3½ to 4 hours on high-heat setting

MAKES:
8 servings

MAKE IT A MEAL:
Smoked turkey and Havarti cheese sandwiches served on marble rye bread

Easy Apple-Cherry Crisp (see recipe, page 280)

SOUPS AND STEWS

Two types of corn add both flavor and body to this pureed soup.

Golden Squash Bowl

1½ pounds butternut squash, peeled, seeded and cut into 1-inch pieces
1 large potato, peeled and cut into 1-inch pieces
1 can (8¼ or 8½ ounces) cream-style corn
1 cup loose-pack frozen whole kernel corn
1 medium-size onion, chopped
1 clove garlic, chopped
½ teaspoon dried leaf sage
¼ teaspoon salt
⅛ teaspoon black pepper
2 cans (14 ounces each) chicken broth
½ cup sour cream
3 strips bacon, crisp-cooked and crumbled

1. In 3½- or 4-quart slow cooker, combine squash, potato, cream-style corn, frozen corn, onion, garlic, sage, salt and pepper. Pour chicken broth over mixture in slow cooker.

2. Cover slow cooker; cook on low-heat setting for 7 to 8 hours or on high-heat setting for 3½ to 4 hours.

3. In small bowl, combine sour cream and about ½ cup of the hot cooking liquid from the slow cooker. Stir into mixture in slow cooker. Cool mixture slightly. Transfer about one-third of the mixture to a blender or food processor. Cover and blend or process until smooth. Transfer pureed mixture to a serving bowl; cover to keep warm. Repeat with remaining mixture in slow cooker, half at a time, until mixture is pureed. Sprinkle each serving with bacon.

Per serving: 130 cal., 4 g total fat (2 g sat. fat), 10 mg chol., 633 mg sodium, 21 g carbo., 2 g fiber, 4 g pro.

Another time, serve this sophisticated soup as the first course for a dinner party.

Thai Winter Squash Soup

2 **pounds butternut squash, peeled and cut into ¾-inch pieces**
2 **cups thinly sliced bok choy**
1 **medium-size onion, cut into thin wedges**
1 **medium-size fresh jalapeño chile, seeded and finely chopped***
½ **teaspoon grated lime zest**
2 **tablespoons lime juice**
1 **teaspoon ground ginger**
3 **cloves garlic, chopped**
½ **teaspoon salt**
2 **cans (14 ounces each) vegetable broth**
1 **cup unsweetened coconut milk**
1 **tablespoon chopped fresh cilantro**
1 **tablespoon chopped fresh basil**

1. In 3½- or 4-quart slow cooker, combine squash, bok choy, onion, chile, lime zest, lime juice, ginger, garlic and salt. Pour vegetable broth over mixture in slow cooker.

2. Cover slow cooker; cook on low-heat setting for 7 to 8 hours or on high-heat setting for 3½ to 4 hours. Stir in coconut milk, cilantro and basil.

. . . .

Per serving: 99 cal., 6 g total fat (5 g sat. fat), 0 mg chol., 557 mg sodium, 12 g carbo., 2 g fiber, 2 g pro.

*Note: Because chiles contain volatile oils that can burn your skin and eyes, avoid direct contact with them as much as possible. When working with chiles, wear plastic or rubber gloves. If your bare hands do touch the chiles, wash your hands and nails well with soap and warm water.

PREP:
30 minutes

COOKER SIZE:
3½- or 4-quart

COOK:
7 to 8 hours on low-heat or 3½ to 4 hours on high-heat setting

MAKES:
8 servings

FREEZE WITH EASE

MAKE IT A MEAL:
Grilled ham and Swiss cheese sandwiches

Purchased miniature fruit tarts

SOUPS AND STEWS

PREP:
20 minutes

COOKER SIZE:
4- to 5-quart

COOK:
8 to 10 hours on low-heat or 4 to 5 hours on high-heat setting

MAKES:
4 to 6 servings

MAKE IT A MEAL:
Baby carrots and/or celery sticks

Purchased corn bread

Purchased carrot cake with cream cheese frosting

Fresh ginger, curry powder and a jalapeño chile deftly season this hearty, meatless soup.

Curried Lentil Soup

2 medium-size sweet potatoes (about 1 pound), peeled and coarsely chopped
1 cup dry brown or yellow lentils, rinsed and drained
1 medium-size onion, chopped
1 medium-size fresh jalapeño chile, seeded and finely chopped*
3 cloves garlic, chopped
3 cans (14 ounces each) vegetable broth
1 can (14½ ounces) diced tomatoes
1 tablespoon curry powder
1 teaspoon finely chopped fresh ginger
  Plain yogurt or sour cream (optional)
  Small fresh chiles and/or crushed red pepper (optional)

1. In 4- to 5-quart slow cooker, combine sweet potatoes, lentils, onion, jalapeño chile and garlic. Add broth, tomatoes with their juices, curry powder and ginger.

2. Cover slow cooker; cook on low-heat setting for 8 to 10 hours or on high-heat setting for 4 to 5 hours. If desired, top each serving with yogurt or sour cream and garnish with chiles and/or crushed red pepper.

· ·

Per serving: 316 cal., 2 g total fat (0 g sat. fat), 0 mg chol., 1,425 mg sodium, 60 g carbo., 18 g fiber, 18 g pro.

*Note: Because chiles contain volatile oils that can burn your skin and eyes, avoid direct contact with them as much as possible. When working with chiles, wear plastic or rubber gloves. If your bare hands do touch the chiles, wash your hands and nails well with soap and warm water.

PREP:
20 minutes

COOKER SIZE:
3½- or 4-quart

COOK:
8 to 9 hours on low-heat or 4 to 4½ hours on high-heat setting

MAKES:
6 to 8 servings

Even kids will eat veggies when they come cloaked in a creamy, cheesy bowlful of soup.

Cheesy Vegetable Soup

3 medium-size potatoes, peeled and chopped
4 carrots, chopped
1 package (16 ounces) loose-pack frozen whole kernel corn
1 large onion, chopped
2 cups water
1 can (10¾ ounces) condensed cream of chicken soup
1 teaspoon dried thyme
¼ teaspoon black pepper
8 ounces American cheese, cubed

1. In 3½- or 4-quart slow cooker, combine potatoes, carrots, frozen corn and onion. Stir in the water, cream of chicken soup, thyme and pepper.

2. Cover slow cooker; cook on low-heat setting for 8 to 9 hours or on high-heat setting for 4 to 4½ hours.

3. Add cheese to hot soup, stirring until melted.

Per serving: 349 cal., 16 g total fat (8 g sat. fat), 40 mg chol., 968 mg sodium, 41 g carbo., 5 g fiber, 14 g pro.

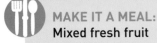

KIDS' FAVORITE!

MAKE IT A MEAL:
Mixed fresh fruit

Refrigerated soft breadsticks, baked

There are many flavors of hummus on the market. For this stew, we recommend the traditional one.

Kielbasa-Chickpea Stew

2 cans (15 ounces each) chickpeas, drained and rinsed
2 medium-size carrots, halved lengthwise, then sliced crosswise ¼ inch thick
2 ribs celery, halved lengthwise, then sliced crosswise ¼ inch thick
1 medium-size onion, coarsely chopped
1 medium-size sweet red pepper, seeded and diced
1 medium-size green pepper, seeded and diced
1 teaspoon dried thyme
½ teaspoon dried basil
¼ teaspoon black pepper
1 package (1 pound) Polish kielbasa, cut into cubes
2½ cups beef broth
1 container (8 ounces) prepared hummus
1 can (6 ounces) tomato paste
½ teaspoon salt

1. Spread chickpeas in 5- or 5½-quart slow cooker. Layer the carrots, celery, onion, sweet red pepper and green pepper on top of the chickpeas. Sprinkle with thyme, basil and black pepper. Arrange cubed kielbasa evenly on top of vegetables. Pour beef broth over.

2. Cover slow cooker; cook on low-heat setting for 10 to 11 hours or on high-heat setting for 5 to 6 hours or until vegetables are tender.

3. If necessary, raise temperature to high-heat setting. Stir hummus, tomato paste and salt into the mixture in the slow cooker. Cover slow cooker; cook for 10 to 15 minutes longer or until heated through.

Per serving: 369 cal., 20 g total fat (6 g sat. fat), 38 mg chol., 1,532 mg sodium, 31 g carbo., 8 g fiber, 18 g pro.

PREP:
30 minutes

COOKER SIZE:
5- or 5½-quart

COOK:
10 to 11 hours on low-heat or 5 to 6 hours on high-heat setting, plus 10 to 15 minutes on high-heat setting

MAKES:
8 servings

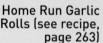

MAKE IT A MEAL:
Home Run Garlic Rolls (see recipe, page 263)

Purchased fudge brownies served with vanilla ice cream

PREP:
35 minutes

COOKER SIZE:
4½- to 5½-quart

COOK:
9 to 10 hours on low-heat or 4½ to 5 hours on high-heat setting

STAND:
10 minutes

MAKES:
6 servings

MAKE IT A MEAL:
Buttermilk Angel Biscuits (see recipe, page 267)

Purchased fruit salad

Vanilla frozen yogurt

Hearty vegetables and chickpeas give this stew texture, substance and protein.

Hearty Chickpea-Vegetable Stew

  1 medium-size sweet potato, peeled and cut into 1-inch cubes
  1 can (15 ounces) chickpeas, drained and rinsed
  1 can (14½ ounces) Mexican-style stewed tomatoes, cut up
1½ cups loose-pack frozen small whole onions
  1 large russet potato, peeled and cut into 1-inch cubes
  1 cup peeled and cubed rutabaga
  1 large sweet red pepper, seeded and coarsely chopped
⅔ cup halved small fresh mushrooms
  1 large carrot, peeled and thinly sliced
  1 rib celery, sliced
  1 can (14 ounces) vegetable broth
  1 can (6 ounces) tomato paste
  2 teaspoons Cajun seasoning
½ teaspoon salt
½ teaspoon black pepper
1½ cups loose-pack frozen whole green beans
½ cup loose-pack frozen peas

1. Lightly coat 4½- to 5½-quart slow cooker with nonstick cooking spray. Add sweet potato, chickpeas, tomatoes with their juices, the onions, russet potato, rutabaga, sweet pepper, mushrooms, carrot and celery to slow cooker. In medium-size bowl, combine vegetable broth, tomato paste, Cajun seasoning, salt and black pepper. Pour over vegetables.

2. Cover slow cooker; cook on low-heat setting for 9 to 10 hours or on high-heat setting for 4½ to 5 hours.

3. Stir frozen green beans and peas into mixture in slow cooker. Cover slow cooker; let stand for 10 minutes before serving.

Per serving: 228 cal., 1 g total fat (0 g sat. fat), 0 mg chol., 1,161 mg sodium, 47 g carbo., 10 g fiber, 9 g pro.

PREP:
15 minutes

COOKER SIZE:
5- to 6-quart

COOK:
4 to 5 hours on low-heat or 2 to 2½ hours on high-heat setting

MAKES:
8 servings

FREEZE WITH EASE

MAKE IT A MEAL:
Croissants served with Brie cheese

Chocolate cherry ice cream served in waffle cones

Garlic and tomatoes star in this take on hearty ham and bean soup.

Navy Bean-Garlic Soup

3 cans (15 to 16 ounces each) navy beans, drained and rinsed
2 cans (14½ ounces each) stewed tomatoes, cut up
2 cans (14 ounces each) chicken broth with roasted garlic or regular chicken broth
2 cups cubed cooked ham
1 can (10¾ ounces) condensed cream of potato soup
4 cloves garlic, chopped
1 teaspoon dried rosemary

1. In 5- to 6-quart slow cooker, combine navy beans, tomatoes with their juices, chicken broth, ham, cream of potato soup, garlic and rosemary.

2. Cover slow cooker; cook on low-heat setting for 4 to 5 hours or on high-heat setting for 2 to 2½ hours.

Per serving: 333 cal., 6 g total fat (2 g sat. fat), 24 mg chol., 2,059 mg sodium, 51 g carbo., 10 g fiber, 21 g pro.

Ten minutes of boiling on the rangetop ensures the black-eyed peas will be tender.

Ham and Black-Eyed Pea Soup

    4 cups water
    ¾ pound dry black-eyed peas (2 cups)
    2 cans (14 ounces each) reduced-sodium chicken broth
    1 cup ham cut into ½-inch pieces
    4 medium-size carrots, cut into ½-inch-thick slices
    2 ribs celery, sliced
    ¼ cup dried minced onion
    1 teaspoon dried sage
    1 teaspoon dried thyme
    ¼ teaspoon cayenne pepper
 1½ cups water
    1 tablespoon lemon juice

1. In 3-quart saucepan, combine the 4 cups water and the black-eyed peas; bring to a boil. Boil, uncovered, for 10 minutes. Drain and rinse.

2. In 4- to 5-quart slow cooker, combine chicken broth, ham, carrots, celery, dried minced onion, sage, thyme and cayenne pepper. Stir in the 1½ cups water. Stir in black-eyed peas.

3. Cover slow cooker; cook on low-heat setting for 9 to 11 hours or on high-heat setting for 4½ to 5½ hours. Stir in lemon juice.

. . . .

Per serving: 131 cal., 2 g total fat (1 g sat. fat), 13 mg chol., 654 mg sodium, 20 g carbo., 5 g fiber, 8 g pro.

PREP:
30 minutes

COOKER SIZE:
4- to 5-quart

COOK:
9 to 11 hours on low-heat or 4½ to 5½ hours on high-heat setting

MAKES:
6 servings

FREEZE WITH EASE

MAKE IT A MEAL:
Home Run Garlic Rolls (see recipe, page 263)

Mixed greens with Thousand Island dressing

Purchased raspberry pie served with vanilla ice cream

PREP:
15 minutes

COOKER SIZE:
3½- or 4-quart

COOK:
6 to 7 hours on low-heat or 3 to 3½ hours on high-heat setting, plus 30 minutes on high-heat setting

MAKES:
6 servings

KIDS' FAVORITE!

MAKE IT A MEAL:
Whole wheat bread slices served with butter

Purchased apple cake served with caramel-swirl ice cream

Why does this recipe call for evaporated milk instead of regular? Because the evaporated milk won't break down during the slow cooking.

Swiss, Ham and Broccoli Chowder

2 cans (10¾ ounces each) condensed cream of celery soup
1 can (12 ounces) evaporated milk
½ cup water
1 package (16 to 20 ounces) refrigerated diced potatoes or 3 cups loose-pack frozen diced hash brown potatoes with onion and peppers, thawed
2 cups diced cooked ham
2 ribs celery, finely chopped
8 ounces process Swiss cheese slices, torn into small pieces
2 cups chopped fresh broccoli or loose-pack frozen chopped broccoli, thawed

1. In 3½- or 4-quart slow cooker, combine cream of celery soup, evaporated milk and the water. Gently stir potatoes, ham and celery into mixture in slow cooker.

2. Cover slow cooker; cook on low-heat setting for 6 to 7 hours or on high-heat setting for 3 to 3½ hours.

3. If necessary, raise temperature to high-heat setting. Stir in Swiss cheese and broccoli. Cover slow cooker; cook for 30 minutes longer.

Per serving: 460 cal., 24 g total fat (13 g sat. fat), 78 mg chol., 2,148 mg sodium, 34 g carbo., 4 g fiber, 24 g pro.

A little prosciutto adds a lot of flavor to this veggie-packed soup.

Zesty Minestrone Soup

- 3 cups packaged coleslaw mix
- 1 large onion, chopped
- 3 medium-size carrots, peeled and chopped
- 1 medium-size yellow squash, halved lengthwise and cut crosswise into ¼-inch-thick slices
- 1 medium-size zucchini, halved lengthwise and cut crosswise into ¼-inch-thick slices
- 1 can (28 ounces) diced tomatoes
- 2 cans (14 ounces each) chicken broth
- 2 cups water
- 1 can (15 ounces) red kidney beans, drained and rinsed
- ¼ pound thinly sliced prosciutto, chopped
- 2 cloves garlic, chopped
- 1½ teaspoons dried Italian seasoning
- 1 teaspoon salt
- ½ teaspoon black pepper
- ¼ teaspoon red pepper flakes
- 1 cup ditalini pasta
  Shaved Parmesan cheese (optional)

1. In 5- or 5½-quart slow cooker, stir together coleslaw mix, onion, carrots, yellow squash, zucchini, tomatoes with their juices, chicken broth, the water, kidney beans, prosciutto, garlic, Italian seasoning, salt, black pepper and red pepper flakes.

2. Cover slow cooker; cook on high-heat setting for 4½ hours.

3. Stir uncooked ditalini into mixture in slow cooker. Cover slow cooker; cook for 30 minutes longer. If desired, top each serving with shaved Parmesan cheese.

Per serving: 222 cal., 4 g total fat (1 g sat. fat), 12 mg chol., 1,367 mg sodium, 34 g carbo., 9 g fiber, 13 g pro.

PREP:
30 minutes

COOKER SIZE:
5- or 5½-quart

COOK:
4½ hours plus 30 minutes on high-heat setting

MAKES:
8 servings

FREEZE WITH EASE

MAKE IT A MEAL:
Cheesy French Bread (see recipe, page 266)

Purchased New York-style cheesecake served with strawberries

PREP:
30 minutes

COOKER SIZE:
3½- or 4-quart

COOK:
8 to 9 hours on low-heat or 4 to 4½ hours on high-heat setting, plus 20 to 30 minutes on high-heat setting

MAKES:
4 servings

MAKE IT A MEAL:
Fruit and Broccoli Salad (see recipe, page 248)

Purchased blueberry pie served with sweetened whipped cream

As summer gives way to fall, simmer a bumper-crop of late-season vegetables slowly in this wonderfully varied soup.

Farmer's Market Vegetable Soup

½ small rutabaga, peeled and chopped (2 cups)
2 large plum tomatoes, chopped
2 medium-size carrots or parsnips, cut into ½-inch pieces
1 large red-skin potato, chopped
2 medium-size leeks, chopped
3 cans (14 ounces each) vegetable broth
1 teaspoon fennel seeds, crushed
½ teaspoon dried sage
¼ to ½ teaspoon black pepper
½ cup tiny bowtie pasta
3 cups torn fresh spinach
  Garlic Toast (recipe follows) (optional)

1. In 3½- or 4-quart slow cooker, combine rutabaga, plum tomatoes, carrots or parsnips, potato and leeks. Add vegetable broth, fennel seeds, sage and pepper.

2. Cover slow cooker; cook on low-heat setting for 8 to 9 hours or on high-heat setting for 4 to 4½ hours. If necessary, raise temperature to high-heat setting. Stir in uncooked pasta. Cover slow cooker; cook for 20 to 30 minutes longer or until pasta is tender. Just before serving, stir in spinach.

3. If desired, serve with Garlic Toast.

Per serving: 198 cal., 2 g total fat (0 g sat. fat), 0 mg chol., 1,313 mg sodium, 41 g carbo., 8 g fiber, 8 g pro.

Garlic Toast: Heat broiler. Brush both sides of eight ½-inch-thick baguette slices with 1 tablespoon garlic-flavor olive oil. Arrange on a baking sheet. Broil 3 to 4 inches from the heat for 1 minute. Turn; sprinkle with 2 teaspoons grated Parmesan cheese. Broil for 1 to 2 minutes longer or until lightly toasted.

PREP:
30 minutes

COOKER SIZE:
4- to 5-quart

COOK:
6 to 8 hours on low-heat or 3 to 4 hours on high-heat setting, plus 15 minutes on high-heat setting

MAKES:
6 servings

MAKE IT A MEAL:
Purchased Waldorf salad

Oyster crackers

Shortbread Brownies (see recipe, page 270)

Ginger, jerk seasoning, lime and garlic turn simple white fish into a tropical delight.

Caribbean Fish Stew

2 **pounds sweet potatoes, peeled and coarsely chopped**
1 **large sweet red pepper, seeded and chopped**
1 **medium-size onion, chopped**
1 **tablespoon finely chopped fresh ginger**
½ **teaspoon grated lime zest**
1 **tablespoon lime juice**
1 **teaspoon Jamaican jerk seasoning**
2 **cloves garlic, minced**
2 **cans (14 ounces each) chicken broth**
1 **can (14½ ounces) diced tomatoes**
1 **pound firm white fish, cut into 1-inch pieces**
2 **tablespoons chopped fresh cilantro**

1. In 4- to 5-quart slow cooker, combine sweet potatoes, sweet pepper, onion, ginger, lime zest, lime juice, jerk seasoning and garlic. Pour chicken broth and tomatoes with their juices over mixture in slow cooker.

2. Cover slow cooker; cook on low-heat setting for 6 to 8 hours or on high-heat setting for 3 to 4 hours.

3. If necessary, raise temperature to high-heat setting. Stir in fish. Cover slow cooker; cook about 15 minutes longer or until fish flakes easily when tested with a fork. Sprinkle each serving with cilantro.

. . . .

Per serving: 232 cal., 5 g total fat (1 g sat. fat), 45 mg chol., 792 mg sodium, 29 g carbo., 4 g fiber, 17 g pro.

Bring-a-Dish Nights

223 Chicken and Pasta Soup

Crock-Full of Reubens 230

239 Cheesy Cauliflower for a Crowd

Multigrain Pilaf with Beans 242

Potluck, party or family gathering—all such occasions call for a big batch of food. These flavorful appetizer, side and main dish recipes all make enough to feed a hungry crowd.

PREP:
25 minutes

COOKER SIZE:
3½- or 4-quart

COOK:
5 to 6 hours on low-heat or 2½ to 3 hours on high-heat setting

MAKES:
7 cups dip

KIDS' FAVORITE!

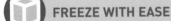

FREEZE WITH EASE

If there's any of this spunky dip left over, spoon it into freezer containers and stash it in the freezer for up to 3 months.

Spicy Sausage Pizza Dip

1 pound bulk Italian sausage
⅔ cup chopped onion
4 cloves garlic, chopped
2 cans (15 ounces each) tomato sauce
1 can (14½ ounces) tomatoes, cut up
1 can (6 ounces) tomato paste
4 teaspoons dried oregano
1 tablespoon dried basil
2 teaspoons sugar
¼ teaspoon cayenne pepper
½ cup chopped pitted ripe olives
  Assorted dippers (such as toasted bread slices sprinkled with Parmesan cheese, breadsticks, breaded mozzarella cheese sticks and/or sweet pepper strips)

1. In large skillet, cook sausage, onion and garlic until sausage is cooked through and onion is tender, stirring to break sausage into bite-size pieces. Drain off fat.

2. In 3½- or 4-quart slow cooker, combine sausage mixture, tomato sauce, tomatoes with their juices, tomato paste, oregano, basil, sugar and cayenne pepper.

3. Cover slow cooker; cook on low-heat setting for 5 to 6 hours or on high-heat setting for 2½ to 3 hours.

4. Stir in olives. Serve with assorted dippers.

Per ¼-cup dip: 70 cal., 4 g total fat (2 g sat. fat), 11 mg chol., 275 mg sodium, 4 g carbo., 1 g fiber, 3 g pro.

PREP:
25 minutes

BAKE:
18 minutes

COOKER SIZE:
3½- or 4-quart

COOK:
3 to 4 hours on low-heat or 1½ to 2 hours on high-heat setting

OVEN:
350°

MAKES:
20 appetizer servings

KIDS' FAVORITE!

FREEZE WITH EASE

The hotter the salsa you use, the spicier these saucy meat tidbits will be.

Mexi Meatballs And Mini Sausages

1 **egg**
¼ **cup packaged plain dry bread crumbs**
¼ **cup finely chopped onion**
3 **cloves garlic, chopped**
¾ **pound ground beef (93% lean)**
¼ **pound chorizo (remove casing, if present)**
1 **jar (16 ounces) salsa**
1 **jar (12 ounces) chili sauce**
1 **package (16 ounces) small cooked smoked sausage links**
2 **tablespoons chopped fresh cilantro**

1. Heat oven to 350°. In medium-size bowl, beat egg with a fork; stir in bread crumbs, onion and garlic. Add ground beef and chorizo; mix well. Shape into 1-inch meatballs (about 38 meatballs).

2. Place meatballs in 15×10×1-inch baking pan. Bake at 350° about 18 minutes or until meatballs are cooked through. Drain off fat. Pat dry with paper towels.

3. In 3½- or 4-quart slow cooker, stir together salsa and chili sauce. Stir in baked meatballs and smoked sausage links.

4. Cover slow cooker; cook on low-heat setting for 3 to 4 hours or on high-heat setting for 1½ to 2 hours. To serve, sprinkle with cilantro. Serve with decorative picks.

Per serving: 160 cal., 11 g total fat (4 g sat. fat), 39 mg chol., 687 mg sodium, 7 g carbo., 1 g fiber, 9 g pro.

PREP:
25 minutes

COOKER SIZE:
Oval 5½-quart

COOK:
4½ hours on low-heat setting

MAKES:
8 servings

FREEZE WITH EASE

Preshredded cheese and ready-made pasta sauce help shave prep time.

Spicy Turkey Lasagna

 1 **pound uncooked ground turkey**
 1 **teaspoon dried oregano**
 ½ **teaspoon salt**
 ¼ **teaspoon red pepper flakes**
 1 **carton (15 ounces) ricotta cheese**
 1 **package (10 ounces) frozen chopped spinach, thawed and squeezed dry**
 1 **package (8 ounces) shredded Italian-blend cheese (2 cups)**
 12 **lasagna noodles, uncooked and broken in half**
 1 **jar (26 ounces) chunky pasta sauce with mushrooms and green peppers**
 ½ **cup water**
    Grated Parmesan cheese (optional)

1. In large nonstick skillet, cook turkey over medium-high heat for 5 to 7 minutes or until cooked through, stirring to break into bite-size pieces. Season with oregano, salt and red pepper flakes. Remove from heat.

2. In medium-size bowl, combine ricotta cheese, spinach and cheese blend.

3. In oval 5½-quart slow cooker, arrange half of the lasagna noodles, overlapping as necessary. Spoon on half of the turkey mixture. Pour on half of the pasta sauce and half of the water. Spread half of the cheese mixture on top. Repeat layering.

4. Cover slow cooker; cook on low-heat setting for 4½ hours.

5. To serve, cut into eight equal pieces. If desired, sprinkle with Parmesan cheese.

. . . .

Per serving: 452 cal., 20 g total fat (10 g sat. fat), 92 mg chol., 781 mg sodium, 39 g carbo., 4 g fiber, 29 g pro.

This make-ahead spaghetti sauce allows the intense flavors of the ingredients to slowly meld together during cooking.

Spaghetti Sauce Italiano

PREP:
25 minutes

COOKER SIZE:
3½- to 4½-quart

COOK:
9 to 10 hours on low-heat or 4½ to 5 hours on high-heat setting

MAKES:
8 servings

1 pound ground beef (93% lean)
½ pound bulk Italian sausage
1 can (28 ounces) diced tomatoes
2 cans (6 ounces each) tomato paste
2 jars (4½ ounces each) sliced mushrooms, drained
1 cup chopped onion
¾ cup chopped green pepper
½ cup dry red wine or water
⅓ cup water
1 can (2¼ ounces) sliced, pitted ripe olives, drained
2 teaspoons sugar
1½ teaspoons Worcestershire sauce
½ teaspoon salt
½ teaspoon chili powder
⅛ teaspoon black pepper
2 cloves garlic, chopped
  Hot cooked spaghetti
½ cup finely shredded Parmesan cheese (2 ounces)

1. In large skillet, cook ground beef and sausage until cooked through, stirring to break into bite-size pieces. Drain off fat.

2. In 3½- to 4½-quart slow cooker, combine meat mixture, tomatoes with their juices, tomato paste, drained mushrooms, onion, green pepper, wine, the water, drained olives, sugar, Worcestershire sauce, salt, chili powder, black pepper and garlic.

3. Cover slow cooker; cook on low-heat setting for 9 to 10 hours or on high-heat setting for 4½ to 5 hours.

4. Serve meat mixture over hot cooked spaghetti. Sprinkle each serving with Parmesan cheese.

- -

Per serving: 416 cal., 16 g total fat (6 g sat. fat), 56 mg chol., 1,212 mg sodium, 41 g carbo., 6 g fiber, 25 g pro.

KIDS' FAVORITE!

FREEZE WITH EASE

PREP:
25 minutes

COOKER SIZE:
5- to 6-quart

COOK:
5 to 6 hours on low-heat or 2½ to 3 hours on high-heat setting

MAKES:
8 servings

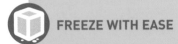

KIDS' FAVORITE!

FREEZE WITH EASE

After a long day, sit down with a steaming bowl of stew that's chock-full of pizza flavors.

Chunky Italian Sausage Stew

2 pounds hot or sweet bulk Italian sausage
¾ pound unsliced pepperoni, cut into ¾-inch chunks
4 large sweet yellow peppers, seeded and cut into thin strips (4 cups)
2 cans (4 ounces each) sliced mushrooms, drained
½ cup finely chopped onion
1 can (2½ ounces) sliced, pitted ripe olives, drained
¼ to ½ teaspoon crushed red pepper (optional)
1 jar (26 ounces) pasta sauce with mushrooms

1. In very large skillet, cook bulk sausage over medium heat until cooked through, stirring to break into bite-size pieces. Drain off fat. In 5- to 6-quart slow cooker, combine cooked sausage, pepperoni, sweet peppers, mushrooms, onion, olives and, if desired, crushed red pepper. Pour pasta sauce over mixture in cooker.

2. Cover slow cooker; cook on low-heat setting for 5 to 6 hours or on high-heat setting for 2½ to 3 hours.

· ·

Per serving: 650 cal., 49 g total fat (17 g sat. fat), 127 mg chol., 1,931 mg sodium, 23 g carbo., 5 g fiber, 29 g pro.

Wonder what to do with leftover chicken or turkey? Chop it and drop it into this pretty, hearty vegetable-pasta broth-based soup.

Chicken and Pasta Soup

2 cans (14 ounces each) chicken broth
1 can (15 ounces) white cannellini beans, drained and rinsed
1 can (14½ ounces) diced tomatoes with basil, garlic and oregano
1 cup loose-pack frozen cut green beans
1 cup sliced carrots
½ cup sliced celery
½ cup chopped onion
¼ teaspoon black pepper
2 cups chopped cooked chicken or turkey
1 cup bowtie pasta
½ cup halved lengthwise and sliced zucchini
Grated Parmesan cheese (optional)

1. In 4- to 5-quart slow cooker, combine chicken broth, cannellini beans, tomatoes with their juices, green beans, carrots, celery, onion and black pepper.

2. Cover slow cooker; cook on low-heat setting for 7 to 8 hours or on high-heat setting for 3½ to 4 hours.

3. If necessary, raise temperature to high-heat setting. Add chicken, uncooked pasta and zucchini to cooker. Cover slow cooker; cook about 20 minutes longer or until pasta is tender. If desired, top each serving with Parmesan cheese.

. . . .

Per serving: 158 cal., 3 g total fat (1 g sat. fat), 32 mg chol., 792 mg sodium, 20 g carbo., 4 g fiber, 16 g pro.

PREP:
20 minutes

COOKER SIZE:
4- to 5-quart

COOK:
7 to 8 hours on low-heat or 3½ to 4 hours on high-heat setting, plus 20 minutes on high-heat setting

MAKES:
6 servings

KIDS' FAVORITE!

FREEZE WITH EASE

PREP:
15 minutes

COOKER SIZE:
3½- to 6-quart

COOK:
6 to 8 hours on low-heat or 3 to 4 hours on high-heat setting

MAKES:
8 servings

KIDS' FAVORITE!

FREEZE WITH EASE

Black-eyed peas, chickpeas and two kinds of beans make this dynamite soup distinctive. Dollops of sour cream will add a cool touch.

Taco-Seasoned Beef Soup

1 pound ground beef
1 can (15 ounces) black-eyed peas
1 can (15 ounces) black beans
1 can (15 ounces) chili beans with chili gravy
1 can (15 ounces) chickpeas
1 can (14½ ounces) Mexican-style stewed tomatoes
1 can (11 ounces) whole kernel corn with sweet peppers
1 package (1¼ ounces) taco seasoning mix
  Sour cream (optional)
  Salsa (optional)
  Tortilla chips (optional)

1. In large skillet, cook ground beef until cooked through, stirring to break into bite-size pieces. Drain off fat. Transfer ground beef to 3½- to 6-quart slow cooker. Stir in black-eyed peas with their liquid, black beans with their liquid, chili beans with chili gravy, chickpeas with their liquid, tomatoes with their juices and corn. Add dry taco seasoning mix; stir until combined.

2. Cover slow cooker; cook on low-heat setting for 6 to 8 hours or on high-heat setting for 3 to 4 hours. If desired, top each serving with a dollop of sour cream and serve with salsa and tortilla chips.

· ·

Per serving: 349 cal., 10 g total fat (3 g sat. fat), 36 mg chol., 1,372 mg sodium, 45 g carbo., 11 g fiber, 25 g pro.

PREP:
25 minutes

COOKER SIZE:
4- to 5-quart

COOK:
6 to 8 hours on low-heat or 3 to 4 hours on high-heat setting

MAKES:
8 servings

If you love Buffalo chicken wings as an appetizer, why not enjoy the same flavors in an entrée?

Buffalo Chicken Drumsticks

16 chicken drumsticks (about 4 pounds), skin removed
1 bottle (16 ounces) Buffalo wing hot sauce (2 cups)
¼ cup tomato paste
2 tablespoons white vinegar or apple cider vinegar
2 tablespoons Worcestershire sauce
1 carton (8 ounces) sour cream
½ cup mayonnaise
½ cup crumbled blue cheese
¼ to ½ teaspoon cayenne pepper

1. Place chicken in a 4- to 5-quart slow cooker. In medium-size bowl, combine hot sauce, tomato paste, vinegar and Worcestershire sauce; pour over chicken.

2. Cover slow cooker; cook on low-heat setting for 6 to 8 hours or on high-heat setting for 3 to 4 hours.

3. Meanwhile, in small bowl, stir together sour cream, mayonnaise, blue cheese and cayenne pepper. Refrigerate until ready to use.

4. Using a slotted spoon, remove chicken from cooker. Skim fat from cooking liquid. Serve chicken with some of the cooking liquid and the blue cheese mixture.

. . . .

Per serving: 366 cal., 24 g total fat (8 g sat. fat), 120 mg chol., 2,036 mg sodium, 6 g carbo., 0 g fiber, 29 g pro.

Here's a cure for ho-hum pasta and meatballs. Liven the dish up with a zippy sauce spiked with beer and ground chipotle chiles.

Chipotle Chile Meatballs

 2 large eggs, lightly beaten
 ⅓ cup ketchup
 ¾ cup quick-cooking rolled oats
 1 to 1¼ teaspoons ground chipotle chiles
 ½ teaspoon garlic powder
 ½ teaspoon salt
 1 pound lean ground beef (93% lean)
 1 pound ground pork
 1 can (12 ounces) beer
 1 cup ketchup
 ¼ cup packed brown sugar
 1 tablespoon quick-cooking tapioca, crushed
 ¼ to ½ teaspoon ground chipotle chiles
    Hot cooked pasta

1. Heat oven to 350°. In large bowl, stir together eggs, the ⅓ cup ketchup, the oats, the 1 to 1¼ teaspoons ground chipotle chiles, the garlic powder and salt. Add beef and pork; mix well. Shape meat mixture into 32 balls. Arrange meatballs in a single layer in a 15×10×1-inch baking pan. Bake, uncovered, at 350° for 25 minutes. Drain off fat.

2. In 3½- or 4-quart slow cooker, combine beer, the 1 cup ketchup, the brown sugar, tapioca and the ¼ to ½ teaspoon ground chipotle chiles. Place meatballs on top of mixture in cooker.

3. Cover slow cooker; cook on low-heat setting for 4 to 5 hours or on high-heat setting for 2 to 2½ hours.

4. Serve meatballs and sauce over hot cooked pasta.

. . . .

Per serving: 481 cal., 19 g total fat (7 g sat. fat), 124 mg chol., 689 mg sodium, 47 g carbo., 2 g fiber, 29 g pro.

PREP:
35 minutes

BAKE:
25 minutes

COOKER SIZE:
3½- or 4-quart

COOK:
4 to 5 hours on low-heat or 2 to 2½ hours on high-heat setting

OVEN:
350°

MAKES:
8 servings

FREEZE WITH EASE

PREP:
25 minutes

MARINATE:
6 to 24 hours

COOKER SIZE:
3½- to 5-quart

COOK:
10 to 12 hours on low-heat or 5 to 6 hours on high-heat setting

MAKES:
8 to 10 servings

 KIDS' FAVORITE!

 FREEZE WITH EASE

Shredded tender pork and onions stuff these tortilla wraps. For even more Caribbean flavor, spoon on avocado dip.

Cuban-Style Pork Wraps

Marinade and Roast:
- ½ cup lime juice
- ¼ cup water
- ¼ cup grapefruit juice
- 3 cloves garlic, chopped
- 1 teaspoon dried oregano
- ½ teaspoon salt
- ½ teaspoon ground cumin
- ¼ teaspoon black pepper
- 2 bay leaves
- 1 boneless pork shoulder roast (about 3 pounds)
- 1 large onion, sliced

Wraps:
- Shredded lettuce (optional)
- Lime wedges (optional)
- Chopped tomato (optional)
- Sour cream (optional)
- Salsa (optional)
- 8 to 10 (10-inch) flour tortillas, warmed

1. **Marinade and Roast:** For marinade, in small bowl, combine lime juice, the water, grapefruit juice, garlic, oregano, salt, cumin, pepper and bay leaves. Trim fat from roast. If necessary, cut roast to fit into 3½- to 5-quart slow cooker. Using a large fork, pierce roast in several places. Place roast in a large plastic food-storage bag set in a deep bowl or baking dish. Pour marinade over roast; seal bag and turn to coat roast. Marinate in refrigerator for 6 to 24 hours, turning bag occasionally.

2. Place onion slices in the 3½- to 5-quart slow cooker. Top with roast and marinade mixture.

3. Cover slow cooker; cook on low-heat setting for 10 to 12 hours or on high-heat setting for 5 to 6 hours.

4. **Wraps:** Transfer roast to cutting board; cool slightly. Skim fat from cooking liquid; keep liquid warm. Remove and discard bay leaves. Using two forks, pull meat apart into shreds. Transfer shredded meat to serving platter. Using a slotted spoon, remove onion from cooking liquid. Transfer onion to same serving platter. If desired, pass lettuce, lime wedges, tomato, sour cream and/or salsa. Serve meat and onion in tortillas.

Per serving: 398 cal., 19 g total fat (6 g sat. fat), 90 mg chol., 420 mg sodium, 27 g carbo., 1 g fiber, 29 g pro.

Simple slow-cooked pork has many fans. In this version, it gets a savory infusion of heat thanks to chiles and hot paprika.

Peppery Pork Sandwiches

1 cup thinly sliced onions
1 boneless pork shoulder roast (2 to 2½ pounds)
1 tablespoon hot paprika
2 cans (14½ ounces each) diced tomatoes
1 can (4 ounces) diced green chiles
2 teaspoons dried oregano
½ to 1 teaspoon black pepper
¼ teaspoon salt
8 or 9 French-style rolls, split and toasted

1. Place onion in 4- to 5-quart slow cooker. Trim fat from roast. Sprinkle roast evenly with paprika. Place roast on onion in cooker. In medium-size bowl, combine tomatoes with their juices, chiles with their juices, oregano, black pepper and salt; pour over mixture in cooker.

2. Cover slow cooker; cook on low-heat setting for 10 to 12 hours or on high-heat setting for 5 to 6 hours.

3. Transfer roast to cutting board, reserving cooking liquid and tomato mixture. When roast is cool enough to handle, use two forks to pull roast apart into shreds; discard any fat. Using a slotted spoon, remove tomatoes and onions from cooking liquid; add to shredded roast. Stir in enough of the cooking liquid to moisten. Spoon roast mixture onto toasted rolls.

Per sandwich: 512 cal., 12 g total fat (3 g sat. fat), 73 mg chol., 1,066 mg sodium, 65 g carbo., 5 g fiber, 33 g pro.

PREP:
25 minutes

COOKER SIZE:
4- to 5-quart

COOK:
10 to 12 hours on low-heat or 5 to 6 hours on high-heat setting

MAKES:
8 or 9 sandwiches

FREEZE WITH EASE

PREP:
20 minutes

COOKER SIZE:
3½- or 4-quart

COOK:
4 to 6 hours on low-heat or 2 to 3 hours on high-heat setting

MAKES:
24 small sandwiches

If your favorite bakery doesn't routinely carry mini rolls, ask them to make some for you.

Crock-Full of Reubens

1 corned beef brisket with spice packet (2 to 3 pounds)
1 jar (16 ounces) sauerkraut, drained
½ cup bottled Thousand Island salad dressing
24 small rye or whole wheat rolls, split and toasted
8 ounces Swiss cheese, thinly sliced
  Bottled Thousand Island salad dressing (optional)

1. Trim fat from brisket. Place brisket in 3½- or 4-quart slow cooker, cutting to fit if necessary. Sprinkle with spices from packet. Spread drained sauerkraut over the brisket. Drizzle the ½ cup salad dressing over all.

2. Cover slow cooker; cook on low-heat setting for 4 to 6 hours or on high-heat setting for 2 to 3 hours.

3. Remove brisket from cooker to cutting board. Thinly slice brisket against the grain. Return sliced brisket to the cooker; stir to combine with the cooking liquid.

4. Using a slotted spoon, spoon corned beef mixture onto toasted rolls. Top each serving with cheese and, if desired, additional salad dressing. If desired, secure with cocktail picks.

Per small sandwich: 231 cal., 13 g total fat (5 g sat. fat), 47 mg chol., 1,165 mg sodium, 17 g carbo., 3 g fiber, 12 g pro.

PREP:
25 minutes

COOKER SIZE:
3½- or 4-quart

COOK:
4½ hours on low-heat
or 2 hours on high-
heat setting

MAKES:
18 sandwiches

With only five ingredients, this streamlined version of all-time-favorite sandwiches lives up to its name.

Easy Cheesy Sloppy Joes

3 pounds ground beef (93% lean)
1 cup chopped onion
2 cans (10¾ ounces each) condensed fiesta nacho cheese soup
¾ cup ketchup
18 hamburger or cocktail buns, split and toasted

1. In a very large skillet or Dutch oven, cook ground beef and onion until meat is cooked through and onion is tender, stirring to break meat into bite-size pieces. Drain off fat.

2. Transfer meat mixture to 3½- or 4-quart slow cooker. Stir in nacho cheese soup and ketchup.

3. Cover slow cooker; cook on low-heat setting for 4½ hours or on high-heat setting for 2 hours. Serve meat mixture in toasted buns.

Per sandwich: 286 cal., 9 g total fat (4 g sat. fat), 45 mg chol., 600 mg sodium, 28 g carbo., 2 g fiber, 21 g pro.

This recipe features both beef and pork, which are cooked to tender perfection and shredded—and it feeds a crowd of hungry tailgaters.

Down-South Barbecue Sandwiches

1½ pounds boneless beef chuck roast
1½ pounds boneless pork shoulder roast
 1 can (6 ounces) tomato paste
½ cup packed brown sugar
¼ cup water
¼ cup apple cider vinegar
 2 tablespoons chili powder
 2 teaspoons Worcestershire sauce
 1 teaspoon dry mustard
16 kaiser rolls or hamburger buns, split and toasted

1. Place beef and pork roasts in 3½- or 4-quart slow cooker, cutting to fit if necessary.

2. In medium-size bowl, combine tomato paste, brown sugar, the water, apple cider vinegar, chili powder, Worcestershire sauce and mustard. Pour over roasts in cooker.

3. Cover slow cooker; cook on low-heat setting for 10 to 12 hours or on high-heat setting for 5 to 6 hours.

4. Remove roasts from slow cooker, reserving sauce. Using two forks, pull meat apart into shreds. Stir shredded meat into reserved sauce in cooker. Serve meat mixture on toasted rolls or buns.

· ·

Per sandwich: 286 cal., 8 g total fat (3 g sat. fat), 56 mg chol., 330 mg sodium, 31 g carbo., 2 g fiber, 21 g pro.

PREP:
20 minutes

COOKER SIZE:
3½- or 4-quart

COOK:
10 to 12 hours on low-heat or 5 to 6 hours on high-heat setting

MAKES:
16 sandwiches

KIDS' FAVORITE!

FREEZE WITH EASE

PREP:
30 minutes

COOKER SIZE:
4- to 5-quart

COOK:
10 to 12 hours on low-heat or 5 to 6 hours on high-heat setting

MAKES:
8 servings

KIDS' FAVORITE!

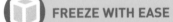

FREEZE WITH EASE

Spritz the tostadas with lime for a fresh finish, or set out a bowl of lime wedges so everyone can spritz to taste.

Adobo Pork Tostadas

1 boneless pork shoulder roast (3 to 3½ pounds)
1 can (15 ounces) tomato sauce
½ cup chicken broth
2 tablespoons finely chopped canned chipotle chiles in adobo sauce*
6 cloves garlic, chopped
½ teaspoon salt
½ teaspoon ground cumin
½ teaspoon ground coriander
¼ teaspoon black pepper
2 cups canned refried beans
16 corn tostada shells
2 cups shredded lettuce
2 cups chopped tomato (3 medium)
2 avocados, halved, seeded, peeled and sliced
2 cups queso fresco cheese, crumbled (8 ounces)
1 carton (8 ounces) sour cream

1. Trim fat from roast. Cut meat into chunks. Place meat in 4- to 5-quart slow cooker. In large bowl, combine tomato sauce, chicken broth, chipotle chiles, garlic, salt, cumin, coriander and black pepper; pour over meat in cooker.

2. Cover slow cooker; cook on low-heat setting for 10 to 12 hours or on high-heat setting for 5 to 6 hours.

3. Using a slotted spoon, remove meat to a platter. When meat is cool enough to handle, use two forks to pull meat apart into shreds. Add 1 cup of the cooking liquid to the meat to moisten. Discard any remaining cooking liquid.

4. Spread refried beans over tostada shells. Top evenly with meat mixture. Divide lettuce, tomato, avocados and cheese evenly among tostadas. Top each serving with sour cream.

Per serving: 655 cal., 32 g total fat (9 g sat. fat), 128 mg chol., 879 mg sodium, 42 g carbo., 9 g fiber, 50 g pro.

*Note: Because chiles contain volatile oils that can burn your skin and eyes, avoid direct contact with them as much as possible. When working with chiles, wear plastic or rubber gloves. If your bare hands do touch the chiles, wash your hands and nails well with soap and warm water.

Plain potatoes take a scrumptious flavor turn when they're slow-simmered with mushrooms, Swiss cheese and garlic.

Hash Browns With Garlic-Mushroom Sauce

PREP:
15 minutes

COOKER SIZE:
3½- or 4-quart

COOK:
8 to 9 hours on low-heat or 4 to 4½ hours on high-heat setting

MAKES:
8 to 10 side-dish servings

1 **package (32 ounces) loose-pack frozen diced hash brown potatoes**
2 **cups shredded Swiss cheese (8 ounces)**
2 **cans (4 ounces each) sliced mushrooms, drained**
1 **tablespoon bottled roasted minced garlic**
1 **can (10¾ ounces) condensed cream of mushroom soup**
¼ **cup water**

1. In 3½- or 4-quart slow cooker, combine frozen potatoes, Swiss cheese, mushrooms and roasted minced garlic. Add cream of mushroom soup and the water; stir to combine.

2. Cover slow cooker; cook on low-heat setting for 8 to 9 hours or on high-heat setting for 4 to 4½ hours. Stir gently before serving.

Per serving: 248 cal., 11 g total fat (6 g sat. fat), 26 mg chol., 482 mg sodium, 26 g carbo., 3 g fiber, 12 g pro.

PREP:
20 minutes

COOKER SIZE:
3½- or 4-quart

COOK:
5 to 6 hours on low-heat setting

MAKES:
12 side-dish servings

KIDS' FAVORITE!

Not just ordinary spuds, these hash browns are dressed up with bacon, leek and three kinds of cheese.

Easy Cheesy Potatoes

- 1 package (28 ounces) loose-pack frozen diced hash brown potatoes with onion and peppers, thawed
- 1 can (10¾ ounces) condensed cream of chicken with herbs soup
- 1 cup finely shredded smoked Gouda cheese (4 ounces)
- 1 cup finely shredded provolone cheese (4 ounces)
- 1 package (8 ounces) cream cheese, cut into cubes
- ¾ cup milk
- ¼ cup sliced leek or thinly sliced scallions
- ½ teaspoon black pepper
- 4 strips bacon, crisp-cooked and crumbled

1. In 3½- or 4-quart slow cooker, combine thawed potatoes, cream of chicken soup, smoked Gouda cheese, provolone cheese, cream cheese, milk, leek and pepper.

2. Cover slow cooker; cook on low-heat setting for 5 to 6 hours.

3. To serve, sprinkle with bacon.

Per serving: 218 cal., 14 g total fat (8 g sat. fat), 41 mg chol., 564 mg sodium, 16 g carbo., 2 g fiber, 9 g pro.

PREP:
10 minutes

COOKER SIZE:
3½- or 4-quart

COOK:
3½ to 4½ hours on low-heat or 1¾ to 2¼ hours on high-heat setting

MAKES:
8 side-dish servings

KIDS' FAVORITE!

Sour cream dip, two types of cheese and mayonnaise turn refrigerated potato wedges into a company-special side dish.

Creamy Potato Wedges

2 **containers (8 ounces each) sour cream chive dip**
1 **cup finely shredded Asiago cheese (4 ounces)**
1 **package (3 ounces) cream cheese, cut up**
½ **cup mayonnaise**
2 **packages (20 ounces each) refrigerated new potato wedges**
   Chopped fresh chives (optional)

1. In 3½- or 4-quart slow cooker, stir together sour cream dip, Asiago cheese, cream cheese and mayonnaise. Stir in potato wedges.

2. Cover slow cooker; cook on low-heat setting for 3½ to 4½ hours or on high-heat setting for 1¾ to 2¼ hours. Stir before serving. If desired, sprinkle with chives.

Per serving: 415 cal., 31 g total fat (14 g sat. fat), 55 mg chol., 835 mg sodium, 23 g carbo., 4 g fiber, 10 g pro.

When you're looking for a classy side to tote to that next potluck, remember this easy-to-make and oh-so-cheesy cauliflower.

Cheesy Cauliflower For a Crowd

8 cups cauliflower flowerets
1 large onion, thinly sliced
½ teaspoon fennel seeds, crushed
1 jar (14 to 16 ounces) Cheddar cheese pasta sauce
Black pepper (optional)

1. In 3½- or 4-quart slow cooker, combine cauliflower, onion and fennel seeds. Pour pasta sauce over all.

2. Cover slow cooker; cook on low-heat setting for 6 to 7 hours or on high-heat setting for 3 to 3½ hours. Stir gently before serving. If desired, sprinkle with pepper before serving.

. . . .

Per serving: 59 cal., 6 g total fat (2 g sat. fat), 16 mg chol., 329 mg sodium, 8 g carbo., 2 g fiber, 3 g pro.

PREP:
20 minutes

COOKER SIZE:
3½- or 4-quart

COOK:
6 to 7 hours on low-heat or 3 to 3½ hours on high-heat setting

MAKES:
10 to 12 side-dish servings

KIDS' FAVORITE!

PREP:
20 minutes

COOKER SIZE:
3½- or 4-quart

COOK:
5 to 6 hours on low-heat setting

STAND:
10 minutes

MAKES:
15 side-dish servings

If you've been invited to a "turkey and all the trimmings" potluck dinner, help out with the trimmings by bringing this elegant rice pilaf.

Wild Rice with Pecans and Cherries

  3 cans (14 ounces each) chicken broth
2½ cups wild rice, rinsed and drained
  1 cup coarsely shredded carrots
  1 jar (4½ ounces) sliced mushrooms, drained
  2 tablespoons butter or margarine, melted
  2 teaspoons dried marjoram
  ¼ teaspoon salt
  ¼ teaspoon black pepper
  ⅔ cup dried tart cherries
  ⅔ cup chopped scallions
  ½ cup coarsely chopped pecans, toasted
    Chopped scallions (optional)

1. In 3½- or 4-quart slow cooker, combine chicken broth, uncooked wild rice, carrots, mushrooms, melted butter, marjoram, salt and pepper.

2. Cover slow cooker; cook on low-heat setting for 5 to 6 hours.

3. Turn off cooker. Stir in dried cherries, the ⅔ cup scallions and the toasted pecans. Cover slow cooker; let stand for 10 minutes. Serve with a slotted spoon. If desired, garnish with additional scallions.

Per serving: 169 cal., 5 g total fat (1 g sat. fat), 4 mg chol., 423 mg sodium, 27 g carbo., 3 g fiber, 5 g pro.

PREP:
20 minutes

COOKER SIZE:
3½- or 4-quart

COOK:
6 to 8 hours on low-heat or 3 to 4 hours on high-heat setting

MAKES:
12 side-dish servings

Wheat berries, barley and wild rice make this dish filling and infinitely interesting.

Multigrain Pilaf With Beans

⅔ cup wheat berries
½ cup regular barley
½ cup wild rice
2 cans (14 ounces each) vegetable broth or chicken broth
2 cups loose-pack frozen sweet soybeans (edamame) or baby lima beans
1 medium-size sweet red pepper, seeded and coarsely chopped
1 medium-size onion, finely chopped
1 tablespoon butter or margarine
¾ teaspoon dried sage
½ teaspoon salt
¼ teaspoon coarsely ground black pepper
4 cloves garlic, chopped

1. Rinse and drain wheat berries, barley and wild rice. In 3½- or 4-quart slow cooker, combine uncooked wheat berries, uncooked barley, uncooked wild rice, broth, soybeans, sweet red pepper, onion, butter, sage, salt, black pepper and garlic.

2. Cover slow cooker; cook on low-heat setting for 6 to 8 hours or on high-heat setting for 3 to 4 hours. Stir before serving.

· ·

Per serving: 169 cal., 4 g total fat (1 g sat. fat), 3 mg chol., 386 mg sodium, 25 g carbo., 5 g fiber, 9 g pro.

PREP:
20 minutes

COOKER SIZE:
3½- or 4-quart

COOK:
5 to 6 hours on low-heat or 2½ to 3 hours on high-heat setting

STAND:
10 minutes

MAKES:
12 side-dish servings

If you like spicy foods, kick this corn up a notch by using cheese with jalapeño chiles.

Spicy Creamed Corn

2 packages (16 ounces each) loose-pack frozen white whole kernel corn (shoepeg corn), thawed
1 can (14¾ ounces) cream-style corn
2 cups shredded Monterey Jack cheese (8 ounces)
1 cup chopped tomato
⅓ cup chopped onion
1 can (4½ ounces) diced green chiles
1½ teaspoons chili powder
½ teaspoon salt
1 carton (16 ounces) sour cream
2 tablespoons chopped fresh cilantro

1. In 3½- or 4-quart slow cooker, combine thawed whole kernel corn, cream-style corn, cheese, tomato, onion, chiles with their juices, chili powder and salt.

2. Cover slow cooker; cook on low-heat setting for 5 to 6 hours or on high-heat setting for 2½ to 3 hours.

3. Gently stir in sour cream and cilantro. Let stand for 10 minutes before serving.

Per serving: 250 cal., 15 g total fat (9 g sat. fat), 33 mg chol., 350 mg sodium, 25 g carbo., 2 g fiber, 9 g pro.

Sides and Desserts

247 Greens and Berry Salad

Quick and Cheesy Veggies 253

263 Home Run Garlic Rolls

Rocky Road Malts 278

Jazz up your slow cooker dinner with these super-simple and decidedly delicious sides and desserts. Most can be prepared from start to finish in less than 30 minutes so you can get the rest of your meal ready while your slow cooker finishes the main dish.

PREP:
30 minutes

CHILL:
4 to 24 hours

MAKES:
20 servings

This easy-to-make salad goes great with sandwiches such as Down-South Barbecue Sandwiches (page 233).

No-Chop Potato Salad

1 package (24 ounces) loose-pack frozen diced hash brown potatoes with onions and peppers
1½ cups thinly sliced celery
1 container (8 ounces) light sour cream chive dip
⅔ cup light mayonnaise or salad dressing
1 tablespoon sugar
1 tablespoon white wine vinegar
1 tablespoon yellow mustard
½ teaspoon salt
3 hard-cooked eggs, coarsely chopped
  Celery leaves (optional)
  Cracked black pepper

1. In large covered saucepan, cook hash brown potatoes in boiling water for 6 to 8 minutes or until tender; drain well. In large bowl, combine potatoes and celery. Set aside.

2. In small bowl, combine sour cream dip, mayonnaise, sugar, white wine vinegar, mustard and salt. Add mayonnaise mixture to potato mixture; toss lightly to coat. Gently fold in hard-cooked eggs. Cover and refrigerate for at least 4 hours or up to 24 hours.

3. Before serving, garnish with celery leaves (if desired) and sprinkle with pepper.

Per serving: 98 cal., 5 g total fat (2 g sat. fat), 43 mg chol., 265 mg sodium, 10 g carbo., 1 g fiber, 2 g pro.

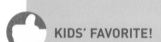

KIDS' FAVORITE!

Dijon mustard adds the perfect zing to the dressing for this pretty red and green salad.

Greens and Berry Salad

START TO FINISH:
15 minutes

MAKES:
4 to 6 servings

1 **package (8 ounces) torn mixed salad greens (about 8 cups)**
½ **cup crumbled blue cheese (optional)**
¼ **of a small red onion, slivered**
1 **cup sliced fresh strawberries and/or fresh raspberries**
1 **package (2 ounces) slivered almonds (⅓ cup), toasted**
¼ **cup bottled balsamic vinaigrette**
1 **teaspoon Dijon mustard**

1. In large salad bowl, combine mixed greens, blue cheese (if desired), red onion, berries and almonds.

2. In small bowl, whisk together vinaigrette and mustard. Pour vinaigrette over greens mixture. Toss to combine. Serve immediately.

. . . .

Per serving: 157 cal., 12 g total fat (1 g sat. fat), 0 mg chol., 215 mg sodium, 11 g carbo., 5 g fiber, 5 g pro.

PREP:
15 minutes

CHILL:
1 to 4 hours

MAKES:
6 to 8 servings

Broccoli slaw can be found near the regular coleslaw mix at the supermarket.

Fruit and Broccoli Salad

½ of a package (16 ounces) broccoli slaw (about 2½ cups)
1 cup seedless red and/or green grapes, halved
1 medium-size apple, cored and chopped
⅓ to ½ cup bottled poppy seed salad dressing
2 medium-size oranges, peeled, seeded and sectioned*
½ cup broken pecans or walnuts, toasted if desired**
 Red Bibb lettuce

1. In large bowl, combine broccoli slaw, grapes and apple. Pour salad dressing over broccoli mixture; add oranges and toss gently to coat. Cover and chill for at least 1 hour or up to 4 hours. Sprinkle with nuts; toss again. Spoon salad into lettuce-lined salad bowls.

Per serving: 234 cal., 16 g total fat (2 g sat. fat), 6 mg chol., 17 mg sodium, 22 g carbo., 3 g fiber, 3 g pro.

*Note: To section oranges, hold peeled oranges over a bowl to catch the juices. Cut down against inside membrane of one segment on both sides and release segment. Repeat with remaining segments, removing any seeds.

**Note: To toast nuts, heat oven to 350°. Spread nuts in a single layer in a shallow baking pan. Bake at 350° for 5 to 10 minutes or until light golden brown, watching carefully and stirring once or twice.

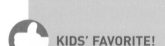

KIDS' FAVORITE!

Take your choice of dill, caraway seeds or celery seeds to season this simple slaw.

Creamy Ranch Coleslaw

1 **bag (16 ounces) coleslaw mix**
½ **cup bottled ranch salad dressing**
¼ **cup shelled sunflower seeds**
2 **teaspoons chopped fresh dill or 1 teaspoon caraway seeds or celery seeds**

1. In large bowl, toss together coleslaw mix, ranch salad dressing, sunflower seeds and dill or caraway or celery seeds. Serve immediately or cover and chill for up to 24 hours.

Per serving: 111 cal., 10 g total fat (1 g sat. fat), 5 mg chol., 131 mg sodium, 5 g carbo., 2 g fiber, 2 g pro.

KIDS' FAVORITE!

Even kids will love broccoli when it's teamed with cheese, bacon and a creamy dressing.

Broccoli-Cheddar Salad

START TO FINISH:
20 minutes

MAKES:
6 servings

4 **cups broccoli flowerets**
1 **small red onion, chopped or cut into thin wedges**
1 **cup cubed Cheddar or smoked Cheddar cheese**
5 **strips bacon, crisp-cooked, drained and crumbled**
½ **cup mayonnaise or salad dressing**
¼ **cup bottled coleslaw salad dressing or buttermilk ranch salad dressing**
2 **tablespoons vinegar**
1 **tablespoon sugar**

1. In large salad bowl, combine broccoli, red onion, cheese and bacon.

2. For dressing, in small bowl, stir together mayonnaise, coleslaw dressing, vinegar and sugar. Pour over broccoli mixture; toss to coat. Serve immediately or cover and chill for up to 2 hours; stir before serving.

Per serving: 330 cal., 30 g total fat (8 g sat. fat), 34 mg chol., 400 mg sodium, 8 g carbo., 2 g fiber, 9 g pro.

KIDS' FAVORITE!

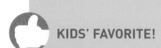

KIDS' FAVORITE!

If you think you'll miss the bread, top the salad with baked whole wheat croutons or serve with fresh crusty rolls.

Super Simple B.L.T. Salad

> 5 cups torn mixed salad greens or fresh spinach
> 2 cups grape tomatoes or cherry tomatoes, halved
> ½ pound bacon (about 10 strips), crisp-cooked, drained and crumbled
> 2 hard-cooked eggs, peeled and chopped
> ⅓ cup bottled poppy seed salad dressing

1. In large bowl, top greens with tomatoes, bacon and chopped eggs. Drizzle with dressing. Toss well.

Per serving: 126 cal., 10 g total fat (3 g sat. fat), 62 mg chol., 231 mg sodium, 4 g carbo., 1 g fiber, 5 g pro.

Nuts add a nice crunch to this side dish. But if only some members of the family care for walnuts, sprinkle them on individual servings.

Quick and Cheesy Veggies

1 package (12 ounces) frozen broccoli and cauliflower in microwaveable steaming bag
1 cup shredded American cheese (4 ounces)
2 tablespoons chopped walnuts, toasted

1. Steam vegetables in microwave following package directions. Transfer vegetables to a large bowl. Stir in cheese; let stand for 1 minute. Toss until cheese is melted and vegetables are coated. Sprinkle with nuts.

Per serving: 158 cal., 11 g total fat (6 g sat. fat), 27 mg chol., 445 mg sodium, 5 g carbo., 2 g fiber, 8 g pro.

KIDS' FAVORITE!

PREP:
15 minutes

BAKE:
30 minutes

OVEN:
350°

MAKES:
4 to 6 servings

All the elements for this classic side dish come from the freezer or a can.

Golden Green Bean Crunch

1 **package (16 ounces) loose-pack frozen French-cut green beans**
1 **can (10¾ ounces) condensed golden mushroom soup**
1 **can (8 ounces) sliced water chestnuts, drained (optional)**
½ **of a can (2.8 ounces) French fried onions (about ¾ cup)**
   or 1 cup chow mein noodles

1. Heat oven to 350°. Cook frozen beans following package directions; drain well. In 1½-quart casserole, stir together beans, golden mushroom soup and, if desired, water chestnuts.

2. Bake, uncovered, at 350° about 25 minutes or until bubbly around edges. Sprinkle with French fried onions. Bake about 5 minutes longer or until heated through.

- -

Per serving: 188 cal., 6 g total fat (1 g sat. fat), 3 mg chol., 719 mg sodium, 27 g carbo., 5 g fiber, 5 g pro.

Toasted nuts and green vegetables are an appealing combination that is quick and easy to put together.

Lemon-Almond Broccoli

½ pound broccoli, cut into ¾-inch pieces, or 2 cups loose-pack
   frozen cut broccoli
1 tablespoon butter or margarine
¾ cup sliced fresh mushrooms
1 scallion, thinly sliced
2 tablespoons slivered almonds or chopped pecans, toasted
½ teaspoon grated lemon zest

1. If using fresh broccoli, in covered medium-size saucepan, cook broccoli in a small amount of boiling lightly salted water about 8 minutes or until crisp-tender. If using frozen broccoli, cook following package directions. Drain well.

2. Meanwhile, for sauce, in small saucepan, melt butter over medium heat. Add mushrooms and scallion; cook until tender, stirring occasionally. Remove from heat. Stir in nuts and lemon zest. Toss with hot drained broccoli.

Per serving: 69 cal., 6 g total fat (2 g sat. fat), 8 mg chol., 34 mg sodium, 4 g carbo., 2 g fiber, 3 g pro.

KIDS' FAVORITE!

Wow—it's astonishing what stirring a bit of cornmeal into this simple side does for its sinfully silky texture!

Buttery Corn Medley

PREP:
15 minutes

COOK:
30 minutes

STAND:
10 minutes

MAKES:
6 servings

5 ears corn, husked and silked, or one package (20 ounces) frozen whole kernel corn
¼ cup (½ stick) butter
2 to 4 tablespoons sugar
1 tablespoon cornmeal
   Salt
   Black pepper

1. If using fresh corn, cut kernels from cobs (you should have about 2½ cups). In large skillet, melt butter over medium-low heat. Stir in corn, sugar and cornmeal. Cover and cook for 30 minutes, stirring occasionally.

2. Season to taste with salt and pepper. Let stand for 10 minutes before serving.

Per serving: 152 cal., 9 g total fat (4 g sat. fat), 22 mg chol., 254 mg sodium, 19 g carbo., 2 g fiber, 2 g pro.

KIDS' FAVORITE!

SIDES AND DESSERTS

PREP:
10 minutes

COOK:
15 minutes

STAND:
5 minutes

MAKES:
8 servings

KIDS' FAVORITE!

This rice is veggie-packed and not too spicy. Lime wedges squeezed over the top just before serving add a special zing.

Mexican-Style Rice

1½ cups long grain white rice
1 can (14½ ounces) Mexican-style stewed tomatoes, cut up finely
1 can (14 ounces) chicken broth
½ cup water
½ cup chopped carrots
½ cup loose-pack frozen peas or chopped zucchini
Lime wedges (optional)

1. In large saucepan, stir together uncooked rice, tomatoes with their juices, chicken broth, the water and carrots. Bring to a boil; reduce heat. Cover and simmer for 15 to 20 minutes or until rice is tender and most of the liquid is absorbed. Stir in peas or zucchini. Let stand, covered, for 5 minutes. Fluff with a fork before serving. If desired, garnish with lime wedges.

· ·

Per serving: 155 cal., 0 g total fat (0 g sat. fat), 1 mg chol., 391 mg sodium, 33 g carbo., 1 g fiber, 4 g pro.

PREP:
20 minutes

COOK:
25 minutes

MAKES:
6 servings

If you want to save a little prep time, you can use canned Mandarin oranges in this recipe.

Rice Pilaf with Oranges and Nuts

1½ cups sliced fresh mushrooms
1 cup sliced celery
1 cup finely chopped onion
1 tablespoon vegetable oil
1 can (14 ounces) chicken broth
⅔ cup water
1 package (6 ounces) long grain and wild rice mix
2 medium oranges, peeled and sectioned,
    or 1 can (11 ounces) Mandarin orange sections, drained
½ cup broken walnuts, toasted

1. In large saucepan, cook mushrooms, celery and onion in hot oil about 5 minutes or until tender. Add chicken broth and the water; bring to a boil. Stir in wild rice mix and seasoning packet; reduce heat. Cover and simmer for 25 to 30 minutes or until rice is tender. Remove from heat. Gently stir in oranges and walnuts.

Per serving: 214 cal., 10 g total fat (1 g sat. fat), 1 mg chol., 673 mg sodium, 29 g carbo., 3 g fiber, 6 g pro.

PREP:
15 minutes

BAKE:
1 hour 5 minutes

OVEN:
300°/375°

MAKES:
10 servings

KIDS' FAVORITE!

Heavy cream and shredded cheese transform refrigerated mashed potatoes into a side dish special enough for a company meal.

Volcano Mashed Potatoes

> 3 packages (20 ounces each) refrigerated mashed potatoes
> ¾ cup heavy cream
> ¾ cup shredded Gruyère, Havarti or American cheese (3 ounces)
>   Freshly cracked black pepper

1. Heat oven to 300°. Spoon potatoes into a 2-quart casserole. Bake, covered, at 300° for 50 minutes.

2. Meanwhile, in medium-size bowl, beat heavy cream with an electric mixer on low to medium speed until soft peaks form (tips curl); fold in cheese.

3. Remove casserole from oven. Raise oven temperature to 375°. Uncover potatoes. Using large spoon, make a hole in the center of the potatoes by pushing from the center to the side. Spoon the whipped cream mixture into the hole. Sprinkle top with cracked black pepper.

4. Bake, uncovered, at 375° for 15 to 20 minutes longer or until top is golden brown.

· ·

Per serving: 312 cal., 20 g total fat (10 g sat. fat), 64 mg chol., 266 mg sodium, 24 g carbo., 3 g fiber, 9 g pro.

Be sure to brush the butter mixture gently over the unbaked rolls so they don't deflate.

Home Run Garlic Rolls

PREP:
20 minutes

RISE:
1½ hours

BAKE:
15 minutes

OVEN:
350°

MAKES:
24 rolls
(12 servings)

1 **loaf (16 ounces) frozen white or whole wheat bread dough, thawed**
1 **tablespoon butter, melted**
2 **cloves garlic, chopped**
2 **tablespoons grated Parmesan cheese**

1. Lightly grease a 13×9×2-inch baking pan; set aside. Shape dough into 24 balls. Place balls in prepared pan. Cover; let rise in warm place until nearly double (1½ to 2 hours).

2. Heat oven to 350°. In small bowl, stir together melted butter and garlic. Brush butter mixture over rolls. Sprinkle with Parmesan cheese. Bake at 350° for 15 to 20 minutes or until golden brown. Remove rolls from pans; cool slightly on a wire rack. Serve warm.

Per serving: 55 cal., 1 g total fat (0 g sat. fat), 2 mg chol., 99 mg sodium, 9 g carbo., 0 g fiber, 1 g pro.

KIDS' FAVORITE!

PREP:
25 minutes

RISE:
30 minutes

BAKE:
12 minutes

OVEN:
400°

MAKES:
24 rolls

KIDS' FAVORITE!

FREEZE WITH EASE

If you like, substitute your favorite herb for the basil. Options include thyme, dill, oregano and rosemary.

Parmesan Dinner Rolls

1   package (16 ounces) hot roll mix
¼   cup finely shredded Parmesan cheese
2   tablespoons sugar
2   tablespoons chopped fresh basil or 1 teaspoon dried basil
1   tablespoon milk
2   tablespoons finely shredded Parmesan cheese

1. In large bowl, prepare hot roll mix following package directions through the resting step, except stir the ¼ cup Parmesan cheese, the sugar and basil into the flour mixture. Divide dough in half.

2. Grease 24 muffin cups (1¾ inches each). Using a knife, divide each dough half into 12 portions (24 portions total). Gently pull each dough portion into a ball, tucking edges beneath. Arrange balls, smooth sides up, in the prepared muffin cups. Cover; let rise in warm place until almost double in size (about 30 minutes).

3. Heat oven to 400°. Using pastry brush, brush roll tops with milk; sprinkle with the 2 tablespoons Parmesan cheese. Bake rolls at 400° for 12 to 15 minutes or until tops are golden brown. Remove rolls from muffin cups. Serve warm.

Per roll: 89 cal., 2 g total fat (0 g sat. fat), 9 mg chol., 145 mg sodium, 15 g carbo., 0 g fiber, 3 g pro.

Make-Ahead Tip: Wrap cooled, baked rolls tightly in aluminum foil. Freeze for up to 2 days. To serve, heat oven to 350°. Reheat the frozen rolls at 350° about 20 minutes or until warm.

KIDS' FAVORITE!

If you prefer, substitute another variety of shredded cheese for the provolone or mozzarella on this gooey bread.

Cheesy French Bread

2 tablespoons (¼ stick) butter, softened
½ of a loaf (1 pound) French bread, halved horizontally
¾ cup shredded provolone or mozzarella cheese (3 ounces)

1. Heat broiler. Spread butter over cut sides of bread. Place bread, cut sides up, on baking sheet. Broil 3 to 4 inches from the heat for 1 to 2 minutes or until browned. Sprinkle with cheese. Broil for 1 to 2 minutes longer or until cheese melts. Cut crosswise into slices to serve. Serve warm.

· ·

Per serving: 281 cal., 13 g total fat (8 g sat. fat), 30 mg chol., 572 mg sodium, 30 g carbo., 2 g fiber, 10 g pro.

If you can't bake these biscuits immediately, cover and chill the dough for up to 24 hours. Roll, cut and bake the biscuits as directed.

Buttermilk Angel Biscuits

PREP:
20 minutes

BAKE:
15 minutes

OVEN:
400°

MAKES:
about 20 biscuits

- 5 **cups all-purpose flour**
- ¼ **cup sugar**
- 1 **tablespoon baking powder**
- 1 **teaspoon baking soda**
- 1 **teaspoon salt**
- 1 **cup solid vegetable shortening**
- 1 **package (¼ ounce) active dry yeast**
- 2 **tablespoons warm water (105° to 115°)**
- 2 **cups buttermilk**

1. Heat oven to 400°. In large bowl, stir together flour, sugar, baking powder, baking soda and salt. Using a pastry blender, cut in shortening until mixture resembles coarse crumbs. Make a well in center of flour mixture; set aside.

2. In medium-size bowl, dissolve yeast in the warm water. Stir in buttermilk. Add buttermilk mixture to well. Using a fork, stir just until moistened.

3. Turn out the dough onto a lightly floured surface. Knead the dough by folding and gently pressing dough for 4 to 6 strokes or just until the dough holds together. Pat or lightly roll the dough to ¾-inch thickness. Cut the dough with a floured 2½-inch biscuit cutter.

4. Place biscuits 1 inch apart on ungreased baking sheet. Bake at 400° for 15 to 18 minutes or until light brown. Remove from baking sheet; serve immediately.

Per biscuit: 225 cal., 11 g total fat (3 g sat. fat), 1 mg chol., 260 mg sodium, 28 g carbo., 1 g fiber, 4 g pro.

KIDS' FAVORITE!

FREEZE WITH EASE

PREP:
15 minutes

BAKE:
10 minutes

COOL:
5 minutes

OVEN:
400°

MAKES:
24 muffins

KIDS' FAVORITE!

FREEZE WITH EASE

Try these terrific muffins with any Southern or south-of-the-border inspired dish.

Southern Corn Bread Mini Muffins

2 tablespoons jalapeño chile jelly
1 egg, lightly beaten
¼ cup buttermilk
1 package (8½ ounces) corn muffin mix
½ cup loose-pack frozen whole kernel corn, thawed
½ cup shredded taco cheese or Cheddar cheese (2 ounces)
¼ cup (½ stick) butter, softened
1 tablespoon honey
Dash cayenne pepper or several dashes hot-pepper sauce

1. Heat oven to 400°. Grease bottoms and halfway up the sides of 24 muffin cups (1¾ inches each); set aside.

2. In microwave-safe bowl, microwave jalapeño jelly on HIGH for 20 to 40 seconds or until melted. Stir in egg and buttermilk. Add dry muffin mix; stir just until moistened. Stir in corn and cheese.

3. Spoon batter into prepared muffin cups, filling each two-thirds full. Bake at 400° for 10 to 12 minutes or until golden brown and a wooden toothpick inserted in centers comes out clean.

4. For butter spread, in small bowl, combine butter, honey and cayenne pepper or hot-pepper sauce; set spread aside.

5. Cool in muffin cups on a wire rack for 5 minutes. Remove from muffin cups; serve warm with butter spread.

Per muffin: 103 cal., 3 g total fat (3 g sat. fat), 22 mg chol., 157 mg sodium, 10 g carbo., 0 g fiber, 1 g pro.

PREP:
20 minutes

BAKE:
48 minutes

OVEN:
350°

MAKES:
24 bars

KIDS' FAVORITE!

FREEZE WITH EASE

Both the shortbread crust and the cocoa brownie layer are studded with bits of semisweet chocolate.

Shortbread Brownies

    1 cup all-purpose flour
    ¼ cup packed brown sugar
    ½ cup (1 stick) butter
    ¼ cup miniature semisweet chocolate pieces
    1⅓ cups granulated sugar
    ¾ cup all-purpose flour
    ½ cup unsweetened cocoa powder
    1½ teaspoons baking powder
    ½ teaspoon salt
    3 eggs
    ⅓ cup butter, melted
    1 tablespoon vanilla extract
    ½ cup miniature semisweet chocolate pieces

1. Heat oven to 350°. Line 9×9×2-inch baking pan with aluminum foil; set aside. For crust, in medium-size bowl, stir together the 1 cup flour and the brown sugar. Using a pastry blender, cut in the ½ cup butter until mixture resembles coarse crumbs. Stir in the ¼ cup chocolate pieces. Press mixture into prepared pan. Bake at 350° for 8 minutes.

2. Meanwhile, in large bowl, stir together granulated sugar, the ¾ cup flour, the cocoa powder, baking powder and salt. Add eggs, the ⅓ cup melted butter and the vanilla extract; using a wooden spoon, beat until smooth. Stir in the ½ cup chocolate pieces. Carefully spread over crust in pan.

3. Bake at 350° for 40 minutes longer. Cool brownies in pan on a wire rack. Lift brownies out of pan by lifting up on foil. Cut into bars.

Per bar: 180 cal., 9 g total fat (4 g sat. fat), 44 mg chol., 121 mg sodium, 23 g carbo., 1 g fiber, 3 g pro.

If desired, top the cupcakes with crushed gingersnaps, a twist of candied lemon peel or snipped spiced gumdrops.

Lemon-Spice Cupcakes

1 **package (2-layer size) lemon cake mix**
1 **can (16 ounces) cream cheese frosting**
1 **teaspoon apple pie spice**

1. Heat oven to 350°. Line 24 muffin cups (2½ inches each) with foil or paper bake cups; set aside. Prepare cake mix following package directions for cupcakes. Spoon batter into prepared muffin cups, filling each muffin cup about one-half to two-thirds full. Bake following package directions. Cool in muffin cups on wire racks for 5 minutes. Remove from muffin cups; cool on wire racks.

2. For frosting, in small bowl, stir together cream cheese frosting and apple pie spice. Spread frosting over each cupcake.

Per cupcake: 183 cal., 5 g total fat (2 g sat. fat), 0 mg chol., 198 mg sodium, 33 g carbo., 0 g fiber, 1 g pro.

PREP:
30 minutes

BAKE:
following package directions

OVEN:
350°

MAKES:
24 cupcakes

KIDS' FAVORITE!

FREEZE WITH EASE

PREP:
30 minutes

BAKE:
following package directions

OVEN:
350°

MAKES:
12 servings

KIDS' FAVORITE!

Be sure to use regular and not the diet version of root beer in this delicously simple cake.

Root Beer Float Cake

1 **package (2-layer size) caramel or yellow cake mix**
  Root beer
1½ **teaspoons vanilla extract**
1 **teaspoon grated lemon zest**
  Celebration Icing (recipe follows)
  Maraschino cherries (optional)

1. Heat oven to 350°. Grease two 8- or 9-inch round cake pans; set aside. Prepare cake mix following package directions, except substitute root beer for the liquid called for and add the vanilla and lemon zest. Pour batter into prepared cake pans. Bake following package directions. Cool in pans on wire racks for 10 minutes. Remove cake layers from pans. Cool completely on wire racks.

2. Fill and frost cooled cake layers with Celebration Icing. If desired, garnish with maraschino cherries.

Celebration Icing: In large bowl, beat ⅔ cup softened butter with an electric mixer on medium speed until smooth. Gradually add 2 cups confectioners' sugar, beating well. Slowly beat in 6 tablespoons root beer and 2 teaspoons vanilla extract. Gradually beat in another 4 cups confectioners' sugar. If necessary, beat in a little more root beer or confectioners' sugar to make icing of spreading consistency.

Per serving: 592 cal., 21 g total fat (9 g sat. fat), 82 mg chol., 368 mg sodium, 100 g carbo., 0 g fiber, 3 g pro.

PREP:
15 minutes

BAKE:
50 minutes

COOL:
1 hour 20 minutes

OVEN:
350°

MAKES:
10 to 12 servings

KIDS' FAVORITE!

If you don't have time to make your own pastry shell, use purchased refrigerated piecrust dough for this luscious dessert.

Brownie and Walnut Pie

½ cup (1 stick) butter
3 ounces unsweetened chocolate, cut up
3 eggs, lightly beaten
1½ cups sugar
½ cup all-purpose flour
1 teaspoon vanilla extract
1 cup chopped walnuts
1 (9-inch) unbaked pastry shell
   Caramel ice cream topping
   Coffee or vanilla ice cream

1. Heat oven to 350°. For filling, in heavy, small saucepan, combine butter and chocolate; melt over low heat, stirring frequently. Cool for 20 minutes.

2. In large bowl, stir together eggs, sugar, flour and vanilla extract. Stir in cooled chocolate mixture and walnuts. Pour filling into pastry shell.

3. Bake at 350° for 50 to 55 minutes or until knife inserted near the center comes out clean. Cool for 1 hour on a wire rack. Serve warm. Drizzle each slice with caramel topping and serve with ice cream.

Per serving: 655 cal., 42 g total fat (19 g sat. fat), 156 mg chol., 193 mg sodium, 65 g carbo., 3 g fiber, 10 g pro.

This is the best fast-fixin' chocolate dessert you'll ever taste!

Fudge Cookies in Chocolate Cream

½ of a package (8 ounces) cream cheese
¼ cup chocolate-flavor syrup
1 teaspoon vanilla extract
½ cup heavy cream
6 fudge-covered chocolate sandwich cookies, chopped
2 fudge-covered chocolate sandwich cookies, halved crosswise

1. In medium-size bowl, beat cream cheese with an electric mixer on medium to high speed for 30 seconds. Beat in chocolate-flavor syrup and vanilla extract until well mixed. Add heavy cream; beat until fluffy. Fold in chopped cookies. Spoon into dessert dishes. Top each serving with a half-cookie.

Per serving: 426 cal., 31 g total fat (15 g sat. fat), 72 mg chol., 253 mg sodium, 39 g carbo., 2 g fiber, 5 g pro.

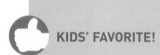

KIDS' FAVORITE!

This is a great way to get your kids to eat more fruit. Let them choose their favorite pudding flavor and their favorite fruits.

Fruity Waffle Bowls

1 package (4-serving size) instant lemon or white chocolate pudding mix
1⅓ cups fat-free milk
1 cup fresh fruit (such as blueberries, kiwifruit wedges, cut-up strawberries, sliced bananas and/or raspberries)
4 waffle ice cream bowls or large waffle ice cream cones

1. Prepare pudding following package directions, except use the 1⅓ cups milk. Spoon fruit and pudding into waffle bowls or cones. Serve immediately.

Per serving: 196 cal., 3 g total fat (1 g sat. fat), 6 mg chol., 399 mg sodium, 40 g carbo., 1 g fiber, 3 g pro.

KIDS' FAVORITE!

KIDS' FAVORITE!

Despite their name, these chocolate peanutty malts go down smooth and creamy.

Rocky Road Malts

1 quart (2 pints) chocolate ice cream
⅓ cup milk
⅓ cup chocolate instant malted milk powder
¼ cup creamy peanut butter
  Milk (optional)
  Marshmallow creme (optional)
  Coarsely chopped peanuts (optional)
  Miniature chocolate sandwich cookies with white filling (optional)
  Tiny marshmallows (optional)

1. In blender, combine half of the ice cream, the ⅓ cup milk, the malted milk powder and peanut butter. Cover; blend until smooth, stopping and scraping down side as necessary. Spoon in remaining ice cream; blend until smooth. If necessary, add enough additional milk to make malts desired consistency.

2. To serve, spoon malts into four glasses. If desired, top with marshmallow creme, chopped peanuts, miniature sandwich cookies and/or tiny marshmallows.

Per serving: 493 cal., 24 g total fat (11 g sat. fat), 47 mg chol., 252 mg sodium, 66 g carbo., 4 g fiber, 11 g pro.

PREP:
5 minutes

BAKE:
20 minutes

OVEN:
375°

MAKES:
6 servings

KIDS' FAVORITE!

Dried fruit adds variety to this easy recipe, and granola makes a super-simple topper compared to the streusel Mom used to make.

Easy Apple-Cherry Crisp

> 2 cans (21 ounces each) apple pie filling
> ¼ cup dried cherries, cranberries or mixed dried fruit bits
> 1½ cups granola
> Vanilla ice cream (optional)

1. Heat oven to 375°. In 2-quart square baking dish, stir together pie filling and dried fruit; sprinkle with granola. Bake, uncovered, at 375° for 20 to 25 minutes or until heated through. Serve warm; if desired, serve with ice cream.

Per serving: 326 cal., 2 g total fat (0 g sat. fat), 0 mg chol., 155 mg sodium, 79 g carbo., 4 g fiber, 3 g pro.

Index

Index

Note: Page numbers in **bold** indicate photographs.

The charts on this page provide a guide for converting measurements from the U.S. customary system, which is used throughout this book, to the metric system.

Product Differences

Most of the ingredients called for in the recipes in this book are available in most countries. However, some are known by different names. Here are some common American ingredients and their possible counterparts:

- Sugar (white) is granulated, fine granulated or castor sugar.
- Powdered sugar is icing sugar.
- All-purpose flour is enriched, bleached or unbleached white household flour. When self-rising flour is used in place of all-purpose flour in a recipe that calls for leavening, omit the leavening agent (baking soda or baking powder) and salt.
- Light-colored corn syrup is golden syrup.
- Cornstarch is cornflour.
- Baking soda is bicarbonate of soda.
- Vanilla or vanilla extract is vanilla essence.
- Green, red, or yellow sweet peppers are capsicums or bell peppers.
- Golden raisins are sultanas.

Volume and Weight

The United States traditionally uses cup measures for liquid and solid ingredients. The chart below shows the approximate imperial and metric equivalents. If you are accustomed to weighing solid ingredients, the following approximate equivalents will be helpful.

- 1 cup butter, castor sugar or rice = 8 ounces = ½ pound = 250 grams
- 1 cup flour = 4 ounces = ¼ pound = 125 grams
- 1 cup icing sugar = 5 ounces = 150 grams

Canadian and U.S. volume for a cup measure is 8 fluid ounces (237 ml), but the standard metric equivalent is 250 ml.

1 British imperial cup is 10 fluid ounces.

In Australia, 1 tablespoon equals 20 ml, and there are 4 teaspoons in the Australian tablespoon.

Spoon measures are used for smaller amounts of ingredients. Although the size of the tablespoon varies slightly in different countries, for practical purposes and for recipes in this book, a straight substitution is all that's necessary. Measurements made using cups or spoons always should be level unless stated otherwise.

Common Weight Range Replacements

Imperial / U.S.	Metric
½ ounce	15 g
1 ounce	25 g or 30 g
4 ounces (¼ pound)	115 g or 125 g
8 ounces (½ pound)	225 g or 250 g
16 ounces (1 pound)	450 g or 500 g
1¼ pounds	625 g
1½ pounds	750 g
2 pounds or 2¼ pounds	1,000 g or 1 Kg

Oven Temperature Equivalents

Fahrenheit Setting	Celsius Setting*	Gas Setting
300°F	150°C	Gas Mark 2 (very low)
325°F	160°C	Gas Mark 3 (low)
350°F	180°C	Gas Mark 4 (moderate)
375°F	190°C	Gas Mark 5 (moderate)
400°F	200°C	Gas Mark 6 (hot)
425°F	220°C	Gas Mark 7 (hot)
450°F	230°C	Gas Mark 8 (very hot)
475°F	240°C	Gas Mark 9 (very hot)
500°F	260°C	Gas Mark 10 (extremely hot)
Broil	Broil	Grill

* Electric and gas ovens may be calibrated using celsius. However, for an electric oven, increase celsius setting 10 to 20 degrees when cooking above 160°C. For convection or forced air ovens (gas or electric) lower the temperature setting 25°F/10°C when cooking at all heat levels.

Baking Pan Sizes

Imperial / U.S.	Metric
9×1½-inch round cake pan	22- or 23×4-cm (1.5 L)
9×1½-inch pie plate	22- or 23×4-cm (1 L)
8×8×2-inch square cake pan	20×5-cm (2 L)
9×9×2-inch square cake pan	22- or 23×4.5-cm (2.5 L)
11×7×1½-inch baking pan	28×17×4-cm (2 L)
2-quart rectangular baking pan	30×19×4.5-cm (3 L)
13×9×2-inch baking pan	34×22×4.5-cm (3.5 L)
15×10×1-inch jelly roll pan	40×25×2-cm
9×5×3-inch loaf pan	23×13×8-cm (2 L)
2-quart casserole	2 L

U.S. / Standard Metric Equivalents

⅛ teaspoon = 0.5 ml	
¼ teaspoon = 1 ml	
½ teaspoon = 2 ml	
1 teaspoon = 5 ml	
1 tablespoon = 15 ml	
2 tablespoons = 25 ml	
¼ cup = 2 fluid ounces = 50 ml	
⅓ cup = 3 fluid ounces = 75 ml	
½ cup = 4 fluid ounces = 125 ml	
⅔ cup = 5 fluid ounces = 150 ml	
¾ cup = 6 fluid ounces = 175 ml	
1 cup = 8 fluid ounces = 250 ml	
2 cups = 1 pint = 500 ml	
1 quart = 1 litre	

FamilyCircle®
cookbook
THE ULTIMATE RECIPE COLLECTION FOR BUSY FAMILIES

Features

- More than 300 delicious recipes that both kids and grown-ups will love

- Advice on every page – cooking hints, timesaving tips and menu suggestions

- Includes express-lane meals, kid-pleasing treats, party foods and desserts

About the Brand

Family Circle celebrates today's family and champions the woman at its center.

Every page provides smart, practical solutions to help you raise a happy, healthy family with a particular emphasis on the concerns of raising tweens and teens.

Family Circle delivers essential advice to you for tough parenting challenges, provides fun suggestions for your family's activities, offers healthy and delicious recipes and showcases projects to create a comfortable home. *Family Circle* helps you look and feel your best by delivering the latest health, diet and fitness news and beauty and fashion tips.

BOOKS

ADT1016_0308